The Wealth Architect

(Volume Two)

Building a Life of Unstoppable Riches

Ted Kiyosaki

TABLE OF CONTENTS

PREFACE

In a world where financial success is often equated with personal fulfillment, the pursuit of wealth remains a central theme in many people's lives. Whether we acknowledge it or not, money permeates nearly every aspect of our existence—our choices, our opportunities, and our sense of security. Yet, despite its ubiquity, the principles that govern true financial prosperity are often misunderstood, underappreciated, or shrouded in mystery. *The Wealth Architect (Vol 2): Building A Life of Unstoppable Riches* was born out of a burning desire to unravel more complexities and offer a clear, practical guide to mastering not just financial independence, but sustainable wealth and lasting abundance.

This book is not just about acquiring wealth—it is about creating a holistic and purposeful relationship with money. Through the years, I have seen many individuals focus solely on accumulating riches, only to find themselves unfulfilled or vulnerable to economic downturns and personal crises. In contrast, those who understand how to build wealth in its truest sense—balancing financial growth with emotional, intellectual, and social well-being—achieve a form of abundance that extends beyond monetary gains.

Why This Book Matters Now

We live in an era of unprecedented access to information and opportunity. The digital revolution has democratized wealth-building tools, making it possible for more people than ever before to take control of their financial futures. Yet, with this flood of information comes confusion. Financial jargon, conflicting advice, and volatile markets can make it difficult to chart a clear path to success. Too often, people find themselves overwhelmed or discouraged before they even begin.

The purpose of this book is to provide a further comprehensive, actionable plan for those who are ready to take their financial journey more seriously. *The Wealth Architect (Vol 2)* is not a get-rich-quick guide; it is a roadmap designed with *The Wealth Architect (Vol 1)* to building enduring wealth and achieving true financial freedom. Whether you are just starting your journey, recovering from financial setbacks, or seeking ways to secure generational wealth, the strategies outlined in the pages of these books will empower you to make informed decisions, and set achievable goals.

What You Will Learn

The Wealth Architect (Vol 2) is structured after *The Wealth Architect (Vol 1)* to guide you through each phase of financial development, from mastering the basics of personal finance to advanced strategies for investment, entrepreneurship, and legacy building. Each chapter offers practical insights, tools, and actionable steps that will help you:

- Develop a Wealth Mindset: The foundation of abundance starts with mindset. We'll explore how to shift from a scarcity mentality to one that fosters growth, opportunity, and resilience in the face of challenges.
- Master the Mechanics of Money: This section focuses on the essentials of cash flow management, savings, and debt elimination. You'll learn how to optimize your income, reduce unnecessary expenses, and create surpluses that fuel wealth-building.
- Build and Protect Wealth: Once the basics are mastered, we move into strategies for investing in stocks, real estate, and businesses, while also focusing on risk management and asset protection

through insurance, diversification, and smart financial planning.

- Achieve Financial Freedom: True wealth is about more than just accumulating assets; it's about creating systems that generate passive income and allow you to live on your terms. We'll explore methods for building multiple streams of income and designing a lifestyle where financial worries are a thing of the past.
- Leave a Legacy: Wealth, when properly managed, can extend beyond your lifetime. The final sections of the book explore how to create generational wealth, ensuring that your success benefits future generations, and how to use your resources to make a lasting impact through philanthropy and purposeful giving.

Who This Book is For

This book is for anyone who desires financial transformation. Whether you are an aspiring entrepreneur, a professional seeking to optimize your financial position, or someone nearing retirement looking to secure your legacy, this book provides the tools and insights you need. You don't need to have a degree in finance or business to understand the concepts presented here. This book is written for individuals at all stages of their financial journey, from beginners to seasoned investors, with clear, actionable steps that demystify the complexities of wealth creation.

It is also important to note that wealth is not just about dollars and cents. The pursuit of abundance involves aligning your financial goals with your personal values, your relationships, and your life's purpose. *The Wealth Architect (Vol 2)* is as much about creating a fulfilling life as it is about growing your bank account.

A Blueprint for Lasting Abundance

Throughout this book, you will be presented with real-world examples, practical exercises, and proven strategies that have helped countless individuals move from financial insecurity to financial freedom. The goal is to fully equip you with the knowledge, tools, and mindset required to creating lasting wealth, no matter your starting point.

As you move forward, remember that the journey to abundance is not linear—it requires persistence, adaptability, and continuous learning which are all covered in this book. There will be challenges and setbacks along the way, but each obstacle presents an opportunity to learn, grow, and strengthen your financial foundation.

I invite you to embark on this great journey with an open mind and a commitment to take action. The principles outlined in this book and its companion-*The Wealth Architect (Vol 1)* have the unequivocal power to transform your financial future.

Ted Kiyosaki

Tallahassee-Florida.

30 January 2025.

FOREWORD

Wealth creation is a topic that transcends time, geography, and socioeconomic status. For centuries, people have sought to understand the secrets behind financial success, riches, and abundance. And yet, in today's modern age—where information is more accessible than ever before—many still find themselves grappling with the complexities of money. Some chase it without purpose, while others see it as a distant, unattainable goal. *The Wealth Architect (Vol 2): Building A Life of Unstoppable Riches* serves as a powerful antidote to this confusion, offering readers a clear, actionable path toward financial mastery.

When I was first introduced to this book, I immediately recognized its value—not just as a guide to accumulating wealth, but as a holistic roadmap to creating a life of purpose, security, and fulfillment. What sets this book apart is the author's profound understanding that true abundance goes beyond mere monetary gains. Abundance is a state of mind, a way of living, and a philosophy that encompasses financial well-being, personal growth, and the ability to positively impact the world around us.

In the pages that follow, you will find a wealth of knowledge that goes far beyond traditional financial advice. You will be introduced to principles that challenge conventional wisdom, urging you to think differently about money, riches, and wealth. The author expertly intertwines practical financial strategies with insights into the mindset and behaviors that are essential for achieving long-term prosperity. It is this combination of mindset, mechanics, and meaning that makes *The Wealth Architect (Vol 2)* a true roadmap to abundance.

The Journey to Financial Mastery

As someone who has spent decades working in the fields of finance, business, and wealth management, I have seen firsthand the transformative power that financial literacy can have on people's lives. I've witnessed individuals from all walks of life—those who once struggled to make ends meet—grow into financially secure, empowered individuals who use their resources to create impact and live meaningful lives. The journey to financial mastery is not an easy one, but it is one that is open to anyone willing to put in the work, make informed decisions, and stay committed to their goals.

What struck me most about this book is its ability to break down complex financial concepts into digestible, actionable steps. Whether you are just beginning your financial journey or are looking to refine and optimize your existing wealth strategies, the insights offered here will guide you toward making smart, informed decisions. This book doesn't just tell you what to do—it teaches you how to think about money in a way that will serve you for life.

More Than Money

What makes *The Wealth Architect (Vol 2)* truly unique is its acknowledgment that wealth, in its most meaningful form, goes beyond accumulating dollars. It delves into the importance of building a balanced, fulfilling life that aligns with your values, passions, and vision for the future. The author reminds us that wealth without purpose is hollow, and that true abundance involves nurturing relationships, maintaining physical and mental health, and creating opportunities for others.

In a world where the pursuit of wealth is often seen as a solitary or self-serving endeavor, this book brings a fresh perspective. It emphasizes the role of **legacy**—the impact we leave behind, the ways in which our wealth can benefit others, and how we can use our resources to foster positive change in our communities and beyond. The author urges you to think not only about how they can enrich their own lives, but also about how their success can be a force for good.

A Blueprint for the Modern World

The Wealth Architect (Vol 2) serves as the perfect companion to *(Vol 1)*, expanding on the foundational principles of wealth building with a clear, step-by-step approach to achieving financial independence. While *The Wealth Architect (Vol 1)* lays out the blueprint for constructing a life of unstoppable riches, *The Wealth Architect (Vol 2)* dives into the practical tools and strategies to help you take control of your finances, create lasting wealth and live life on your terms. Together, these books form a powerful duo that equips you with both the mindset and the roadmap for financial freedom.

The modern financial landscape is more complex than ever before. With the rise of digital currencies, global markets, and technological advancements, wealth creation has evolved into a multifaceted endeavor. For many, navigating this evolving terrain can feel overwhelming. *The Wealth Architect (Vol 2)* provides clarity in this complexity. It demystifies the noise, giving you a framework to understand and capitalize on new opportunities in today's financial world.

In particular, I found the chapters on financial technology (FinTech) and digital assets to be invaluable. As the world continues to move toward automation, artificial intelligence, and cryptocurrency, the need for financial adaptability and digital literacy becomes ever more apparent. This book offers a thoughtful exploration of these trends, equipping you with the tools you need to stay ahead in an increasingly digital economy.

The Author's Expertise

Throughout this book and its companion the author demonstrates a deep understanding of not only financial systems but also human behavior. Their unique approach draws from years of experience in finance, business, and personal development, and the results are books that are as much about wealth-building as they are about personal transformation. The author's expertise is evident in every chapter, from their knowledge of investment strategies to their insights on the psychology of money.

One of the book's greatest strengths is its focus on the **wealth mindset**. In a society where instant gratification often overshadows long-term thinking, the author encourages you to cultivate patience, resilience, and discipline. By focusing on mindset, the book teaches that financial success is not just a matter of luck or external circumstances—it is the result of intentional, strategic actions grounded in a solid understanding of one's goals and values.

A Path to True Abundance

It is often said that knowledge is power, but knowledge without action is meaningless. *The Wealth Architect (Vol 2)* empowers you to take actionable steps toward financial abundance, but it also serves as a reminder that wealth is a journey, not a destination. It is about building a life that is rich not only in financial resources but in purpose, relationships, and personal fulfillment.

As you get on this great journey through the pages of this amazing book, I encourage you to take your time with each concept and reflect on how it applies to your own lifespan. This is not a book to be skimmed or rushed through. It is a comprehensive guide meant to inspire thoughtful consideration and meaningful action.

In closing, I would like to offer my deepest gratitude to **Ted Kiyosaki** for creating such a transformative and impactful work. *The Wealth Architect (Vol 2)* has the potential to change lives—not just by teaching you how to accumulate money, but by showing you how to create a life of true abundance.

This is more than just a book about finances—it is a guide to a richer, more fulfilling existence.

Professor Mike Carnegie

Olympia, Washington

23 February 2025.

INTRODUCTION

Welcome to *The Wealth Architect (Vol 2)*, your guide to mastering the art of personal finance and creating a life of financial independence. This book was designed to provide the visionary blueprint for constructing lasting wealth and abundance. It takes a more granular approach, focusing on the actionable steps that will allow you to take control of your financial destiny.

In a world where financial freedom often feels elusive, this book will immensely equip you with a formula that simplifies complex concepts, breaks down barriers, and empowers you to make informed, strategic financial decisions. Whether you are just starting out or are well on your way to financial independence, this guide is designed to meet you where you are.

What You Will Gain from This Book

We will explore the essential pillars of wealth creation—earning, saving, investing, and protecting your assets—while also delving into the psychological, emotional, and behavioral aspects that so often determine success or failure in personal finance. Through practical strategies, real-life case studies, and clear financial tools, you will learn how to take ownership of your financial future, turning your dreams into actionable, achievable goals.

This book complements the broader philosophy of building unstoppable riches by focusing on day-to-day tactics, habits, and decisions. Here, you will learn not only how to grow your wealth, but how to maintain and multiply it in a sustainable way. With *The Wealth Architect (Vol 2)*, you won't just build wealth—you'll create a financial ecosystem that enables you to live on your own terms, free from worry and rich in opportunity.

The Path to Abundance

As you embark on this journey, remember: financial freedom is not just about accumulating money, but about creating the life you've always envisioned. This book will provide the roadmap, the tools, and the mindset to help you unlock that potential. Together with *The Wealth Architect (Vol 1)*, you now have everything you need to chart your course toward a life of wealth, control, and unbounded possibility.

As we continue this journey with in this path, you'll discover that the strategies within are not just theoretical frameworks, but practical tools that can be immediately applied to your financial life. This book delves deeper into the daily actions, habits, and systems that are essential for building and sustaining wealth, creating a solid foundation for long-term financial success. While *The Wealth Architect (Vol 1)* emphasizes the broader architecture of wealth-building, this companion book breaks down the "how" behind financial independence, helping you to take manageable steps toward a life of abundance.

One of the key distinctions that this book offers is its focus on financial empowerment—giving you the knowledge and confidence to make sound financial decisions. This includes a detailed look at budgeting systems that align with your goals, investment strategies that are tailored to your risk tolerance, and methods for controlling debt so that it doesn't control you. You'll also learn how to automate wealth-building habits, making financial success a natural outcome of your daily routine.

This book recognizes that wealth is personal. Financial freedom doesn't look the same for everyone. For some, it may mean early retirement, while for others, it's the ability to pursue passion projects without worrying about money. No matter your goals, this book will help you align your financial habits with the life you want to live. You'll gain clarity on your financial freedom number, establish clear savings targets, and learn how to structure your finances so that they support the lifestyle of your dreams.

At its core, it is about more than just managing money—it's about reclaiming your time and your choices. With each chapter, you'll become more adept at understanding financial principles, applying them to real-life situations, and achieving financial resilience in an ever-changing world. And as a complement to (*Vol 1)*, this book brings the bigger picture into sharper focus, transforming the pursuit of wealth into a purposeful and intentional journey.

By combining the visionary strategies of *the Vol 1* with the practical, actionable steps in this *Vol 2*, you'll be well-equipped to take charge of your finances and create the life you truly desire. Whether you're looking to escape the 9-to-5 grind, secure your family's financial future, or simply live with more freedom and choice, this formula will guide you every step of the way.

With this book in your hands, the path to financial freedom is no longer a distant dream—it is within reach. Now is the time to take control, start building, and unlock the extraordinary life that financial independence can offer.

CHAPTER ONE

ACHIEVING FINANCIAL FREEDOM

This chapter discusses financial independence and how to design a life where money works for you, rather than the other way around.

Defining Financial Freedom

- The difference between financial security, financial independence, and true freedom

Achieving financial freedom is a journey, but there are distinct stages along the way. Understanding the differences between **financial security**, **financial independence**, and **true financial freedom** is crucial for setting clear goals and knowing where you are on your path to financial empowerment. Each stage represents a different level of financial stability, autonomy, and personal freedom.

1. Financial Security: The Foundation of Stability

Financial security is the first step on the journey to financial freedom. It means having the financial resources to meet your basic needs without constant stress or uncertainty about your financial future. Financial security doesn't necessarily imply wealth, but it provides peace of mind that your essentials—such as housing, food, healthcare, and education—are covered, even in the event of a job loss or emergency.

Key Characteristics of Financial Security:

- Basic Needs Covered: You have enough income or savings to comfortably cover your essential living expenses—housing, utilities, food, transportation, and healthcare.

- Emergency Fund: You have an established emergency fund, typically covering 3-6 months of living expenses, which provides a cushion against unexpected financial setbacks such as job loss or medical emergencies.
- Debt Management: While you may still have some debt (e.g., a mortgage, car loan), it is manageable and does not significantly hinder your ability to meet monthly financial obligations.
- Income Reliability: You rely on a steady income, such as employment or other reliable income sources, to maintain your lifestyle.

Achieving Financial Security:

To achieve financial security, it's essential to focus on building a strong financial foundation. This includes creating a budget that aligns with your priorities, saving consistently, reducing high-interest debt, and creating an emergency fund to safeguard against unforeseen circumstances.

Importance of Financial Security:

Financial security provides peace of mind and a sense of control over your life. It’s a critical foundation because without financial security, any future pursuit of wealth or independence can be undermined by unexpected financial disruptions. It represents stability, and it's the foundation upon which the pursuit of greater financial independence is built.

2. Financial Independence: The Power of Choice

Financial independence is the next stage, and it represents having enough passive or semi-passive income streams to cover your expenses without being reliant on a paycheck or full-time employment. Financial independence gives you more autonomy over your life choices—whether that means continuing to work, pursuing personal passions, or simply enjoying more time with loved ones.

Key Characteristics of Financial Independence:

- Income Exceeds Expenses: You have enough passive income (e.g., investment returns, rental income, or dividends) to cover all your living expenses without having to rely on a job or active labor.
- Debt-Free or Low Debt: Financial independence typically involves being free of high-interest debt or significantly reducing liabilities, allowing your money to work for you rather than being tied up in obligations.
- Freedom to Choose Work: You may choose to work, but it's optional rather than a necessity. Employment becomes something you do for fulfillment, passion, or enjoyment, not because you need the paycheck.
- Future Security: You are prepared for future financial needs, such as healthcare in retirement or legacy planning, and have investments or income streams that ensure long-term financial sustainability.

Achieving Financial Independence:

To reach financial independence, individuals must focus on building passive income streams through smart investments, such as stocks, bonds, real estate, or business ventures. Controlling expenses, diversifying income, and adopting long-term financial planning strategies are crucial to reaching this milestone.

Importance of Financial Independence:

Financial independence is often seen as the ultimate goal for many individuals because it provides freedom from the financial constraints of traditional employment. It grants the luxury of choosing how to spend your time and resources, whether that means traveling, starting a new business, or simply living life on your terms. However, it's still a stage on the journey to true financial freedom, as it may require ongoing management of investments and finances.

3. True Financial Freedom: The Pinnacle of Wealth and Autonomy

True financial freedom represents the highest level of financial success and personal autonomy. It goes beyond simply having enough money to cover your living expenses—it means having the financial abundance to live a life without limits, to pursue passions, philanthropy, or even create a legacy, all without any financial stress or constraints. True financial freedom is often accompanied by a sense of purpose and fulfillment, where money is no longer a concern, and personal values and desires shape your life decisions.

Key Characteristics of True Financial Freedom:

- Abundance Beyond Needs: You have more than enough wealth to cover both your needs and desires, with significant financial flexibility to pursue any life goals without worry about the cost.
- Completely Debt-Free: You are entirely debt-free, including mortgages or other long-term obligations. Your assets generate wealth independently, and your lifestyle is fully self-sustaining.

- Unlimited Choices: True financial freedom means having the time, resources, and energy to pursue any opportunity, hobby, or philanthropic endeavor without the constraints of financial concerns. You can travel the world, start passion projects, or focus on personal growth.
- Generational Wealth: True financial freedom often involves creating and preserving wealth that extends beyond your lifetime, ensuring that future generations benefit from your financial success.
- Impact and Legacy: Many people who achieve true financial freedom focus on making a positive impact on the world through philanthropy, social entrepreneurship, or creating a lasting legacy.

Achieving True Financial Freedom:

Reaching this level involves not only maximizing passive income streams and investments but also carefully structuring your life around personal fulfillment. Wealth management, tax planning, and estate planning become important tools for ensuring that your assets continue to grow and serve your life's purpose, even into future generations.

Importance of True Financial Freedom:

True financial freedom is the ultimate goal for those who desire complete autonomy over their lives. It allows individuals to transcend financial concerns entirely and focus on making an impact, living authentically, and enjoying a life of purpose and meaning. At this stage, wealth becomes a tool for self-expression and contribution, rather than a necessity for survival.

Each stage—financial security, financial independence, and true financial freedom—represents a progressively greater degree of financial control, freedom, and flexibility. **Financial security** ensures stability and peace of mind by covering basic needs, while **financial independence** provides the ability to choose how you live without being tied to a paycheck. **True financial freedom**, the pinnacle, allows you to live life on your terms, free from any financial constraints, and to make a meaningful impact on the world.

Understanding these stages helps clarify where you are on the journey and what steps are needed to reach the next level. Financial freedom is not a one-size-fits-all concept—it is a deeply personal experience, shaped by individual goals, values, and ambitions. Whether your ultimate vision involves early retirement, global travel, or philanthropic endeavors, moving from financial security to true financial freedom requires discipline, planning, and the right mindset.

- How Much Is Enough? Calculating Your Financial Freedom Number

Achieving financial freedom starts with knowing exactly how much wealth is necessary to sustain the lifestyle you desire without the need to actively work for income. This crucial figure, often referred to as your "financial freedom number", represents the amount of money that, once accumulated, allows your investments and passive income to cover all of your living expenses indefinitely. Calculating this number requires a deep understanding of your financial goals, projected expenses, investment returns, and desired quality of life.

1. Defining Your Desired Lifestyle and Future Goals

The first step in determining your financial freedom number is TO understand the lifestyle you want to live once you reach financial independence. This includes everyday expenses, leisure activities, travel, healthcare, and even philanthropic or legacy goals. Your number will vary significantly based on your lifestyle choices, so it's essential to be honest about what you want and how much it will cost.

Assess Your Current and Future Living Expenses

Estimate your monthly and annual living expenses, factoring in both current and future needs. This should include:

- Housing: Mortgage or rent, property taxes, utilities, maintenance, and potential upgrades.
- Healthcare: Insurance premiums, medical expenses, long-term care, and wellness-related costs.
- Transportation: Car payments, fuel, public transport, maintenance, and future purchases.
- Food and groceries: Daily meals, dining out, and grocery shopping.
- Leisure and travel: Hobbies, vacations, and other activities that contribute to your quality of life.
- Miscellaneous expenses: Any additional costs such as education, insurance, taxes, or personal care.

It's crucial to forecast future costs, including inflation and possible changes in lifestyle, as these will impact your financial freedom number.

2. Estimating Passive Income Streams

To achieve financial freedom, your passive income streams—derived from investments, real estate, businesses, or other sources—should generate enough cash flow to cover your expenses. Estimate how much you expect to generate from various income sources:

- Investment returns: Dividends, capital gains, and interest from stocks, bonds, mutual funds, ETFs, and other assets.
- Real estate income: Rental income from properties, real estate investment trusts (REITs), or real estate partnerships.
- Business income: Profit from businesses or side ventures, especially if they continue to generate revenue with minimal involvement.
- Royalties and intellectual property: Income from books, patents, software, or other intellectual assets.
- Pension and social security: If you expect to receive pension payments or social security benefits, factor these into your passive income plan.

Your goal is to ensure that these streams can generate sufficient income over time to meet your desired living expenses.

3. Calculating Your Financial Freedom Number: The 25x Rule

One of the most widely used methods for calculating your financial freedom number is the **25x rule**. This formula estimates how much you need to have invested to generate a sustainable income that covers your annual expenses.

Formula:
Financial Freedom Number = Annual Expenses × 25

This rule is based on the **4% safe withdrawal rate**—the idea that you can safely withdraw 4% of your total investment portfolio each year without depleting your savings. For example, if your annual living expenses are $80,000, your financial freedom number would be:

$80,000 × 25 = $2,000,000

This means you would need to accumulate $2 million in assets to sustain a withdrawal rate of 4%, providing you with $80,000 per year indefinitely.

Adjusting for Risk and Variability

The 25 x rule assumes a moderate risk tolerance and investment returns. However, it's essential to account for factors like market volatility, inflation, and individual risk tolerance. If you prefer a more conservative approach, you may opt for a 30x multiple, or lower your withdrawal rate to 3.5% to reduce the risk of running out of money.

4. Factoring in Inflation and Market Volatility

When calculating your financial freedom number, it's critical to account for inflation, which can erode the purchasing power of your savings over time. A typical inflation rate of 2–3% annually means that expenses will rise, and your financial plan must accommodate this increase.

Adjusting for Inflation

If you expect annual expenses to rise due to inflation, consider adding an inflation adjustment to your financial freedom number. You can do this by estimating your expenses in today's dollars and then using a **future value calculation** to project how much you'll need in the future.

Formula:-
Future Value of Expenses = Current Expenses × (1 + inflation rate)^number of years

For example, if your current annual expenses are \$80,000, and you plan to retire in 20 years with an assumed inflation rate of 3%, the future value of your expenses will be:

\$80,000 × (1 + 0.03)^20 ≈ \$144,800

This means that you would need around \$144,800 per year in future dollars to maintain the same lifestyle. Using the 25x rule, this translates to a financial freedom number of **\$144,800 × 25 = \$3,620,000**.

5. Considering Longevity and Healthcare Costs

Another critical aspect of calculating your financial freedom number is accounting for potential **longevity** and increasing healthcare costs as you age. The longer you live, the more savings you will need to support yourself, particularly if healthcare expenses rise significantly.

Longevity Planning

Since you cannot predict exactly how long you will live, it is wise to plan for a long retirement, possibly up to 30 or 40 years. This requires not only building a robust investment portfolio but also having access to healthcare savings accounts, long-term care insurance, or other healthcare plans that mitigate out-of-pocket medical expenses.

Rising Healthcare Costs

Healthcare costs typically increase as people age, so it's essential to factor in these rising expenses. Consider strategies such as maximizing contributions to tax-advantaged healthcare accounts (such as HSAs) and including healthcare cost buffers in your overall financial freedom number.

6. Reviewing and Revising Your Financial Freedom Number

Your financial freedom number is not a static figure; it may change over time based on shifts in your income, lifestyle, or market conditions. It's important to **review and adjust** your plan regularly to stay on track.

Annual Financial Reviews

- Review and update your expenses and income projections annually.
- Reassess your investment portfolio to ensure it aligns with your financial freedom goals.
- Make adjustments based on changes in inflation rates, market performance, or lifestyle shifts.

Adapt to Life Changes

- Unexpected expenses (e.g., medical bills, emergencies) can require you to revise your financial freedom number upward.
- Lifestyle upgrades (e.g., luxury travel, second homes) may necessitate a larger financial cushion.
- Early retirement plans may require more aggressive saving and investing strategies to reach your financial freedom number sooner.

Calculating your financial freedom number is a critical step in achieving financial independence. By understanding your current and future expenses, factoring in inflation, and building diversified passive income streams, you can reach a point where your wealth works for you, allowing you to live the life you desire without financial worry. The key is to continually review, adjust, and refine your approach as you move closer to your financial goals.

- Aligning Lifestyle Goals with Financial Goals

Achieving true financial freedom involves more than simply accumulating wealth; it's about designing a lifestyle that reflects your values, aspirations, and personal well-being. This balance between lifestyle goals and financial goals is key to long-term satisfaction and fulfillment. Without alignment, even significant financial success may not translate into happiness or freedom.

1. Defining Lifestyle Goals

Your lifestyle goals encompass the vision of how you want to live, your personal aspirations, and what brings you joy and satisfaction. These could include:

- Travel and Experiences: If exploring new places or engaging in unique experiences is a priority, your financial planning should accommodate the cost of regular travel or adventurous activities.
- Work-Life Balance: Some people prioritize career growth, while others value more time for family, hobbies, or relaxation. Defining your work-life balance goals helps in determining how much you need to earn or invest to sustain the lifestyle you desire.
- Health and Wellness: For those who prioritize health and wellness, financial goals might involve allocating more resources to premium healthcare, fitness programs, or mental well-being activities.
- Family and Legacy: Lifestyle goals often include providing for family members, whether that means saving for children's education, planning family

vacations, or building a financial legacy for future generations.

2. Establishing Clear Financial Objectives

Financial goals are concrete targets related to wealth accumulation, financial security, and independence. To align them with your lifestyle, you should consider:

- Short-Term Goals: These could include buying a home, paying off debt, or saving for a large purchase (e.g., a car or vacation). Aligning these goals with your immediate lifestyle desires ensures your financial resources are focused on what matters most in the near term.
- Long-Term Goals: Retirement, achieving financial independence, or leaving a legacy are longer-term goals. Understanding the kind of lifestyle you want in retirement, for example, will help you set savings and investment targets that match your future aspirations.
- Emergency Funds and Financial Security: Building a robust safety net is crucial for peace of mind. Aligning this with lifestyle goals ensures that you have the right amount of liquidity to weather life's uncertainties without disrupting your quality of life.

3. Balancing Enjoyment with Delayed Gratification

It's essential to find a balance between enjoying life today and saving for the future. The concept of delayed gratification, where you sacrifice short-term pleasures for long-term benefits, is important but should not come at the cost of present fulfillment.

- Budget for Joy: Build a financial plan that allocates resources for both necessities and personal enjoyment. By budgeting for hobbies, entertainment, and experiences, you ensure that you're not missing out on life while still working towards financial independence.

- Investing in Experiences: Research shows that spending on experiences tends to bring more lasting happiness than spending on material possessions. Aligning your financial goals with this idea can help you prioritize meaningful experiences, whether it's travel, time with loved ones, or personal growth opportunities.

4. Aligning Your Spending Habits with Your Core Values

Lifestyle and financial alignment come down to how you manage your spending. Ask yourself:

- Are your daily and monthly expenses reflective of what truly matters to you?
- Are you spending on things that enhance your life, or do you find yourself buying items that offer little long-term value? Redirecting spending towards what aligns with your values ensures that you're using your financial resources in a way that maximizes happiness and fulfillment.

5. Setting Lifestyle-Compatible Financial Targets

- Defining Your "Enough": Calculating your financial freedom number involves understanding how much is enough to support your desired lifestyle. This could mean determining how much passive income you need, or what net worth allows you to live comfortably without the pressure of earning more.
- Lifestyle Inflation Awareness: As your income grows, it's easy to fall into the trap of lifestyle inflation—spending more as you earn more. To maintain alignment between financial and lifestyle

goals, be conscious of unnecessary upgrades and changes that don't align with your long-term values.

6. The Role of Financial Planning in Supporting Lifestyle Goals

Proper financial planning serves as the blueprint for aligning your financial means with your lifestyle desires. A comprehensive plan should include:

- Budgeting: Creating a budget that reflects your values and aspirations ensures that your money is going towards activities and goals that matter most to you.
- Investing for Growth: Investments that generate wealth over time allow you to support a lifestyle of freedom and independence. Whether it's through passive income streams, long-term investments, or business ventures, growing your assets are essential to sustaining your lifestyle.
- Flexibility in Plans: Life changes, and so do your goals. A flexible financial plan will allow you to adapt to new desires or priorities without derailing your path to financial freedom.

7. Revisiting and Reassessing Goals Periodically

Both lifestyle and financial goals should be revisited regularly to ensure they remain aligned. Major life events—such as marriage, having children, or career changes—often require adjustments in both your personal and financial plans. Continual alignment ensures that your financial progress supports your evolving vision of an ideal life.

Achieving financial freedom is not solely about accumulating wealth; it's about using that wealth to live the life you desire. Aligning lifestyle goals with financial objectives ensures that the effort you put into building financial security results in a life of purpose, satisfaction, and balance. By making intentional financial choices that reflect your values, you can create a sustainable pathway to both wealth and fulfillment.

Passive Income Strategies for Freedom

- Rental income, dividend stocks, royalties, and other passive income sources

Passive income refers to earnings generated with minimal effort or active involvement. These streams allow you to build wealth over time and achieve financial freedom, as they continue to flow even when you're not actively working. Establishing multiple sources of passive income is a critical element in reaching long-term financial independence. Let's explore key passive income strategies, including rental income, dividend stocks, royalties, and other opportunities.

1. Rental Income: Creating Wealth Through Real Estate

Rental income from real estate is one of the most well-known and effective methods of generating passive income. When structured correctly, it can provide a steady cash flow and long-term capital appreciation.

- ❖ Types of Rental Properties:
    - Residential properties: Single-family homes, multi-family units, or apartment buildings offer recurring monthly income, provided the property is rented.
    - Commercial properties: Leasing spaces to businesses can offer

longer-term leases and potentially higher returns, though the risks and capital requirements may also be greater.

- Vacation rentals: Platforms like Airbnb have enabled property owners to generate income through short-term rentals. These require more active management than long-term rentals but can generate significantly higher returns in the right markets.

❖ Advantages of Rental Income:

- Appreciation and Equity Building: Real estate tends to appreciate over time, allowing landlords to build equity in their properties while collecting rental income.
- Tax Benefits: Real estate investors can deduct expenses such as mortgage interest, property taxes, repairs, and depreciation from their taxable income.
- Inflation Hedge: Rental prices often rise with inflation, providing protection against rising costs and maintaining the real value of income.

❖ Considerations:

- Property Management: Managing rental properties can require significant time, especially if you have multiple units. Outsourcing to a property management company can

help make it more passive but will reduce your profits.
- Location Matters: Location significantly impacts rental demand and property appreciation. High-demand areas offer higher returns but often come with higher upfront costs.

2. Dividend Stocks: Earning While You Hold

Dividend stocks are a powerful form of passive income that allows investors to earn a share of company profits without selling their shares.

- What Are Dividend Stocks?:
  Dividend stocks represent shares of companies that distribute a portion of their profits to shareholders in the form of regular dividend payments. These payments are often made quarterly.
- Types of Dividend Stocks:
  - Blue-Chip Stocks: These are shares in large, established companies with a history of stable dividends. Examples include companies like Johnson & Johnson, Coca-Cola, and Procter & Gamble.
  - High-Yield Stocks: These offer higher dividend payouts but often come with greater risks. They are typically found in sectors like energy, utilities, and real estate.
  - Dividend Growth Stocks: These stocks come from companies that consistently increase their dividends

year after year, providing both income and potential capital gains.

- ❖ Advantages of Dividend Stocks:
    - o Regular Income: Investors can receive predictable income without selling their stocks, allowing for long-term wealth accumulation.
    - o Compounding Power: By reinvesting dividends back into additional shares, you can harness the power of compounding to grow your wealth exponentially over time.
    - o Tax Efficiency: Qualified dividends in many countries are taxed at lower rates than regular income, making them a tax-efficient source of passive income.
- ❖ Considerations:
    - o Market Volatility: Dividend payouts are not guaranteed, and in times of financial strain, companies may reduce or suspend dividends.
    - o Sector Concentration: Many high-dividend companies come from a few sectors like energy or utilities. Over-reliance on one sector can expose investors to heightened risks.

3. Royalties: Earning from Intellectual Property

Royalties provide another source of passive income, particularly for those involved in creative or intellectual property fields.

- What Are Royalties?:
  Royalties are payments made to individuals or businesses for the ongoing use of their intellectual property. This could include works of art, music, books, patents, or software.
- Types of Royalties:-
  - Book Royalties: Authors earn royalties when their books are sold, whether through traditional publishers or self-publishing platforms like Amazon Kindle Direct Publishing.
  - Music Royalties: Musicians earn royalties whenever their music is played, purchased, streamed, or used commercially.
  - Patent Royalties: Inventors or patent holders earn royalties when companies use their patented technology or processes in production.
  - Franchise Royalties: Franchise owners receive royalties from franchisees who pay for the right to use their brand, products, or business systems.
- Advantages of Royalties:
  - Long-Term Income: Once intellectual property is created, it can generate income for years or even decades, with little to no ongoing effort from the creator.
  - Scalability: Intellectual property can be sold or licensed multiple times

without additional cost, allowing for scalable income.

- Considerations:
    - Upfront Effort: While royalties can generate passive income over time, creating intellectual property (like writing a book or developing a product) requires significant upfront effort.
    - Market Saturation: Intellectual property must remain valuable over time, and in some cases, royalties may diminish if market trends change or if the intellectual property becomes less relevant.

4. Other Passive Income Sources

In addition to rental income, dividends, and royalties, there are numerous other passive income opportunities that can contribute to long-term financial freedom.

- Peer-to-Peer Lending: Through peer-to-peer lending platforms, individuals can lend money to others and earn interest on the loans. This allows for diversification of passive income streams, though it comes with default risk.
- Affiliate Marketing: Affiliate marketing allows individuals to earn commissions by promoting other companies' products online. This is common among bloggers, influencers, and content creators who have established an audience.
- Automated Online Businesses: E-commerce platforms, drop-shipping

businesses, or subscription-based services can be highly automated, providing recurring income without active daily involvement.

- REITs (Real Estate Investment Trusts): REITs allow individuals to invest in large-scale real estate portfolios without directly owning property. They pay out regular dividends, making them a passive income source similar to dividend stocks.

5. Creating a Passive Income Portfolio

Building a robust passive income portfolio involves diversifying your income sources across different asset types and investment vehicles. This diversification helps reduce risk and ensure that income continues to flow even if one source is affected by economic shifts.

- Diversification: Spreading passive income streams across real estate, stocks, intellectual property, and peer-to-peer lending can ensure financial stability.
- Reinvestment: A key strategy for growing passive income is reinvesting earnings from one source into other income-generating assets. For example, dividends from stocks can be reinvested into rental properties or additional stocks.
- Long-Term Focus: Passive income strategies often take time to build. They require upfront investment—whether that's money, time, or intellectual capital—but with patience, they can create financial independence and freedom.

Passive income sources such as rental income, dividend stocks, royalties, and other streams play a significant role in achieving financial freedom. These strategies, when employed thoughtfully, provide ongoing income, build wealth, and reduce reliance on active labor. By diversifying income streams, automating where possible, and continually reinvesting returns, individuals can establish a sustainable path to long-term financial independence.

- Steps to Transition from Active to Passive Income Reliance

Transitioning from reliance on active income—where you trade time for money—to passive income, where your investments and assets generate income with minimal day-to-day involvement, is a key step toward financial freedom. This shift requires a strategic approach, disciplined financial management, and patience to build a sustainable income portfolio. Below are the critical steps involved in transitioning from active to passive income reliance.

1. Evaluate Your Current Financial Position

Before starting the transition to passive income, it is essential to assess your current financial standing. Understanding where you are financially will allow you to create a clear roadmap for your transition.

- ❖ Calculate Net Worth: Assess your assets (savings, investments, real estate) minus your liabilities (debts, loans) to determine your net worth. This provides a baseline for your financial health.
- ❖ Analyze Cash Flow: Review your monthly income versus expenses. Determine how much disposable income you can allocate toward building passive income streams.

- Review Debt Obligations: Paying down high-interest debt should be a priority before moving to passive income strategies. Reducing debt improves your cash flow and reduces financial risk.

2. Set Clear Financial Goals

To successfully shift to passive income reliance, you need clear, actionable goals. These goals will guide your investment strategy and help you stay focused on the long-term vision.

- Define Your Passive Income Target: Calculate how much passive income you need to cover your basic living expenses, including housing, food, transportation, and lifestyle preferences. This is the foundation of financial independence.
- Establish a Timeline: Set realistic time frames for achieving your passive income goals. Consider how much you can invest monthly and how long it will take for your passive income to match or exceed your active income.
- Break Down Milestones: Break your larger passive income goals into smaller, manageable milestones. For example, you might aim to replace 20% of your active income within the first two years and 50% within five years.

3. Start Building Passive Income Streams Alongside Active Income

The best time to start building passive income streams is while you are still relying on active income. This reduces the pressure on your passive investments and allows you to reinvest profits.

- Invest in Dividend-Paying Stocks: Begin by investing in reliable, dividend-paying stocks that provide a regular income stream. Dividend reinvestment can significantly accelerate wealth accumulation over time.
- Explore Real Estate Opportunities: If possible, invest in rental properties or Real Estate Investment Trusts (REITs) for stable cash flow. Starting small with residential properties can help you gain experience before expanding into larger investments.
- Monetize Skills Through Intellectual **Property**: If you have specialized knowledge or creative skills, consider creating content that generates royalties. This could include writing a book, developing an online course, or licensing software.
- Automate and Outsource: Consider building online businesses that can be automated or outsourced, such as e-commerce, drop-shipping, or affiliate marketing. These ventures require an upfront time investment but can generate passive income once established.

4. Reinvest Passive Income to Accelerate Growth

In the early stages of building passive income, reinvesting earnings is crucial to accelerating growth. Reinvestment enables you to compound returns and build multiple streams of income.

- Dividend Reinvestment: Use dividend reinvestment plans (DRIPs) to automatically reinvest dividends into purchasing additional shares, which further increases future dividend payments.

- ❖ Real Estate Reinvestment: Any surplus rental income after expenses should be reinvested into property improvements or saved for purchasing additional properties. This increases the value of your assets and boosts long-term cash flow.
- ❖ Scale Intellectual Property: Expand the reach of intellectual property like online courses or digital products by reinvesting profits into marketing, advertising, or additional content creation to boost sales.

5. Diversify Your Passive Income Portfolio

Diversification is key to reducing risk and ensuring consistent passive income. By spreading your investments across different assets, you can protect against market fluctuations and income interruptions.

- ❖ Real Estate: Diversify by investing in various types of properties—residential, commercial, vacation rentals—or through REITs. Diversification across markets can also provide protection against local downturns.
- ❖ Stock Market: Balance your portfolio with a mix of high-yield dividend stocks, index funds, bonds, and growth stocks. Consider low-cost exchange-traded funds (ETFs) for broad market exposure and reduced risk.
- ❖ Peer-to-Peer Lending and Crowdfunding: Consider diversifying into peer-to-peer lending platforms or real estate crowdfunding, where small investments are pooled to finance loans or properties.

These offer attractive returns, though they carry more risk.

- ❖ Business Income: If you own a business or side hustle, ensure it doesn't rely on one single product, service, or market. This can help maintain a stable cash flow even when some areas experience a downturn.

6. Systematize and Automate Your Passive Income

As your passive income grows, it's important to automate processes to minimize the time spent managing these income streams. Automation frees you from day-to-day involvement, allowing you to truly experience the freedom passive income offers.

- ❖ Automate Investments: Set up automated monthly contributions to your brokerage or retirement accounts. Automating your investments ensures consistent growth without relying on manual transactions.
- ❖ Hire Property Managers: For real estate investments, hiring a property management company allows you to outsource tenant management, repairs, and rent collection, making your rental income more passive.
- ❖ Outsource Business Operations: If you have a side business, consider hiring virtual assistants, marketing professionals, or freelancers to handle routine operations. This allows you to focus on scaling the business rather than running it day-to-day.

7. Transition Gradually to Passive Income Reliance

Transitioning from active to passive income should be a gradual process. As your passive income streams increase, you can begin to reduce your reliance on active income sources. This shift can happen over several years, depending on your goals and financial situation.

- Maintain a Balance Between Active and Passive Income: Don't rush to quit your job or active income source until you have sufficient passive income to cover your living expenses. Continue reinvesting passive income for further growth.
- Track Your Progress: Regularly review your passive income growth and compare it to your financial goals. If necessary, adjust your strategy or timeline to ensure you stay on track.
- Reduce Active Income Gradually: As your passive income increases, consider transitioning to part-time work or taking on fewer clients in your business. This allows for a smoother transition while still maintaining some active income.

8. Achieve Financial Freedom with Passive Income

Once your passive income covers your living expenses and exceeds your active income, you've achieved financial freedom. This milestone allows you to fully transition away from active work if desired, focusing on lifestyle, personal goals, or further wealth-building pursuits.

- Live Off Passive Income: At this stage, you can live entirely off your passive income streams. Continue to monitor your investments and diversify to protect against risk.
- Pursue Passion Projects: With financial freedom, you can pursue personal

interests, travel, or philanthropic ventures without worrying about income generation.

- Legacy Planning: Consider estate planning and succession strategies to ensure that your wealth is preserved and passed down to future generations.

Transitioning from active to passive income reliance is a strategic, long-term process that requires planning, discipline, and diversification. By building multiple streams of passive income, reinvesting profits, and gradually reducing your reliance on active income, you can achieve financial freedom. Automation and outsourcing play a key role in making this transition seamless, allowing you to enjoy the benefits of a self-sustaining income without being tied to daily work.

- Maintaining Wealth Once Financial Freedom is Achieved

Achieving financial freedom through passive income streams is a significant milestone, but maintaining that wealth requires consistent effort, discipline, and a strategic mindset. While reaching financial freedom allows for greater flexibility and lifestyle choices, it also comes with the responsibility of ensuring that the wealth generated is preserved, protected, and continues to grow over time. Below are the key strategies for maintaining wealth once financial freedom is achieved.

1. Diversify Your Income Streams

Diversification is crucial not only for building wealth but also for maintaining it. Once financial freedom is achieved, relying on just one or two sources of passive income could expose you to undue risk, particularly if market conditions shift.

- Expand Income Sources: Continuously explore new avenues to diversify income streams. This can include real estate investments, dividend-paying stocks, peer-to-peer lending, royalties, and other alternative investment options.
- Invest in Various Asset Classes: Spread your investments across different asset classes, such as stocks, bonds, real estate, and commodities. This ensures that if one market faces downturns, your overall wealth remains protected by other more stable or countercyclical investments.
- Geographical Diversification: Consider diversifying across different geographical regions. Investments in international markets can protect your wealth from localized economic downturns and provide opportunities in emerging economies.

2. Regularly Rebalance Your Portfolio

Wealth preservation involves actively managing and rebalancing your investment portfolio to align with evolving financial goals and market conditions. Rebalancing helps maintain an optimal balance between risk and return.

- Review Asset Allocation: Periodically assess your asset allocation to ensure it aligns with your risk tolerance and financial objectives. As you age or your financial situation changes, it might be wise to shift from higher-risk investments (such as equities) to more conservative ones (such as bonds).
- Capture Gains and Reinforce Stability: Rebalancing allows you to capture gains

from outperforming assets and reinvest them into underperforming or stable assets. This helps maintain portfolio stability and capitalize on market opportunities.

3. Implement a Solid Tax Strategy

Minimizing tax liabilities is critical for maintaining wealth. Without a well-designed tax strategy, capital gains, dividends, and other forms of passive income can be heavily taxed, diminishing your wealth over time.

- Tax-Advantaged Accounts: Utilize tax-advantaged accounts such as Individual Retirement Accounts (IRAs), 401(k)s, or Roth IRAs to grow your investments tax-free or tax-deferred. This allows your investments to compound more efficiently.
- Optimize Tax Harvesting: Tax-loss harvesting can offset gains from other investments, reducing your overall tax burden. This strategy involves selling investments at a loss to balance out taxable gains.
- Utilize Trusts and Estate Planning: For long-term wealth preservation, consider setting up trusts or charitable donations to reduce tax exposure and ensure that wealth is passed to future generations without being eroded by taxes.

4. Protect Against Inflation

Inflation is a silent threat to long-term wealth. If your investments do not outpace inflation, the purchasing power of your wealth will diminish over time.

- Invest in Inflation-Protected Securities: Consider allocating part of your portfolio to Treasury Inflation-Protected Securities (TIPS) or other inflation-linked bonds that rise with inflation, ensuring your wealth retains its value.
- Real Estate as an Inflation Hedge: Real estate is often seen as a hedge against inflation because property values and rental income tend to increase with inflation, helping to protect purchasing power.
- Diversify into Commodities: Commodities like gold, oil, and agricultural products also tend to perform well during inflationary periods and can serve as a safeguard against inflation-driven depreciation of currency.

5. Adopt a Conservative Withdrawal Strategy

After reaching financial freedom, determining how much to withdraw from your investments while maintaining the longevity of your wealth is critical.

- Use the 4% Rule: A conservative rule of thumb is to withdraw no more than 4% of your investment portfolio annually. This is designed to ensure that your portfolio lasts throughout your lifetime, even with inflation.
- Adjust Withdrawals Based on Market Conditions: In years of economic downturn or poor portfolio performance, consider reducing your withdrawal amount to avoid depleting your principal. During boom years, you can withdraw slightly more, but be mindful of preserving long-term capital.
- Maintain a Cash Buffer: Keep a portion of your wealth in easily accessible cash or

liquid assets to cover living expenses and emergencies. This allows you to avoid selling long-term investments at inopportune times.

6. Keep Emergency Funds in Place

Even with substantial passive income and diversified investments, maintaining a solid emergency fund is vital. Economic or personal crises can arise, and having a financial safety net ensures that you can weather these without tapping into long-term investments.

- ❖ Reassess Emergency Fund Size: After achieving financial freedom, your emergency fund may need to be larger to account for a higher lifestyle cost or greater investment exposure. Ensure the fund covers 6–12 months of living expenses.
- ❖ Separate Emergency Funds from Investments: Keep emergency funds in a separate, easily accessible account. Avoid using these funds for high-risk or illiquid investments, as they are meant to protect against immediate financial needs.

7. Continue Building Passive Income

Reaching financial freedom doesn't mean stopping the pursuit of more income. Continuously seeking new opportunities to increase passive income streams helps maintain financial security and growth.

- ❖ Reinvest Surplus Income: Even after reaching your financial freedom target, reinvest a portion of your passive income to grow your wealth further. This could be in the form of real estate acquisitions, dividend-paying stocks, or other passive income-generating assets.

- ❖ Consider Passive Business Ventures: Explore more passive forms of entrepreneurship, such as franchising or buying into businesses that don't require day-to-day involvement. These ventures can add to your income streams while diversifying your assets.

8. Monitor Expenses and Avoid Lifestyle Inflation

Maintaining wealth is not just about managing investments but also about controlling spending. One of the biggest threats to lasting financial freedom is lifestyle inflation, where increased wealth leads to higher spending that outpaces income.

- ❖ Create a Realistic Spending Plan: Even with significant wealth, having a budget ensures that your spending remains in check. Review expenses regularly and identify any unnecessary costs that can be minimized without sacrificing quality of life.
- ❖ Avoid Debt Accumulation: After achieving financial freedom, it's important to avoid accumulating unnecessary consumer debt, which can erode your financial position. Continue prioritizing debt-free living unless leveraging debt strategically for investments.

9. Safeguard Wealth with Insurance

Preserving wealth also requires safeguarding it from unforeseen risks such as accidents, lawsuits, or health issues. Proper insurance coverage is essential in mitigating these risks.

- Life and Health Insurance: Ensure that you and your dependents are covered by adequate life and health insurance to protect against costly medical bills or the financial impact of unexpected loss.
- Property and Liability Insurance: Protect your assets—homes, businesses, vehicles—with appropriate insurance coverage. Additionally, consider umbrella liability insurance to cover any claims that exceed the limits of your other insurance policies.
- Long-Term Care Insurance: As you age, long-term care insurance can protect your wealth from the potentially significant cost of nursing homes, assisted living, or in-home care.

10. Develop an Estate Plan to Protect Generational Wealth

Once you've achieved financial freedom, the next step is ensuring that your wealth is preserved for future generations. Estate planning is key to avoiding legal complications, minimizing taxes, and ensuring that your heirs can effectively manage the wealth you've built.

- Create a Will and Trusts: A will and trusts can ensure that your assets are transferred to your beneficiaries according to your wishes. Trusts can also help reduce tax liabilities and protect assets from creditors.
- Educate the Next Generation: Preparing your heirs for wealth management is crucial. Teach them the principles of financial literacy, investing, and wealth preservation to ensure that they can

effectively manage the inheritance and continue the legacy.

Maintaining wealth after achieving financial freedom requires ongoing discipline, careful risk management, and strategic diversification. By continuously managing income streams, minimizing risks, protecting against inflation, and focusing on long-term goals, you can preserve and grow your wealth for the future. Additionally, safeguarding your wealth through insurance, estate planning, and proper tax strategies ensures that your financial success can be passed on to future generations, allowing you to truly enjoy the freedom you've worked hard to achieve.

CHAPTER TWO

LEGACY AND GENERATIONAL WEALTH

This chapter focuses on building a legacy that lasts, with an emphasis on transferring wealth across generations.

Teaching Financial Literacy to Your Next Generation

Empowering the Next Generation: Teaching Kids about Money

- The role of financial education within families

Financial education is one of the most powerful tools that families can use to empower future generations and ensure long-term financial stability. Teaching financial literacy to children and young adults not only equips them with the skills needed to manage money responsibly, but it also lays the foundation for creating generational wealth, instilling a sense of financial independence, and fostering disciplined habits. The role of financial education within families is pivotal, as it directly influences how young individuals perceive, manage, and grow their finances throughout their lives.

1. Establishing Core Financial Values and Habits Early

- ❖ Instilling the Value of Money: Financial education within families helps children understand the value of money from an early age. Lessons on budgeting, saving, and distinguishing between wants and needs teach them the importance of prioritizing spending and avoiding wasteful behaviors.
- ❖ Developing Healthy Financial Habits: Just as daily habits shape overall lifestyle, financial habits shape a person's financial future. Parents can model and instill positive financial habits, such as setting aside money for savings or investments regularly, delaying gratification, and making thoughtful purchases.
- ❖ Avoiding Common Pitfalls: Financial mistakes such as overspending, accumulating debt, or neglecting savings can easily be avoided when financial education starts at home. Families play a key role in teaching children how to make informed financial decisions, reducing the likelihood of costly errors later in life.

2. Building a Strong Financial Foundation for Future Independence

- ❖ Basic Financial Skills: Teaching children basic financial skills such as creating a budget, managing a bank account, and understanding credit cards are essential for their financial independence. These skills provide the practical tools needed to navigate the financial systems they will encounter as adults.

- ❖ Understanding Financial Responsibility: By giving children an allowance, involving them in family financial decisions, or encouraging them to earn their own money, parents can teach the responsibility that comes with managing finances. This early exposure fosters an understanding of work and reward and helps children appreciate the effort that goes into earning money.
- ❖ Goal Setting and Planning: Financial education can teach young individuals to set financial goals—whether saving for a toy as a child or a college fund as a teenager—and make plans to achieve them. Understanding the process of setting and achieving financial goals sets the groundwork for more complex financial planning in the future, such as buying a home or investing for retirement.

3. Promoting Financial Discipline and Delayed Gratification

- ❖ Understanding the Importance of Saving: One of the key lessons of financial literacy is the value of saving. Children who learn the importance of saving early on are better equipped to handle financial challenges in adulthood. Parents can emphasize the importance of saving a portion of allowances or income, illustrating how savings can accumulate over time.
- ❖ Encouraging Delayed Gratification: Financial education teaches children to delay immediate gratification in favor of long-term benefits, a crucial skill for wealth

building. Whether saving for a larger purchase or avoiding debt by waiting until they can afford something, this principle fosters patience and long-term financial thinking.

- ❖ Managing Temptation: In a consumer-driven society, it is easy to fall into the trap of impulse buying or living beyond one's means. By teaching financial discipline, families can help children resist the temptation to overspend and make impulsive financial decisions.

4. Introducing the Concepts of Investing and Wealth Growth

- ❖ Teaching the Power of Compounding: Introducing young people to the concept of compounding interest can transform their understanding of wealth creation. Financial education helps children understand that investing early can lead to significant growth in their wealth over time, reinforcing the importance of saving and investing regularly.
- ❖ Exploring Investment Options: Financial education within families can introduce children to basic investment vehicles such as savings accounts, stocks, and bonds. By exposing them to these concepts early, families can spark an interest in investing and wealth growth, allowing young adults to develop a more advanced financial strategy as they age.
- ❖ Risk and Reward in Investing: Educating children about the risks and rewards associated with investing encourages them to make informed decisions. Teaching them to balance risk through diversification and

to focus on long-term gains rather than quick profits promotes a healthier financial mindset.

5. Preparing for Financial Challenges and Emergencies

- ❖ Building an Emergency Fund: One of the most important lessons financial education provides is the need for an emergency fund. Families can emphasize the importance of having financial resources available to handle unexpected expenses, whether it's a medical emergency, car repair, or job loss. This prepares young people for financial resilience in challenging times.
- ❖ Teaching Risk Management: Financial education should also include lessons on risk management. Children and young adults can learn about insurance, the importance of mitigating financial risks, and the role of preparing for uncertain events. This knowledge empowers them to make wise decisions in adulthood.
- ❖ Developing a Plan for Debt Management: Educating young individuals on responsible borrowing and the dangers of high-interest debt can prevent them from falling into the debt trap. Understanding how debt works, the cost of interest, and strategies for paying off loans are vital lessons that help children manage financial challenges more effectively.

6. Shaping an Entrepreneurial and Wealth-Building Mindset

- Encouraging Entrepreneurship: Financial education within families can foster an entrepreneurial spirit by encouraging children to think creatively about how to generate income. Whether it's starting a small business, selling products, or offering services, these early experiences can ignite a lifelong entrepreneurial mindset.
- Teaching Wealth-Building Strategies: Financial literacy is not just about managing money but about growing wealth. Families can teach children how to leverage different financial instruments, like investments, real estate, or even starting a business, to build long-term wealth. This shifts the focus from simply earning a salary to creating multiple streams of income and building generational wealth.
- Instilling a Growth Mindset: Financial education also includes teaching children the importance of continued learning, adaptability, and resilience in the face of challenges. Developing a growth mindset helps children see financial setbacks as opportunities for growth rather than failures, encouraging them to take calculated risks and pursue new ventures.

7. Creating a Legacy of Financial Responsibility

- Passing on Financial Values: The role of financial education within families goes beyond immediate learning; it is about creating a legacy of financial responsibility that can be passed down to future generations. When parents model good financial behavior and teach their children to do the same, they instill values that can be carried forward to benefit their descendants.

- ❖ Wealth Preservation Across Generations: Families that prioritize financial education can ensure that their wealth is preserved and grown across multiple generations. Teaching children about estate planning, trusts, and responsible inheritance management ensures that the wealth created by one generation is not lost by the next.
- ❖ Encouraging Charitable Giving and Social Responsibility: Financial education within families can also instill a sense of social responsibility. By teaching children about charitable giving, philanthropy, and the importance of contributing to their communities, families can foster not just personal wealth but also a culture of generosity and social impact.

8. Promoting Open Financial Discussions and Transparency

- ❖ Encouraging Open Conversations About Money: Financial education within families can be strengthened by fostering open discussions about money. Parents who are transparent about their financial decisions, including successes and failures, create an environment where children feel comfortable asking questions and learning from real-life examples.
- ❖ Demystifying Financial Concepts: Many financial topics—such as taxes, investments, and retirement planning—can

seem overwhelming or abstract to young individuals. By regularly discussing these concepts at home, families can help break down complex financial ideas into simpler, more understandable terms. This proactive approach demystifies financial management and makes it accessible for all family members.

- ❖ Collaborative Financial Planning: Families can engage children in financial decision-making processes, from planning vacations within a budget to discussing household expenses. This collaborative approach teaches responsibility and encourages children to think critically about money management, reinforcing the importance of budgeting, saving, and investing as family-wide values.

9. Leveraging Technology for Financial Literacy

- ❖ Using Financial Apps and Tools: Today's digital tools can play a significant role in teaching financial literacy. Parents can introduce their children to financial management apps that track spending, savings, and investments, offering hands-on learning experiences. These tools provide real-time insights and foster active engagement with personal finances.
- ❖ Online Resources and Courses: In addition to family-led financial education, parents can leverage online resources to teach financial literacy. From webinars to online courses on investing, saving, and budgeting, these platforms offer a wealth of knowledge. Encouraging children and young adults to engage with these

resources allows them to take ownership of their financial education.

- ❖ Simulating Real-World Financial Scenarios: Families can use technology to simulate real-world financial scenarios, such as budgeting for a large purchase, comparing investment returns, or creating mock portfolios. These exercises allow young individuals to apply their financial knowledge in a risk-free environment, helping them develop confidence in making financial decisions.

10. Preparing for Financial Independence in Adulthood

- ❖ Teaching Debt Management Skills: As young adults prepare for independence, families should emphasize the importance of managing debt responsibly. Lessons on student loans, mortgages, and credit card use can help individuals navigate common financial milestones without falling into harmful debt cycles. Understanding how to balance borrowing with repayment is crucial for maintaining financial health.
- ❖ Encouraging Early Investment in Retirement Funds: One of the most impactful lessons families can teach is the value of early retirement planning. By encouraging children to open retirement accounts such as IRAs or 401(k)s as soon as they start earning, families can help them take advantage of compound interest over time, securing their financial future.
- ❖ Guiding the Transition to Independent Budgeting: As children move into adulthood, transitioning from a family-supported budget to managing their own income and expenses can be a challenge.

Parents can guide this transition by helping young adults set realistic budgets based on their earnings, savings goals, and living expenses, ensuring that financial independence starts on a strong footing.

Financial education within families is one of the most powerful tools for empowering future generations. By teaching children about money management, investing, saving, and the importance of financial responsibility, families ensure that wealth is not only accumulated but preserved and grown over time. A strong foundation in financial literacy equips young individuals with the skills they need to achieve financial independence, build generational wealth, and navigate the complex financial landscape with confidence. By instilling these values early and promoting continuous learning, families can create a lasting legacy of financial success for generations to come.

- Practical Strategies for Raising Financially Responsible Children

Raising financially responsible children is a vital aspect of ensuring their long-term success and independence. Instilling sound money management habits at an early age helps children develop the necessary skills and mindset to make informed financial decisions throughout their lives. Below are practical strategies to teach financial responsibility to the next generation.

1. Start with Age-Appropriate Financial Concepts

- Introduce Basic Concepts Early: Teaching children about money doesn't have to wait until they're adults. Simple concepts, such as identifying coins, understanding that money is exchanged for goods and services, and recognizing the value of saving, can be introduced as early as kindergarten.

- Gradual Introduction to Complex Topics: As children grow older, parents can gradually introduce more complex financial topics, such as budgeting, the importance of investing, and how debt works. Tailoring financial education to each child's age and maturity level ensures that they build a solid foundation over time.

2. Teach the Value of Work and Earning Money

- Encourage Earning through Chores and Jobs: Giving children the opportunity to earn their own money through age-appropriate jobs, such as household chores, neighborhood tasks (mowing lawns, walking dogs), or part-time work for older teens, teaches them the value of work. Earning their own money helps children understand that income comes as a result of effort and responsibility.
- Create a Connection between Effort and Rewards: Parents can emphasize that the amount of money earned is tied to the quality or quantity of work performed. This helps children learn the importance of diligence, reliability, and performance in financial success.

3. Introduce Budgeting Early On

- Use Allowances as a Teaching Tool: One of the simplest ways to teach financial responsibility is through the use of an allowance. Giving children a set amount of money each week or month and encouraging them to budget for desired purchases, savings, and donations helps them practice managing their own money.

- ❖ Separate Money into Categories: Parents can teach children to divide their allowance or earnings into categories such as saving, spending, and giving. For example, setting aside 10% for savings, 10% for charitable giving, and the rest for discretionary spending. This introduces the concept of budgeting, prioritizing financial goals, and living within one's means.

4. Teach the Importance of Saving

- ❖ Open a Savings Account: Parents can help children open a savings account as early as possible. Watching their savings grow over time fosters a sense of accomplishment and encourages responsible saving habits.
- ❖ Incentivize Saving: To make saving more appealing, parents can offer to match a percentage of the money saved, turning it into a fun challenge. This can also introduce children to the concept of interest and compounding, giving them a real-world lesson on the power of long-term savings growth.

5. Introduce Goal Setting and Delayed Gratification

- ❖ Encourage Setting Short- and Long-Term Goals: Teaching children to save for specific goals—whether it's a toy they want or a larger purchase such as a bike—helps them understand the value of delayed gratification. It also teaches them how to prioritize their financial goals and make decisions based on the future rather than instant gratification.

- ❖ Demonstrate the Rewards of Waiting: Parents can show children how patience pays off by helping them track their progress toward financial goals. Seeing their savings grow and eventually reach their goal reinforces the positive aspects of saving and delaying unnecessary spending.

6. Explain the Concept of Needs vs. Wants

- ❖ Help Children Differentiate between Needs and Wants: Teaching children to distinguish between essential expenses (needs) and non-essential purchases (wants) is a critical life skill. Encouraging them to think before making a purchase helps them develop a thoughtful approach to spending.
- ❖ Use Real-Life Examples: Parents can explain their own financial decisions in terms of needs and wants. For instance, discussing why the family chooses to save for future expenses rather than spending money on luxury items demonstrates financial discipline and planning.

7. Introduce the Concept of Investing

- ❖ Explain the Basics of Investing: As children grow older, parents can introduce the basics of investing. Concepts such as risk, reward, and the importance of time in building wealth can be explained in simple terms. Parents can also simulate investment scenarios using mock portfolios or through stock market games, giving children hands-on experience.

- ❖ Encourage Long-Term Thinking: Teaching children that investments are long-term commitments helps them understand the value of patience and strategic financial planning. Showing them how investments grow over time, even with ups and downs, reinforces the importance of holding onto assets and thinking beyond short-term gains.

8. Teach About Responsible Borrowing and Debt

- ❖ Explain the Costs of Borrowing: As children become teenagers and start using credit cards or borrowing money, it's essential to teach them about responsible borrowing. Discuss how interest rates work and the potential pitfalls of accumulating debt. Real-life examples can be used to illustrate how borrowing can either help or hurt one's financial health depending on how it's managed.
- ❖ Demonstrate the Impact of Credit Scores: Explaining how borrowing decisions impact credit scores, and how credit scores affect financial opportunities, is critical for young adults as they prepare for major life expenses, such as buying a home or car. Understanding the importance of maintaining a good credit score will help them manage their debt responsibly.

9. Lead by Example

- ❖ Model Responsible Financial Behavior: Children learn by watching their parents.

Leading by example—whether through saving, budgeting, or discussing financial goals—will have a significant impact on their understanding of financial responsibility. Demonstrating healthy money habits in everyday life reinforces the lessons being taught.

- Discuss Family Financial Decisions: Parents can involve their children in family financial discussions, explaining how certain financial decisions are made. This transparency helps children understand the reasoning behind financial choices and how to balance short-term and long-term goals.

10. Encourage Financial Independence

- Give Responsibility for Personal Expenses: As children become older, parents can encourage financial independence by giving them responsibility for managing certain personal expenses, such as clothing, entertainment, or mobile phone bills. This teaches them the importance of managing money carefully and prioritizing needs over wants.
- Support Entrepreneurial Efforts: Encouraging children to start small businesses, such as selling crafts, tutoring, or mowing lawns, fosters an entrepreneurial mindset. It also teaches them valuable skills such as customer service, cost management, and profitability, laying the foundation for future financial independence.

11. Use Real-Life Financial Simulations

- Financial Simulations and Games: Using financial board games, apps, or simulations can make learning about money fun and engaging. Games like Monopoly or digital financial simulators allow children to practice decision-making and experience the consequences of their financial choices in a low-risk environment.
- Create Family Financial Challenges: Parents can organize challenges where family members compete to save the most money or achieve specific financial goals. This turns financial education into a fun, collaborative process that encourages friendly competition and reinforces key financial lessons.

12. Encourage Giving and Social Responsibility

- Teach the Value of Philanthropy: Teaching children about giving and charitable donations helps them understand the importance of social responsibility. Whether it's donating a portion of their earnings or participating in community service, this instills a sense of empathy and the idea that financial success can be used for the greater good.
- Incorporate Giving into Financial Lessons: Parents can encourage children to set aside a portion of their allowance or earnings for charitable causes. This reinforces the value of sharing wealth and makes children more mindful of their role in helping others and making a positive impact.

Teaching financial responsibility to children is a gradual process that involves introducing age-appropriate financial concepts, modeling good financial behavior, and providing opportunities for hands-on learning. By starting early, encouraging saving and goal setting, and instilling the value of work, parents can set their children on the path to long-term financial success. When children learn to manage their money responsibly from a young age, they are better equipped to make informed financial decisions and achieve financial independence as they grow into adulthood.

Leaving a legacy

- Philanthropy and Giving Back: Using Wealth for a Greater Purpose

Philanthropy is a powerful way to use wealth for a greater purpose, extending its impact beyond personal and familial benefit. It enables individuals and families to leave a lasting legacy, promoting social change, improving lives, and contributing to the broader community. By integrating philanthropic goals into wealth management strategies, high-net-worth individuals can align their financial success with a commitment to making the world a better place.

1. Defining Your Philanthropic Vision

❖ Clarifying Core Values and Mission: The foundation of any effective philanthropic effort is a clear understanding of the values and mission that drive it. What causes or issues are most important to you or your family? Whether it's education, health care, environmental sustainability, or poverty alleviation, focusing on areas that resonate deeply will create a more meaningful impact. This vision also serves as a guide for making strategic decisions about where and how to give.

- ❖ Establishing a Purpose-Driven Legacy: Philanthropy offers an opportunity to build a legacy that transcends financial wealth. By contributing to social causes and positively affecting lives, individuals can ensure that their name is associated with more than just material success. Establishing charitable foundations, scholarships, or community programs can extend your influence well beyond your lifetime.

2. Integrating Philanthropy into Financial and Estate Planning

- ❖ Creating a Charitable Giving Strategy: Strategic philanthropy involves more than just writing checks. It requires thoughtful planning to ensure that donations are impactful and align with long-term financial goals. A charitable giving strategy should address key questions such as how much to give, how often, and which organizations to support. This can involve ongoing annual donations, one-time endowments, or planned giving as part of estate distribution.
- ❖ Philanthropy in Estate Planning: Philanthropy can play a central role in estate planning, especially for those looking to use their wealth to create enduring social value. Charitable giving through wills and trusts not only ensures that causes you care about are supported after your passing but can also provide significant tax advantages. Donations to charitable organizations, whether through cash gifts or

appreciated assets, can reduce the taxable value of your estate.

- ❖ Establishing Donor-Advised Funds (DAFs) and Foundations: Donor-Advised Funds and private foundations are powerful vehicles for structured giving. A DAF allows individuals to make a charitable contribution, receive an immediate tax benefit, and then recommend grants to charitable organizations over time. Foundations, on the other hand, offer more control over how donations are allocated and allow families to institutionalize their philanthropic efforts for generations. These structures create a sustainable approach to giving, ensuring long-term support for chosen causes.

3. The Financial and Social Benefits of Philanthropy

- ❖ Tax Incentives for Charitable Giving: Philanthropy can yield significant tax benefits, both during one's lifetime and posthumously. Charitable contributions are generally tax-deductible, which can reduce income taxes in the year of the donation. For high-net-worth individuals, this can be a strategic way to mitigate capital gains taxes by donating appreciated assets such as stocks or real estate. Additionally, bequests to charitable organizations can reduce estate taxes, ensuring more of your wealth goes to meaningful causes rather than to the government.
- ❖ Enhanced Reputation and Social Responsibility: Philanthropy is not just about financial benefit; it also enhances personal and corporate reputation. Engaging in charitable efforts can elevate

an individual's or family's social standing, positioning them as responsible stewards of their wealth. For business owners, a commitment to corporate social responsibility (CSR) can improve brand perception and foster loyalty among customers and employees.

4. Involving Future Generations in Philanthropy

- Fostering a Culture of Giving: One of the most powerful aspects of philanthropy is its ability to inspire future generations to carry on a legacy of giving. Involving children and grandchildren in charitable decision-making helps instill values of generosity, responsibility, and social awareness. It also fosters financial literacy by teaching them how to manage wealth in a way that balances personal gain with community impact.
- Passing on the Mantle of Philanthropy: As part of succession planning, families can create a framework for how future generations will continue the family's charitable mission. This may involve mentoring younger family members on the importance of philanthropy, introducing them to the causes the family supports, and eventually giving them a more active role in managing charitable endeavors.

5. Maximizing Impact through Targeted Giving

- Choosing the Right Causes and Organizations: Philanthropy is most impactful when donations are directed toward organizations with a proven track record of success and financial responsibility. Conducting due diligence on charities, including reviewing their financial statements and impact reports, is essential to ensuring that donations are used effectively. Donors should consider not only the cause they are passionate about but also the specific ways in which the organizations they support are addressing that issue.

- ❖ Sustainable and Strategic Giving: Sustainable philanthropy involves giving in a way that creates lasting impact, rather than short-term fixes. For instance, supporting education through scholarships or funding initiatives that foster long-term community development can create generational change. Strategic philanthropy might also include giving to organizations that tackle systemic issues, such as funding research for policy change or supporting innovative solutions to global challenges.

6. Innovative Approaches to Philanthropy: Impact Investing and Social Entrepreneurship

- ❖ Impact Investing: For those who want their investments to align with their philanthropic goals, impact investing offers a way to generate financial returns while promoting social or environmental benefits. Impact investments are typically made in sectors such as renewable energy, affordable housing, or sustainable agriculture. Unlike traditional philanthropy, which is based on donations, impact investing seeks both financial gain and measurable positive outcomes in society.

- Supporting Social Entrepreneurs: Social entrepreneurship blends business acumen with social responsibility, offering sustainable solutions to societal problems. Supporting social enterprises through grants, investments, or mentorship is an innovative way to ensure your philanthropic efforts generate self-sustaining impact. By fostering businesses that tackle issues like poverty, education, or healthcare, donors can multiply the effect of their giving over time.

7. Balancing Personal Philanthropy with Broader Social Impact

- Personal Fulfillment through Giving: Beyond financial benefits, philanthropy can bring deep personal fulfillment. Using wealth to address pressing societal issues, improve the lives of others, and support causes that resonate with personal values creates a sense of purpose and legacy. Many philanthropists find that giving back enriches their lives, bringing greater meaning to their financial success.
- Measuring and Managing Impact: To ensure philanthropy is as effective as possible, it's important to measure the outcomes of charitable donations. This can involve working with organizations to track progress and milestones or supporting initiatives that publish annual impact reports. By continually assessing the effectiveness of their giving, philanthropists can make more informed decisions about how to allocate resources and refine their strategies over time.

8. Leaving a Legacy of Generosity

- Building Enduring Institutions: One of the most profound ways to leave a legacy through philanthropy is by building enduring institutions. This might involve founding a school, funding a hospital wing, or establishing a foundation that continues to support chosen causes for decades or centuries. These structures can ensure that your name and values are remembered long after you're gone, providing ongoing support to the causes you care most about.
- Influencing Positive Social Change: True philanthropic legacies are built on creating lasting positive social change. Whether through large-scale giving or smaller, targeted donations, individuals have the opportunity to shape the future by addressing systemic issues and improving the quality of life for future generations. By focusing on sustainable solutions, philanthropists can contribute to long-term progress in areas such as education, healthcare, poverty alleviation, and environmental protection.

Philanthropy is an essential component of leaving a lasting legacy. It provides a way to use wealth for a greater purpose, improving lives and contributing to the well-being of society. By developing a thoughtful and strategic approach to giving, integrating philanthropy into estate planning, and involving future generations, individuals can ensure their wealth not only benefits their family but also creates meaningful, long-lasting social impact. Through strategic philanthropy, impact investing, and fostering a culture of giving, individuals can align their financial success with the creation of a better world, ultimately leaving a legacy that extends far beyond personal wealth.

- Building a Legacy That Transcends Material Wealth

When we think of leaving a legacy, it is often associated with passing on financial assets, properties, or material wealth to future generations. However, a truly meaningful legacy transcends monetary inheritance. It encompasses values, principles, and life lessons that can shape future generations in ways far more impactful than wealth alone. Building a legacy that goes beyond material possessions involves nurturing a legacy of knowledge, ethics, family culture, social impact, and stewardship—ensuring that your influence continues to inspire long after you're gone.

1. Instilling Core Values and Principles

- ❖ At the heart of a legacy that transcends material wealth is the transfer of values and principles. This includes fostering a sense of responsibility, integrity, empathy, and hard work in the next generation. These are the traits that build resilient individuals who can navigate life's challenges while maintaining strong moral character. Teaching family members the importance of these values, alongside financial education, ensures that wealth is managed with purpose and responsibility.
- ❖ A legacy rooted in principles can provide the emotional and ethical foundation for managing the wealth you leave behind. When future generations are equipped with integrity and accountability, they are more likely to use inherited wealth for positive purposes, avoiding common pitfalls like

entitlement, mismanagement, or financial dependency.

2. Creating a Culture of Generational Stewardship

- ❖ Stewardship refers to the responsible management of resources, including both material wealth and the intangible assets of knowledge and relationships. Building a legacy that transcends wealth means creating a family culture of stewardship, where each generation learns to value, protect, and grow what has been passed down to them. This is not just about financial wealth but also about taking care of family heritage, traditions, and the community.
- ❖ Stewardship also extends to environmental and social responsibilities. As the world increasingly focuses on sustainability, leaving a legacy that promotes environmental stewardship can be a powerful way to influence future generations. By modeling responsible consumption, giving back to the environment, and investing in sustainable practices, you ensure that your legacy contributes to a healthier planet and society.

3. Passing on Knowledge and Wisdom

- ❖ One of the most valuable assets you can pass on is knowledge. Sharing personal experiences, successes, failures, and lessons learned throughout life equips future generations with the wisdom they need to make informed decisions. Whether through mentoring, storytelling, or written reflections, ensuring that your life's insights are accessible to your family members can have a profound and lasting impact.
- ❖ Some families formalize this process by creating family governance structures, such as family

councils, family constitutions, or written legacy letters, where core values, family mission, and financial education are documented. This creates a blueprint for future generations to follow, ensuring that the family legacy continues to thrive, even as family members grow and change.

4. Empowering Future Generations Through Education

- Education is a key pillar of any meaningful legacy. By investing in the education and personal development of the next generation, you equip them with the skills and knowledge necessary to continue building upon the foundation you've created. This investment can take many forms, from funding formal education to offering opportunities for experiential learning in business, philanthropy, or other areas.
- Education is not only about acquiring knowledge; it's also about fostering a lifelong curiosity and passion for growth. Encouraging future generations to continuously seek knowledge and adapt to changing circumstances will empower them to thrive in a rapidly evolving world.

5. Philanthropy and Social Impact

- Another way to build a legacy that transcends wealth is through philanthropy. By dedicating resources to causes you care about, you create a ripple effect of positive change in the world. Engaging in philanthropy can also instill a sense of purpose and social responsibility in your family members, encouraging them to give back and make a difference in their communities.
- Philanthropy can take many forms, such as establishing a family foundation, funding scholarships, supporting social enterprises, or

contributing to local and global charities. A legacy rooted in philanthropy not only impacts the world but also reinforces the values of generosity, compassion, and social responsibility within the family.

6. Fostering Relationships and Community

- Material wealth can only go so far in creating a lasting legacy. Relationships, both within the family and the community, are what truly keep a legacy alive. Building strong family ties and a sense of unity fosters emotional wealth that far surpasses material assets. A legacy of love, support, and connectedness within the family creates an environment where future generations can thrive both emotionally and financially.
- In addition to family bonds, being actively involved in your community and fostering relationships outside of the family is equally important. These relationships create a broader network of support and collaboration, reinforcing the idea that wealth is not just about accumulation but also about sharing resources, knowledge, and opportunities with others.

7. Encouraging a Life of Purpose and Fulfillment

- Finally, building a legacy that transcends material wealth involves encouraging future generations to pursue lives of purpose and fulfillment. By modeling a life driven by passion, service, and meaningful work, you inspire others to find their own sense of purpose. When wealth is used as a tool to facilitate personal growth, creativity, and the pursuit of passions, it becomes a source of empowerment rather than an end goal.

❖ Encouraging future generations to focus on their passions and pursue fulfilling careers or social causes ensures that wealth serves as a vehicle for enhancing life experiences, rather than being an anchor that limits personal freedom or happiness.

Building a legacy that transcends material wealth is about creating a lasting impact through values, stewardship, education, philanthropy, and meaningful relationships. It involves nurturing a mindset that views wealth as a tool for empowerment, social good, and personal growth, rather than an end in itself. By focusing on the intangible elements of legacy—values, wisdom, and purpose—you leave behind something far more enduring than money: a blueprint for living a meaningful, impactful life that future generations can build upon and contribute to.

- The Ultimate Fulfillment of Abundance: Impact, Influence, and Community Support

When it comes to leaving a legacy, abundance is not just measured by the amount of wealth accumulated or assets transferred. The true fulfillment of abundance lies in the lasting impact one makes on others, the influence exerted on future generations, and the community support cultivated over time. Abundance, in this context, goes beyond financial success to encompass contributions that uplift society, inspire individuals, and create sustainable systems of support for the wider community. This ultimate fulfillment of abundance serves as the capstone of a legacy, reflecting the true value of wealth and success in the broader spectrum of human achievement.

1. Redefining Abundance: From Material Wealth to Meaningful Impact

- The Shift from Accumulation to Contribution: Many people equate abundance with financial wealth, but true abundance is often realized through the impact one has on the world. The highest form of wealth is not just having more, but doing more with what you have. This shift in focus, from accumulating resources to using those resources to create meaningful change, defines the ultimate fulfillment of abundance. When wealth is directed toward improving the lives of others, fostering innovation, and supporting communities, it transcends its material limitations.
- Creating Positive Change through Influence: Influence is a powerful tool for legacy-building. Individuals who understand the far-reaching consequences of their decisions and actions often leverage their wealth and success to advocate for important social causes, support innovation, and promote education. Influencing future generations to adopt ethical practices, embrace creativity, and pursue community-centric goals is an enduring way to ensure that your legacy continues to shape the world long after your financial wealth has been passed on.

2. Impact as a Measure of True Success

- Philanthropy and Social Impact: One of the most effective ways to translate financial wealth into lasting abundance is through philanthropic endeavors. Strategic philanthropy that focuses on systemic, long-term change—whether in education, healthcare, environmental sustainability, or economic development—can lead to profound social impact. Establishing charitable foundations, funding scholarships, or supporting grassroots organizations that tackle critical issues allows individuals to use their financial resources to leave a legacy of positive change.

- Empowering Others to Achieve Success: True abundance is not just about your own success but about empowering others to succeed as well. Mentorship programs, vocational training initiatives, or educational opportunities aimed at marginalized or underserved communities create a ripple effect that multiplies your impact. By helping others break through barriers to achieve their own success, you contribute to a legacy of empowerment, fostering a culture of achievement that continues to grow with each successive generation.
- Sustainable Giving: Sustainable philanthropy focuses on creating solutions that have a long-lasting impact, rather than temporary fixes. By investing in projects that aim for self-sufficiency, community resilience, and long-term outcomes, you ensure that the contributions you make continue to benefit society for years, if not generations. Supporting initiatives that address the root causes of societal challenges—rather than just their symptoms—aligns with the principles of sustainable wealth and long-term impact.

3. Influence through Thought Leadership and Social Advocacy

- ❖ Advocating for Systemic Change: Beyond financial contributions, true influence often comes through advocacy for systemic change. This might involve pushing for policy reforms, supporting educational movements, or using your platform to raise awareness around critical issues like climate change, social justice, or economic inequality. By using your influence to address societal gaps and injustices, you not only leave behind a legacy of wealth but also a legacy of progressive change.
- ❖ Thought Leadership and Innovation: Thought leaders who use their success and influence to drive innovation or contribute to knowledge leave behind intellectual legacies. Whether through writing, public speaking, or creating spaces for dialogue, thought leaders inspire others to think differently, embrace change, and pursue new ideas. By fostering a culture of innovation and intellectual curiosity, you create an enduring legacy that influences industries, communities, and the world at large.
- ❖ Community Leadership and Role Modeling: Leadership within your community or industry can also extend your influence. By setting an example of ethical leadership, community involvement, and social responsibility, you inspire others to adopt similar values. Being a role model means more than financial leadership—it means demonstrating how wealth and influence can be used for the greater good, creating a

ripple effect that transforms others' approach to success and abundance.

4. The Importance of Community Support in Legacy Building

- ❖ Investing in Your Community: Community support is a cornerstone of any lasting legacy. Building programs, organizations, or businesses that benefit your local or global community creates a tangible, lasting impact. Supporting infrastructure, local economies, or community-focused nonprofits ensures that the community thrives and prospers. This not only reinforces your legacy within the community but also builds long-term, sustainable growth that benefits many.
- ❖ Building Networks of Support and Collaboration: Strong communities are built on networks of support, cooperation, and collaboration. Using your resources to foster environments where others can collaborate—whether through shared workspaces, business incubators, or educational programs—leads to collective success. A legacy built on community support fosters a culture of cooperation, where individuals uplift each other to achieve common goals.
- ❖ Creating Enduring Institutions: Some of the most enduring legacies are physical institutions such as schools, libraries, or hospitals, which can serve communities for generations. These structures symbolize long-term commitment and provide ongoing value. By creating or supporting institutions that are vital to community development, health, and education, you ensure that your

resources contribute to a greater social fabric that stands the test of time.

5. Impact, Influence, and Fulfillment: The Three Pillars of Abundance

- ❖ Achieving the Ultimate Fulfillment of Abundance: The ultimate fulfillment of abundance is not solely about wealth accumulation but how that wealth is utilized to create a lasting **impact**. True abundance comes from contributing to the greater good, influencing future generations, and empowering communities to succeed. In this sense, wealth becomes a vehicle for meaningful change rather than just a measurement of success.
- ❖ Legacy of Influence: A legacy of influence is one where your ideas, principles, and vision continue to shape the world. By focusing on education, advocacy, and mentorship, your influence spreads, inspiring others to adopt the same ethos of abundance and responsibility.
- ❖ Community as the Ultimate Measure: Finally, the strength and prosperity of the communities you support serve as the ultimate testament to your legacy. Whether local or global, communities that thrive because of your contributions are living symbols of your abundance.

6. Creating Enduring Social Systems: Generational Change through Legacy

- ❖ Sustaining Impact Over Time: Building a legacy that endures requires a commitment to sustainable systems that support long-term change. Instead of providing short-term solutions, true legacy-builders focus on creating frameworks and institutions that solve problems at their root. This may include setting up educational systems, funding scientific research, or creating social programs aimed at improving health and well-being. These initiatives continue to yield benefits long after the founder's involvement, thus ensuring that their legacy is a catalyst for generational improvement.

- Influencing Generational Behavior: A legacy rooted in abundance goes beyond wealth transfer. It involves imparting values, behaviors, and mindsets that influence future generations. Teaching the next generation to view wealth as a tool for making a positive impact in the world helps shape how they manage, grow, and distribute the resources they inherit. This influence can result in families and communities that prioritize giving, innovation, and ethical leadership, carrying forward the principles of abundance over time.
- Institutional and Systemic Contributions: Establishing systems that promote long-term societal benefit—such as healthcare facilities, research institutions, or public infrastructure—cements your legacy as one that contributed to the fabric of society. Institutions that reflect your values and mission create enduring social systems that enable progress, innovation, and inclusivity, providing a foundation for continued societal growth.

7. Aligning Wealth with Purpose and Passion

- ❖ Philanthropy as a Reflection of Personal Values: True legacy-building aligns personal wealth with passion and purpose. Many individuals choose to support causes that are close to their hearts, whether it's environmental conservation, educational access, or public health. By directing resources toward the things they care deeply about, they ensure that their wealth serves a purpose beyond material accumulation. This alignment of wealth with passion not only adds personal fulfillment but also inspires others to see the power of wealth as a vehicle for good.
- ❖ Purpose-Driven Leadership: Leaders who build legacies through purpose-driven decisions inspire others to follow in their footsteps. Leadership that prioritizes societal impact over personal gain sets a new standard for success, influencing industries, businesses, and communities to adopt a more holistic view of success. This form of leadership, centered on ethical decision-making, inclusivity, and sustainability, creates ripples that affect society at large, establishing a legacy that inspires positive action long after the individual has stepped back from the spotlight.
- ❖ Purposeful Wealth Management: Managing wealth with purpose means using financial resources to achieve goals that extend beyond personal comfort. Purposeful wealth management may include allocating a portion of wealth toward social causes, supporting underserved communities, or investing in businesses that align with

social responsibility and sustainability. By intentionally managing wealth in a way that reflects broader goals for societal good, individuals create a legacy that reflects their commitment to making a lasting difference.

8. Community Development and Empowerment: Uplifting Others for Collective Success

- Empowering Underserved Communities: A meaningful legacy is often characterized by the ability to uplift those who have been marginalized or underserved. Many legacy-builders focus on empowering communities through initiatives that provide access to education, healthcare, and economic opportunities. By creating pathways for others to succeed, individuals can ensure that their wealth helps level the playing field, reducing disparities and fostering inclusive prosperity. Empowering communities to be self-sustaining and resilient contributes to a legacy of equity and shared success.
- Strengthening Local Economies: Investing in community infrastructure and local economies can be a powerful way to create long-lasting social impact. Supporting local businesses, creating jobs, and contributing to economic development in underdeveloped areas are direct ways to ensure that wealth leaves a lasting mark. Legacies built on community empowerment create opportunities for collective success, where entire regions experience growth and improvement because of the resources and initiatives provided.
- Collaborating for Broader Impact: Collaboration is a key component of

community-focused legacy building. Working with other philanthropists, nonprofits, and governmental organizations allows for the pooling of resources and expertise to achieve greater impact. Collaborative efforts aimed at solving large-scale problems—such as poverty, climate change, or public health—amplify the impact of individual wealth and create synergies that lead to lasting, transformative change.

9. Inspiring Others through Generosity and Vision

- Leaving a Legacy of Generosity: Generosity is at the heart of building a lasting legacy. Individuals who make giving a central part of their life's work inspire others to do the same. Generosity that comes in the form of financial support, time, mentorship, and ideas creates a culture of giving that perpetuates itself. When others are inspired to give because of the generosity they have witnessed, the ripple effect of giving ensures that the legacy of abundance grows exponentially.
- Visionary Leadership and Innovation: Legacy-builders often have the ability to envision a future where wealth can be used for broader societal good. By pursuing innovative solutions to pressing challenges, these individuals drive progress and inspire others to think creatively about how to use wealth and influence. Visionary leadership creates a roadmap for others to follow, leaving behind not just material wealth, but also a legacy of creative thinking, problem-solving, and a commitment to progress.

- Personal Influence as a Catalyst for Social Change: Influence plays a powerful role in leaving a legacy. Whether through direct mentorship, public advocacy, or thought leadership, individuals who use their platforms to inspire others leave an indelible mark. Personal influence becomes a catalyst for change when it sparks new ideas, motivates collective action, or challenges societal norms. A legacy of influence ensures that your ideas, values, and vision continue to shape the world long after your time.

10. Sustaining Legacy through Family and Successive Generations

- Passing Down Values Alongside Wealth: To ensure the sustainability of a legacy, it's essential to pass down not only wealth but also the values and principles that guide its use. Teaching younger generations about the responsibility that comes with wealth—along with the importance of giving, ethical leadership, and social impact—ensures that your legacy remains intact. Successive generations who understand these values will continue to build upon the foundation of abundance you established.
- Creating Family Governance Systems: Family governance systems, such as family councils or mission statements, can help maintain alignment within families when managing wealth across generations. These systems provide a framework for making decisions about how wealth is invested, distributed, and used for social good.

CHAPTER THREE

THE GLOBAL PERSPECTIVE ON WEALTH

Understanding how global trends and economic systems influence personal wealth is crucial in today's interconnected world. This chapter explores global financial opportunities, challenges, and strategies for leveraging international markets.

The Impact of Globalization on Wealth

- How Globalization Has Transformed Wealth Creation and Distribution

Globalization, the process of increased interconnectedness among countries, economies, and cultures, has fundamentally reshaped the way wealth is created and distributed across the world. Over the last few decades, it has driven rapid changes in markets, industries, and individual financial opportunities. This section explores the transformative role of globalization in wealth creation, its impact on the distribution of wealth, and the opportunities and challenges it presents for individuals and economies alike.

1. Globalization as a Catalyst for Wealth Creation

- ❖ Expansion of International Markets: Globalization has opened up access to international markets, allowing businesses to scale beyond their domestic borders. This increased access to new consumer bases, suppliers, and resources has fueled growth for multinational corporations and small businesses alike. As a result, individuals and companies can tap into a much larger global customer base, significantly increasing revenue potential.

- Technological Advancements and Innovation: One of the most significant drivers of globalization is technological advancement. Innovations in transportation, communication, and digital infrastructure have enabled businesses to operate globally with ease. The rise of the internet, cloud computing, and mobile technology has allowed entrepreneurs to access international customers, investors, and talent without the constraints of geography. This digital transformation has led to the creation of new industries, such as e-commerce and fintech, enabling individuals to create wealth in ways that were previously unimaginable.
- Global Supply Chains: Globalization has revolutionized supply chains, enabling companies to source raw materials and manufacture products from different parts of the world where it is most cost-effective. This has lowered production costs and increased profit margins for companies, contributing to wealth generation. Additionally, individuals involved in managing and optimizing global supply chains—logistics, finance, procurement, and more—have benefited from lucrative careers and entrepreneurial ventures.
- Access to Capital and Investment Opportunities: Globalization has made it easier for businesses and individuals to access global capital markets. Investors can now allocate capital to emerging markets, international stocks, bonds, and alternative assets, broadening the avenues for wealth accumulation. This cross-border flow of investment has spurred economic growth in developing countries while

providing high returns for investors. Venture capital, private equity, and foreign direct investments have flourished due to the global reach of financial markets.

2. The Changing Landscape of Wealth Distribution

- Widening Income and Wealth Inequality: Despite the wealth-creating opportunities globalization has brought, it has also contributed to widening income and wealth inequality, both within and between countries. Highly skilled workers, entrepreneurs, and investors in developed nations have generally reaped more benefits from globalization, while unskilled or low-wage workers in both developed and developing nations have faced job displacement and wage stagnation. In some regions, globalization has led to the concentration of wealth in the hands of a few, exacerbating inequality.
- Emergence of New Economic Powers: Globalization has shifted wealth and economic power from traditionally dominant economies to emerging markets, such as China, India, Brazil, and Southeast Asia. These countries have seen significant growth in their middle classes, as well as an increase in high-net-worth individuals (HNWIs) and billionaires. This redistribution of wealth across borders has altered the global financial landscape, with emerging markets becoming key players in global trade and investment.
- Job Creation and Outsourcing: While globalization has led to job displacement in some industries due to outsourcing, it has also created new opportunities in sectors

such as technology, finance, and services. Countries like India, the Philippines, and Vietnam have become hubs for outsourced services, such as IT support, software development, and customer service, contributing to economic growth and rising living standards in these regions. At the same time, companies in developed nations have benefited from cost savings by outsourcing non-core functions.

- Impact on Small and Medium Enterprises (SMEs): Globalization has leveled the playing field for SMEs, allowing them to compete in international markets without needing the same resources as large corporations. E-commerce platforms, global payment systems, and digital marketing tools have enabled SMEs to access global markets and consumers directly, thus driving wealth creation for smaller players. However, increased competition from global firms can also challenge SMEs to maintain market share in their home countries.

3. Opportunities and Challenges in a Globalized Economy

- Opportunities for Individuals: Globalization has democratized access to information, education, and financial tools. With the rise of online learning platforms, individuals can now acquire skills and knowledge from anywhere in the world, enhancing their career prospects and earning potential. Similarly, retail investors can easily access international financial markets through online brokerage platforms, diversifying their investment portfolios. Entrepreneurs can also leverage global talent pools and resources to build scalable businesses.

- ❖ Challenges of Competition and Volatility: With globalization comes increased competition. Companies must compete not only with local rivals but also with international corporations that may have more resources or better technology. This heightened competition can reduce profit margins and pressure companies to innovate continuously. Moreover, globalization makes local economies more susceptible to global market volatility, as financial crises or economic slowdowns in one country can have ripple effects worldwide, affecting wealth stability.
- ❖ Cultural and Social Impacts on Wealth Distribution: Globalization has led to cultural exchange and greater access to global markets, but it has also created challenges in terms of wealth distribution. In some cases, local traditions and practices may be disrupted by global economic forces, leading to social tensions and economic imbalances. On the other hand, global migration has allowed individuals to move across borders in search of better economic opportunities, contributing to wealth redistribution across regions.

4. Strategies for Leveraging Globalization to Build Wealth

- ❖ International Diversification: For investors, diversifying across global markets is essential for managing risk and capitalizing on the benefits of globalization. By spreading investments across different regions, sectors, and asset classes, individuals can reduce exposure to domestic economic downturns and take advantage of growth opportunities in other countries.

- Leveraging Technological Platforms: Individuals and businesses must leverage technological platforms to access global markets, sell products, and engage with international audiences. E-commerce, digital payments, and global logistics systems allow for seamless international trade and commerce. Additionally, platforms that facilitate remote work and international collaboration can help individuals and companies tap into global talent and expertise.
- Continuous Learning and Up-skilling: As globalization continues to evolve, individuals must adapt by continuously learning and upgrading their skills. Workers in industries impacted by automation and outsourcing should consider transitioning to sectors where globalization creates demand, such as technology, healthcare, or renewable energy. Entrepreneurs and business leaders need to stay informed about global market trends, consumer preferences, and technological advancements to remain competitive.
- Building Strategic Partnerships: Globalization has opened the door to strategic international partnerships. Entrepreneurs can collaborate with overseas manufacturers, distributors, or joint venture partners to expand their business operations. Such partnerships provide access to local expertise and resources, enabling businesses to scale faster and tap into new markets while mitigating the risks of entering unfamiliar territories.

5. Globalization and the Future of Wealth Creation

- The Rise of the Global Digital Economy: The digital economy, driven by advances in artificial intelligence, blockchain, and the internet of things (IoT), is set to redefine wealth creation. These technologies will continue to break down barriers to entry, allowing entrepreneurs to create wealth through digital platforms, virtual currencies, and decentralized business models. As more industries become digitized, individuals will need to understand how to position themselves within this rapidly changing global landscape.
- Sustainability and Social Responsibility: Globalization is increasingly intertwined with sustainability and corporate social responsibility. Investors are paying more attention to environmental, social, and governance (ESG) factors when making investment decisions. Companies that prioritize sustainability are more likely to attract global investors, making it crucial for individuals to consider how their wealth-building strategies align with global environmental and social trends.
- Global Collaboration and Wealth Distribution: As global challenges such as climate change, poverty, and inequality persist, international collaboration will become increasingly important in ensuring fair wealth distribution. Governments, international organizations, and private enterprises will need to work together to create policies and frameworks that promote inclusive wealth creation, bridging the gap between developed and developing nations.

6. Government Policies and Wealth Distribution

- Trade Agreements and Tariffs: Trade policies, including tariffs and international trade agreements, have a direct influence on wealth creation and distribution. Free trade agreements, such as NAFTA and the European Union's single market, have enabled the free flow of goods and services across borders, allowing companies to access larger markets and reducing costs for consumers. On the other hand, protectionist policies and tariffs can restrict trade and affect industries dependent on global supply chains, potentially leading to wealth disparities.
- Taxation and Wealth Redistribution: Governments play a significant role in wealth redistribution through taxation policies. Progressive tax systems, where higher income earners are taxed at higher rates, are designed to reduce inequality and fund social programs. Similarly, capital gains taxes, estate taxes, and corporate taxes can influence the accumulation and distribution of wealth across a population. In contrast, tax havens and loopholes exploited by multinational corporations and the ultra-wealthy can exacerbate inequality by enabling them to avoid contributing their fair share to the economy.
- Social Safety Nets and Public Services: Governments also influence wealth distribution by providing social safety nets and essential public services. Investments in education, healthcare, infrastructure, and social welfare programs help improve living standards and create opportunities for upward mobility. However, disparities in access to quality services can perpetuate cycles of poverty and

inequality, particularly in regions where globalization has left some populations behind.

7. Global Institutions and Wealth Regulation

- International Monetary Fund (IMF) and World Bank: These global institutions play critical roles in stabilizing economies and promoting economic growth in developing countries. By providing loans, financial aid, and technical assistance, they help nations build infrastructure, strengthen governance, and foster economic development, contributing to global wealth distribution. However, the conditions attached to IMF and World Bank loans, such as austerity measures, can sometimes lead to social unrest and increased inequality if not managed carefully.
- World Trade Organization (WTO): The WTO facilitates global trade by setting rules and resolving disputes between countries. By promoting free and fair trade, it helps ensure that countries can access international markets, thus supporting wealth creation. The organization's focus on reducing trade barriers and tariffs has played a significant role in the growth of emerging economies. Nevertheless, critics argue that some WTO policies can disproportionately benefit wealthier nations while leaving poorer countries at a disadvantage.
- United Nations and Sustainable Development Goals (SDGs): The United Nations (UN) has taken an active role in promoting sustainable and equitable wealth distribution through its Sustainable Development Goals. The SDGs aim to eradicate poverty, reduce inequality, and promote inclusive economic growth by 2030. Governments, corporations, and

individuals are encouraged to contribute to these global objectives, ensuring that the benefits of globalization are more evenly distributed and sustainable.

8. Future Trends in Globalization and Wealth Distribution

- The Shift toward Decentralized Finance (DeFi): The rise of decentralized finance, enabled by blockchain technology, is poised to disrupt traditional financial systems and democratize access to wealth-building tools. DeFi allows individuals to participate in financial markets without the need for intermediaries, such as banks or brokerage firms. This has the potential to lower barriers to entry for wealth creation, particularly in regions where access to traditional banking and investment services is limited. However, it also introduces new risks, such as cybersecurity vulnerabilities and regulatory uncertainty.
- The Impact of Automation and Artificial Intelligence (AI): As automation and AI continue to reshape industries, they will impact wealth creation and distribution in both positive and negative ways. Automation can lead to increased productivity and economic growth, creating new industries and opportunities for wealth accumulation. However, it also has the potential to displace jobs, particularly in manufacturing and low-skill sectors, exacerbating income inequality. Governments and businesses will need to implement policies and training programs to ensure that workers can transition to new roles in the evolving global economy.
- Climate Change and Sustainability: Globalization has also brought attention to the urgent need for sustainability in wealth

creation. Climate change, resource depletion, and environmental degradation pose significant challenges to long-term wealth generation. Countries and companies that prioritize sustainable practices, such as renewable energy, resource efficiency, and circular economies, are likely to be better positioned for future wealth creation. Sustainable investing and green finance are emerging trends that will shape the future of wealth distribution, as investors increasingly prioritize environmental, social, and governance (ESG) factors.

9. Adapting to a Globalized Future

- Embracing Digital Transformation: To thrive in a globalized economy, individuals and businesses must embrace digital transformation. Leveraging digital platforms, cloud computing, and artificial intelligence will be essential for accessing global markets, optimizing operations, and staying competitive. Moreover, individuals will need to develop digital literacy and technical skills to capitalize on emerging opportunities in the digital economy.
- Navigating Global Risks: Globalization has interconnected economies to the extent that shocks in one region can have ripple effects across the world. As a result, individuals and businesses must prepare for global risks, such as financial crises, pandemics, or geopolitical tensions. Diversifying investments across different countries, sectors, and asset classes is a critical strategy for mitigating these risks and preserving wealth in an unpredictable global environment.
- Fostering Global Collaboration: In an increasingly interconnected world, global collaboration will be essential for addressing

shared challenges and ensuring that the benefits of globalization are widely distributed. Governments, businesses, and individuals must work together to create frameworks that promote inclusive growth, reduce inequality, and address global challenges, such as climate change and poverty.

Globalization has transformed the landscape of wealth creation and distribution, offering unprecedented opportunities while also presenting significant challenges. The interconnectedness of global markets, the rise of technology, and the shift in economic power to emerging markets have created new avenues for wealth accumulation. However, they have also contributed to widening inequality and economic volatility.

For individuals, businesses, and policymakers, the key to navigating this globalized world is adaptability. By embracing technological advancements, investing in continuous learning, and adopting strategies for global diversification, individuals can harness the benefits of globalization. At the same time, governments and international institutions must play their part in ensuring that wealth distribution is fair, sustainable, and inclusive, so that the promise of globalization can be realized by all.

The future of wealth creation in a globalized world will be shaped by digital innovation, sustainable practices, and global collaboration. Those who stay informed and adaptable to these changing dynamics will be best positioned to not only accumulate wealth but also contribute to a more equitable and prosperous global society.

- Identifying Opportunities in Emerging Markets

As globalization continues to reshape the global economy, emerging markets present some of the most attractive opportunities for wealth creation. These markets, characterized by rapid economic growth, increasing urbanization, and rising consumer spending, offer unique potential for both investors and businesses. However, identifying and capitalizing on opportunities in emerging markets requires a deep understanding of the local economies, cultural dynamics, and geopolitical risks.

1. Why Emerging Markets Matter

Emerging markets have become a key driver of global economic growth, contributing to a larger share of global GDP and offering a favorable environment for businesses and investors looking for growth. According to the International Monetary Fund (IMF), emerging and developing economies are expected to grow at a faster pace than developed economies, driven by favorable demographics, urbanization, and industrialization.

Some key reasons why emerging markets are important for wealth creation include:

- Rapid Economic Growth: Countries like China, India, Brazil, and several Southeast Asian and African nations are experiencing faster growth rates than their developed counterparts. This growth is fueled by increasing consumer demand, industrial expansion, and improving infrastructure.
- Rising Middle Class: Many emerging markets are witnessing the rise of a sizable middle class, which creates demand for consumer goods, financial services, healthcare, and technology. This growing population offers significant opportunities for businesses targeting these sectors.

- Untapped Resources and Innovation: Emerging markets are often rich in natural resources, such as oil, minerals, and agriculture, providing attractive investment opportunities. Additionally, many of these markets are leapfrogging traditional development paths by adopting innovative technologies, particularly in fintech, e-commerce, and clean energy sectors.

2. Key Sectors for Wealth Creation in Emerging Markets

While emerging markets offer broad opportunities across many industries, several key sectors have shown significant potential for wealth creation:

- Technology and Digital Innovation: Technology-driven sectors, such as e-commerce, fintech, mobile banking, and digital healthcare, are rapidly expanding in emerging markets. For example, in Africa, mobile payments have revolutionized access to financial services, with companies like M-Pesa in Kenya transforming the landscape. In Southeast Asia, the rise of e-commerce platforms like Shopee and Lazada reflects the growing demand for online retail and digital services.
- Consumer Goods and Retail: As incomes rise and populations urbanize, demand for consumer goods, fast-moving consumer goods (FMCG), and luxury products is on the rise. Multinational companies like Unilever, Procter & Gamble, and Nestlé have expanded their operations in emerging markets to meet this demand. Additionally, the shift toward online shopping and digital marketing has made it easier for businesses to reach consumers.
- Infrastructure and Construction: Emerging markets are investing heavily in infrastructure, including transportation, energy, and housing. These large-

scale infrastructure projects create opportunities for companies in construction, engineering, logistics, and real estate. For instance, China's Belt and Road Initiative has spurred infrastructure investments across Asia, Europe, and Africa, creating numerous opportunities for international partnerships and investments.

- Healthcare and Pharmaceuticals: As healthcare needs grow in tandem with rising populations and economic prosperity, healthcare and pharmaceutical companies stand to benefit. Increased demand for medical services, health insurance, and innovative pharmaceutical products opens new avenues for wealth creation. Companies providing telemedicine, low-cost healthcare solutions, and vaccines are particularly well-positioned to capitalize on this trend.
- Renewable Energy and Sustainability: Many emerging markets are embracing renewable energy technologies and sustainability practices to address climate change and reduce dependence on fossil fuels. Countries like India and Brazil have ramped up investments in solar, wind, and hydropower energy. These investments present opportunities in the renewable energy value chain, including manufacturing, distribution, and financing of green technologies.

3. Strategies for Identifying Opportunities in Emerging Markets

Successfully identifying opportunities in emerging markets requires a strategic approach that includes research, risk assessment, and partnerships. The following strategies can help investors and businesses unlock the potential of these rapidly growing economies:

- Market Research and Local Knowledge: Deep market research is critical for understanding the nuances of local economies and industries. Investors and businesses must pay attention to consumer preferences, regulatory environments, and competitive landscapes. Partnering with local firms or consultants with a strong understanding of the region can help mitigate risks and identify untapped opportunities.
- Government Policies and Incentives: Emerging markets often introduce policies and incentives to attract foreign direct investment (FDI). Understanding these policies can help investors capitalize on favorable tax regimes, trade agreements, and incentives in sectors such as technology, energy, and manufacturing. Monitoring geopolitical developments, such as trade agreements and government support for certain industries is essential to identifying lucrative investment opportunities.
- Cultural and Social Dynamics: In emerging markets, understanding local cultures, values, and business practices is essential for success. Misreading cultural nuances can lead to costly missteps, while aligning products and services with local preferences can drive growth. Additionally, companies that demonstrate social responsibility and engage with communities can enhance their brand reputation and loyalty in these markets.
- Monitoring Demographic Trends: Demographic factors, such as population growth, age distribution, urbanization, and educational attainment, can provide insights into emerging market opportunities. Countries with younger, more urbanized populations often exhibit higher demand for technology, education, and financial services. Monitoring these trends can help

investors and businesses anticipate shifts in demand and position themselves to meet emerging needs.

4. Risks in Emerging Markets

While emerging markets offer substantial growth potential, they also present unique risks that must be carefully managed:

- Political Instability: Emerging markets can be subject to political instability, corruption, and weak governance structures. Changes in government, policy shifts, or social unrest can negatively affect investments. Conducting a thorough risk analysis of the political landscape is essential before entering these markets.
- Currency and Inflation Risk: Exchange rate volatility and inflation can erode returns on investments in emerging markets. High inflation can also lead to rising costs of goods and services, which may impact consumer spending and business profitability. Hedging against currency risk and monitoring economic indicators are vital strategies for mitigating these risks.
- Regulatory and Legal Challenges: Navigating the regulatory environment in emerging markets can be complex. Compliance with local laws, environmental regulations, and intellectual property protections can pose challenges. It is crucial to work with legal experts and local partners to understand regulatory frameworks and ensure compliance.
- Infrastructure and Operational Challenges: In some emerging markets, underdeveloped infrastructure, unreliable utilities, and logistical challenges can hinder operations. Businesses

must be prepared to invest in infrastructure or work around these limitations by adopting innovative approaches, such as leveraging mobile technology or distributed networks.

5. Global Investors' Role in Emerging Market Wealth Creation

Global investors play a critical role in the development of emerging markets, providing capital, expertise, and technology that can accelerate economic growth. By investing in high-growth sectors and fostering innovation, investors can contribute to job creation, infrastructure development, and the expansion of consumer markets.

Moreover, the rise of emerging market-focused exchange-traded funds (ETFs), mutual funds, and private equity investments has made it easier for individual and institutional investors to access these markets. These investment vehicles provide diversification, allowing investors to benefit from the growth of multiple emerging economies while mitigating individual country risk.

6. Navigating Technological Advancements in Emerging Markets

One of the most compelling trends shaping emerging markets today is the rapid adoption of technology. Emerging markets are not only embracing technological advancements but in many cases, they are skipping over traditional development paths and leapfrogging directly into the digital age. This trend presents unique opportunities for investors and businesses, especially in sectors such as fintech, e-commerce, healthcare, and telecommunications.

Fintech and Financial Inclusion

Financial technology (fintech) is revolutionizing financial services in emerging markets. In regions where traditional banking infrastructure is underdeveloped, fintech solutions are providing access to financial services such as payments, savings, credit, and insurance. Mobile payment platforms like M-Pesa in Kenya and Paytm in India have rapidly expanded financial inclusion, enabling millions of unbanked individuals to participate in the formal economy.

Investors can capitalize on this trend by focusing on fintech startups and companies that provide digital banking, peer-to-peer lending, mobile wallets, and crypto currency solutions. Moreover, the demand for microfinance and small-business lending is rising in many emerging economies, offering another avenue for investment.

E-commerce and Digital Transformation

As internet access expands in emerging markets, e-commerce is experiencing explosive growth. Consumers in these regions are increasingly turning to online platforms for shopping, banking, and accessing services. Southeast Asia, for example, has seen a surge in online retail, with platforms like Shopee and Tokopedia dominating the market. Similarly, Latin America's e-commerce sector is booming, with companies like MercadoLibre leading the charge.

Businesses that can provide logistics, last-mile delivery, and digital marketing services are well-positioned to benefit from the rise of e-commerce in emerging markets. Furthermore, investors should consider opportunities in companies that develop mobile-friendly platforms and digital payment solutions, as mobile penetration is often higher than fixed broadband access in these regions.

Healthcare Technology and Telemedicine

Healthcare innovation in emerging markets is increasingly focused on leveraging technology to bridge gaps in access and affordability. Telemedicine, digital health platforms, and mobile health applications are gaining traction, particularly in regions with limited healthcare infrastructure. In countries like India and Brazil, healthcare startups are using technology to provide remote consultations, diagnostics, and prescription services, particularly in rural or underserved areas.

For investors and entrepreneurs, healthcare technology presents an opportunity to not only generate returns but also address critical societal needs. Investing in telemedicine platforms, medical supply chains, and digital healthcare solutions can yield both financial and social returns, while also improving the overall quality of life in these regions.

Telecommunications and Connectivity

Improved telecommunications infrastructure is a key enabler of economic growth in emerging markets. As governments and private companies invest in expanding mobile networks and internet connectivity, previously disconnected regions are gaining access to global markets and digital services. The deployment of 5G technologies, in particular, is expected to unlock new opportunities for innovation across industries such as manufacturing, transportation, and education.

Investors should consider the telecommunications sector as a critical pillar of emerging market growth. Companies that provide telecom infrastructure, satellite communications, and digital services are likely to experience sustained demand as connectivity becomes more widespread.

8. Overcoming Challenges in Emerging Market Investment

While emerging markets offer tremendous potential for wealth creation, they also come with inherent risks. Navigating these challenges requires a proactive approach to risk management and a willingness to adapt to changing circumstances.

Volatility and Market Fluctuations

Emerging markets tend to experience greater volatility than developed markets due to factors such as political instability, currency fluctuations, and external economic shocks. Investors need to be prepared for short-term market swings and focus on long-term growth potential. One way to mitigate risk is through diversification—spreading investments across multiple sectors and countries to reduce exposure to any single market or industry.

Political and Regulatory Risk

Political risk is a significant concern in many emerging markets, where governance structures may be weaker and prone to sudden changes. Investors must stay informed about the political landscape, particularly regarding shifts in government policy, trade relations, and regulatory frameworks. Establishing strong relationships with local partners and consultants can help mitigate these risks by providing on-the-ground insights and timely updates.

Cultural and Ethical Considerations

Cultural sensitivity is critical when operating in emerging markets. Understanding local business practices, social norms, and consumer preferences can make the difference between success and failure. Additionally, investors and businesses should be aware of ethical considerations, such as labor practices, environmental impact, and corporate governance. Companies that prioritize corporate social responsibility (CSR) and sustainable practices are more likely to build trust with local communities and regulators, enhancing their long-term prospects.

Currency Risk and Inflation

Emerging markets often experience currency volatility and higher inflation rates, which can erode returns on investments. Hedging against currency risk by investing in foreign exchange derivatives or focusing on markets with relatively stable currencies can help protect investors from losses. Monitoring inflation trends and interest rate policies in target markets is also essential to make informed investment decisions.

9. Future Trends and Opportunities in Emerging Markets

Looking ahead, several key trends are expected to shape the future of emerging markets, offering continued opportunities for wealth creation:

- Green Energy and Sustainability: As global efforts to combat climate change intensify, emerging markets are increasingly investing in renewable energy sources such as solar, wind, and hydropower. Countries like India, China, and Brazil are at the forefront of the green energy transition, offering investment opportunities in clean energy technologies, infrastructure, and carbon trading.

- Urbanization and Smart Cities: Rapid urbanization is driving demand for smart city solutions in emerging markets. Governments and private companies are investing in technologies that improve urban mobility, energy efficiency, waste management, and public safety. Companies providing innovative solutions in these areas can tap into the growing need for sustainable urban development.
- Digital Finance and Blockchain: The adoption of blockchain technology and digital currencies is gaining momentum in emerging markets, particularly in regions where traditional banking systems are underdeveloped. Blockchain's potential to streamline cross-border payments, enhance supply chain transparency, and enable decentralized finance (DeFi) presents exciting opportunities for investors.
- Agricultural Innovation: Agriculture remains a cornerstone of many emerging economies, and technological advancements in this sector are opening new avenues for wealth creation. Precision farming, sustainable agriculture practices, and agritech innovations are helping to increase productivity and improve food security. Investors can benefit from supporting startups and businesses focused on modernizing agriculture in emerging markets.

Emerging markets are fast becoming critical engines of global growth, offering investors and businesses unparalleled opportunities for wealth creation. By carefully analyzing economic, political, and technological trends, and by taking a proactive approach to risk management, businesses and investors can unlock significant value in these dynamic regions.

From technology-driven sectors like Fintech and e-commerce to more traditional industries such as infrastructure and healthcare, the potential for growth in emerging markets is vast. With a strategic and informed approach, investors and entrepreneurs can harness the transformative power of globalization, drive innovation, and create sustainable wealth in the economies of the future.

- The Rise of the Global Middle Class and Its Impact on Wealth Strategies

Globalization has led to one of the most significant economic shifts in recent history: the rapid growth of the global middle class. According to estimates from the World Bank and other institutions, over half of the world's population now belongs to the middle class, with the majority of this growth happening in emerging economies. This expanding demographic has fundamentally altered wealth strategies for businesses, investors, and policymakers. Understanding the rise of the global middle class is critical for developing wealth-building approaches that align with changing consumption patterns, economic shifts, and investment opportunities.

1. The Global Middle Class: A Demographic Transformation

The middle class, generally defined as individuals or households with sufficient income for discretionary spending beyond basic needs, is no longer confined to developed economies. Over the past few decades, countries like China, India, Brazil, and Indonesia have experienced rapid economic growth, leading to a significant expansion of their middle-class populations. McKinsey Global Institute estimates that by 2030, 3 billion more people will join the middle class, largely from Asia.

This demographic shift represents more than just an increase in wealth—it signals a transformation in global consumption patterns. Middle-class consumers typically demand higher-quality goods and services, including education, healthcare, financial services, and lifestyle products. This growth has major implications for wealth creation and distribution on both a local and global scale.

2. Consumption-Driven Wealth Creation

The rise of the global middle class is driving consumption in key industries, providing new opportunities for businesses and investors. In emerging markets, demand for consumer goods, housing, automobiles, and technology products is surging. Companies that cater to the growing purchasing power of middle-class consumers can significantly increase revenue streams and expand their market reach.

- ❖ Consumer Goods and Retail: Middle-class consumers are more likely to spend on branded goods, personal care items, electronics, and luxury products. Businesses that understand and adapt to local preferences can capitalize on this increasing demand. For example, multinational corporations like Unilever and Procter & Gamble have successfully expanded their presence in emerging markets by tailoring products to meet the specific needs and tastes of these consumers.
- ❖ Real Estate and Housing: The global middle class is driving demand for urban housing, both as homeowners and renters. Real estate developers and investors have responded by

building affordable housing in rapidly urbanizing regions. Additionally, there's a growing market for second homes and investment properties, as middle-class households look to secure financial assets beyond their primary residences.

- Healthcare and Education: As incomes rise, the middle class seeks better access to quality healthcare and education. This has led to an increase in private healthcare providers, hospitals, and educational institutions in many emerging markets. Companies operating in these sectors stand to benefit from both government and private sector investment in infrastructure and services.

3. The Impact on Global Investment Strategies

The growth of the global middle class is reshaping investment strategies, particularly for long-term wealth creation. Investors are now eyeing emerging markets as high-potential opportunities for capital growth due to the expanding middle-class consumer base. However, this also requires a nuanced approach to risk management and diversification.

- Emerging Market Investments: As emerging markets continue to grow, they offer opportunities for higher returns, especially in sectors such as retail, technology, financial services, and healthcare. Private equity, venture capital, and public market investments focused on consumer-driven industries are attracting global investors. For example, China's rise as a middle-class powerhouse has led to massive investments in companies like Alibaba and Tencent, which cater to the digital and consumer needs of this demographic.

- Sector Diversification: The rise of the middle class is affecting multiple sectors beyond just consumer goods. Investors are exploring industries such as infrastructure, transportation, and renewable energy in emerging markets, where rising incomes create demand for better roads, airports, clean energy, and smart cities. Infrastructure investments, particularly in countries undergoing urbanization, are seen as key to supporting middle-class growth while offering long-term returns.

4. New Opportunities in Financial Services

The middle class is typically more financially active than lower-income groups, requiring access to a broad range of financial services such as savings, credit, insurance, and investments. This has led to a burgeoning market for financial products tailored to middle-class households.

- Insurance and Wealth Management: As middle-class consumers accumulate wealth, they seek ways to protect and grow it. Insurance products, from health and life insurance to property coverage, are increasingly in demand. Similarly, wealth management services are expanding to help these consumers invest in stocks, mutual funds, and retirement planning. Financial institutions that provide accessible and affordable products will gain a competitive edge.
- Fintech Innovations: Technology-driven financial services, or fintech, are playing a major role in meeting the needs of the emerging middle class. Digital banking, mobile payments, and peer-to-peer lending

platforms have become popular in regions with less developed banking infrastructure. Fintech solutions offer consumers easier access to financial services, while investors can take advantage of this high-growth sector by supporting innovative startups and scalable business models.

5. Challenges and Risks in Global Middle-Class Growth

While the rise of the global middle class presents numerous opportunities, it also brings challenges that need to be considered when formulating wealth strategies.

- Income Inequality and Social Tensions: The uneven distribution of wealth, even among growing middle-class populations, can lead to social and political instability. Policymakers and businesses need to address these disparities by ensuring that economic growth benefits a broader segment of the population. Failure to do so can result in protests, populist movements, and other risks that may negatively impact business operations and investment returns.
- Environmental Sustainability: Rapid urbanization and increased consumption can lead to environmental degradation, particularly in emerging markets. The middle class's growing demand for energy, transportation, and consumer goods puts additional pressure on natural resources. Investors and businesses must adopt sustainable practices to mitigate environmental risks and promote long-term economic growth.

- Global Economic Fluctuations: The global middle class is not immune to economic downturns, and shifts in the global economy, such as trade wars, inflation, and currency fluctuations, can impact consumer confidence and spending power. A well-diversified portfolio and strategies that account for both regional and global economic conditions are essential to managing these risks.

6. Strategies for Leveraging the Global Middle-Class Boom

To effectively harness the growth of the global middle class, businesses and investors must adopt forward-thinking strategies that align with evolving consumer needs and global market dynamics.

- Localization: While the global middle class is expanding, cultural and economic differences across regions require businesses to localize their offerings. Companies must tailor their products, marketing, and distribution strategies to fit the preferences and income levels of middle-class consumers in different countries.
- Technology and Innovation: Adopting cutting-edge technology and embracing digital transformation are essential for reaching and serving middle-class consumers. Companies that invest in e-commerce, mobile platforms, and data-driven marketing will be well-positioned to capture market share in emerging regions.
- Sustainable Business Practices: Emphasizing environmental sustainability

and corporate social responsibility (CSR) is crucial for maintaining long-term growth. Middle-class consumers are increasingly concerned about environmental issues, and businesses that incorporate sustainable practices into their operations can build stronger brand loyalty.

The rise of the global middle class represents a powerful force driving economic growth, wealth creation, and investment opportunities across the world. As this demographic continues to expand, businesses and investors must strategically position themselves to tap into new markets, diversify their portfolios, and address the unique needs and challenges of middle-class consumers. By recognizing and capitalizing on these trends, wealth creators can build lasting value and contribute to sustainable global prosperity.

Investing in Global Markets

- Overview of Global Financial Markets: Opportunities in Stocks, Bonds, and Real Estate Abroad

As globalization continues to reshape economies and connect markets, investing beyond domestic borders has become an essential strategy for wealth creation and risk management. Access to international markets provides investors with opportunities to diversify their portfolios, capitalize on emerging trends, and potentially enhance returns. The three primary global asset classes—stocks, bonds, and real estate—offer various entry points for investors seeking exposure to both developed and emerging markets.

1. Global Stock Markets: Unlocking Growth Potential Beyond Borders

Global stock markets provide a gateway to investing in companies that operate across different regions and industries. While domestic stocks may offer stability and familiarity, global stocks allow investors to tap into the growth trajectories of companies based in other countries, often operating in industries or sectors not prevalent in their home market.

- Developed Markets: Developed markets such as the U.S., Europe, and Japan offer access to well-established multinational corporations. These markets are typically more stable, with companies that have a global footprint, providing both steady growth and dividend income. For example, companies like Nestlé (Switzerland), Toyota (Japan), and Siemens (Germany) are industry leaders with extensive international operations.
- Emerging Markets: Emerging markets such as China, India, Brazil, and Southeast Asia present opportunities for higher growth but with increased volatility and risk. These economies are expanding rapidly, fueled by urbanization, industrialization, and a growing middle class. Emerging market equities can offer substantial returns in industries like technology, infrastructure, and consumer goods. Companies like Alibaba (China), Reliance Industries (India), and Vale (Brazil) are examples of high-growth firms that operate in these regions.
- International Mutual Funds and ETFs: For investors who prefer not to select individual stocks, mutual funds and exchange-traded funds (ETFs) focused on international markets offer a diversified approach to global equity

investing. Funds like the Vanguard FTSE All-World ex-US ETF provide exposure to both developed and emerging markets, helping investors balance risk while capturing international growth potential.

2. Global Bond Markets: Income, Stability, and Diversification

Global bond markets offer investors a way to diversify their fixed-income portfolios, gain exposure to foreign interest rates, and hedge against domestic market volatility. Bonds issued by governments and corporations around the world provide varying degrees of risk and return, depending on the issuing country's economic health and creditworthiness.

- Sovereign Bonds: Bonds issued by foreign governments—particularly those in developed economies such as Germany, the UK, and Japan—are generally considered stable and lower risk. Sovereign bonds from these nations offer relatively low yields but provide a safe haven for investors seeking to preserve capital while earning a modest return. In contrast, bonds from emerging economies like Mexico, Indonesia, or South Africa offer higher yields but come with greater political and economic risks.
- Corporate Bonds: International corporate bonds provide an opportunity to earn higher yields than sovereign bonds while still maintaining exposure to the stability of global markets. Companies issuing bonds in developed countries often have strong credit ratings and established track records. For example, bonds issued by European or

Japanese corporations can provide stable income with less risk than equities.

- Emerging Market Debt: Bonds issued by governments and corporations in emerging markets offer attractive yields due to the higher risk associated with these economies. Investors can benefit from the higher interest rates, but they must also be prepared for potential currency fluctuations and political instability that can impact bond prices. Emerging market debt funds, such as the iShares Emerging Markets Bond ETF, offer exposure to a broad range of countries, balancing the risks and rewards across multiple economies.

3. Global Real Estate: Expanding Investment Horizons

International real estate offers investors another avenue to diversify their portfolios and generate income through property ownership or real estate investment trusts (REITs). Global real estate investments provide exposure to both residential and commercial properties, allowing investors to benefit from capital appreciation, rental income, or dividends.

- Residential Real Estate: Investing in residential properties abroad, particularly in high-demand urban areas, offers opportunities for both rental income and property value appreciation. Cities like London, Paris, Singapore, and Sydney attract investors due to their strong rental markets, high demand for housing, and stable legal frameworks. Additionally, emerging markets like Dubai, Bangkok, and Mexico City provide higher growth potential due to increasing urbanization and demand for modern housing.

- ❖ Commercial Real Estate: Global commercial real estate, such as office buildings, shopping centers, hotels, and industrial properties, offers stable cash flows through long-term lease agreements. Key commercial hubs like New York, Hong Kong, and Frankfurt remain popular with institutional investors for their business-friendly environments and high demand for commercial spaces. Meanwhile, growing economies like China and India are witnessing a surge in demand for industrial and office spaces, driven by economic expansion and urbanization.
- ❖ Real Estate Investment Trusts (REITs): For those seeking exposure to global real estate without the complexities of direct property ownership, REITs offer a convenient alternative. Global REITs pool investors' capital to purchase income-generating properties across multiple regions, providing diversification and liquidity. International REITs like the SPDR Dow Jones International Real Estate ETF allow investors to access both developed and emerging markets while benefiting from dividend income generated by rental properties.

4. Key Considerations for Investing in Global Markets

While global financial markets offer vast opportunities, investors must consider the risks and complexities associated with investing abroad.

- ❖ Currency Risk: Exchange rate fluctuations can significantly impact the returns of international investments. A weakening domestic currency can enhance returns on foreign investments when converted back to the investor's currency, while a strengthening domestic currency can reduce those gains. Currency hedging strategies or investing in funds that manage currency risk can help mitigate these impacts.
- ❖ Geopolitical Risks: Investing in foreign markets exposes investors to political instability, regulatory changes, and government interventions that can affect market performance. For example, sudden changes in trade policies or nationalization of industries in emerging markets can pose risks to foreign investors. Staying informed about the political and economic climate of the countries in which investments are made is critical to managing this risk.
- ❖ Legal and Regulatory Differences: Different countries have varying legal systems, property rights, and tax regulations, which can affect the ease of doing business or investing. Investors must familiarize themselves with these regulations and, where necessary, seek legal or financial advice to navigate foreign markets effectively.

5. The Strategic Importance of Global Diversification

Diversifying across global financial markets provides a way to reduce portfolio risk by spreading investments across different economies, sectors, and asset classes. Global diversification allows investors to capture growth from different regions, ensuring that underperformance in one market can be offset by gains in another.

- ❖ Economic Cycles: Different countries and regions experience economic cycles at different times, allowing investors to capitalize on the growth of one market while others are in downturns. For example, during a slowdown in the U.S. economy, emerging markets in Asia or Latin America may still experience robust growth, providing alternative sources of returns.
- ❖ Sectorial Growth: International markets provide access to industries that may not be prominent in an investor's home country. For example, European markets offer significant opportunities in green energy, while Asian markets are leaders in technology and manufacturing. By diversifying across sectors, investors can benefit from global economic trends and innovation.

Investing in global financial markets—whether through stocks, bonds, or real estate—offers investors a unique opportunity to enhance returns, diversify risks, and capitalize on global growth. By understanding the dynamics of international markets and carefully managing the associated risks, investors can build resilient, globally diversified portfolios that support long-term wealth creation. As the global economy continues to evolve, the ability to navigate international investment opportunities will remain an essential component of a successful financial strategy.

- Benefits and Risks of Diversifying into International Investments

Diversifying into international investments has become an increasingly important strategy for investors seeking to enhance portfolio performance, mitigate risk, and capitalize on global economic opportunities. As globalization continues to integrate markets, investing beyond domestic borders opens doors to new growth prospects, while also presenting unique challenges. Understanding both the benefits and risks of international diversification is critical for developing a well-rounded investment strategy.

- Benefits of Diversifying into International Investments

1. Access to High-Growth Markets
    - Emerging Markets Opportunities: Many emerging economies, particularly in Asia, Africa, and Latin America, are experiencing rapid growth driven by industrialization, urbanization, and a rising middle class. Countries such as China, India, and Brazil offer substantial growth potential, especially in sectors like technology, infrastructure, and consumer goods. By investing in these markets, investors can gain exposure to higher returns that may not be available in mature economies.
    - Sectorial Diversification: International investments also provide access to industries and sectors that may be underrepresented or not available in a domestic market. For example, European markets are known for their strength in green energy and luxury goods, while Asian markets lead in technology and manufacturing. Diversifying into these sectors can offer significant growth potential for investors looking to capitalize on global trends.

2. Geographic Diversification
    - Reducing Country-Specific Risk: By spreading investments across multiple countries and regions, investors can reduce the impact of economic downturns or political instability in any one country. Geographic diversification ensures that underperformance in one market is offset by gains in another. For instance, while a domestic market may face a recession, international markets may continue to perform well, providing a counterbalance to portfolio losses.
    - Access to Different Economic Cycles: Different countries and regions experience economic cycles at varying times. While one economy may be in a period of contraction, another may be expanding. For example, during the 2008 global financial crisis, some emerging markets were more resilient than developed economies. By investing in a broad range of countries, investors can benefit from growth across different economic cycles.
3. Enhanced Portfolio Returns
    - Higher Yield Potential: International investments, particularly in emerging markets, often offer higher yield potential compared to domestic investments. This can be particularly true for international equities and bonds. Companies in high-growth markets, or sovereign debt from countries with higher interest rates, can provide better returns than similar investments in developed economies.
    - Currency Diversification: Holding investments in different currencies can further enhance returns if the foreign currency appreciates relative to the

investor's domestic currency. For instance, if an investor holds stocks in a European company and the Euro strengthens against the U.S. dollar, the investment's value increases when converted back to dollars.

4. Broader Investment Choices
    - Expanding Beyond Domestic Markets: Diversifying into international investments allows investors to choose from a broader pool of assets, including stocks, bonds, real estate, and alternative investments. International markets offer opportunities to invest in industries or sectors that are not prevalent in the domestic economy, such as natural resources in Latin America, financial services in Europe, or consumer technology in Asia.
    - International Mutual Funds and ETFs: For those who may not have the expertise or resources to research individual international stocks or bonds, mutual funds and exchange-traded funds (ETFs) focused on global markets offer a diversified and professionally managed option. These funds allow investors to gain exposure to global markets without the need for extensive knowledge of individual markets.

❖ Risks of Diversifying into International Investments

1. Currency Risk
    - Impact of Currency Fluctuations: One of the primary risks of international investing is exposure to currency fluctuations. Changes in exchange rates can significantly affect the value of an investment. For example, if an investor holds a European stock and the Euro weakens against the U.S. dollar, the value of the investment will decrease when

converted back to dollars, even if the stock price remains stable.

- Currency Hedging: Investors can mitigate currency risk by using hedging strategies, such as currency futures or purchasing funds that hedge against currency movements. However, hedging can add complexity and costs to an investment strategy.

2. Political and Economic Risks
    - Political Instability: International investments, particularly in emerging markets, are subject to political risks, such as changes in government policies, nationalization of industries, or political unrest. Political instability can lead to market volatility and negatively impact investments. For instance, sudden changes in trade policies or regulatory frameworks can disrupt business operations, leading to financial losses for investors.
    - Economic Uncertainty: Economic conditions in foreign markets, such as inflation, interest rates, and fiscal policies, can also influence investment performance. In some emerging markets, economic data may be less reliable, making it harder to assess the financial health of the market. Investors must be aware of the potential for economic shocks, such as currency devaluation or sovereign debt defaults.
3. Legal and Regulatory Challenges
    - Different Legal Frameworks: Investing in foreign markets means dealing with different legal systems, regulations, and tax policies. Investors must be aware of property rights, corporate governance standards, and local tax laws that may affect the return on their investments. For

instance, some countries have strict capital controls or restrictions on foreign ownership that can limit investment opportunities or make it difficult to repatriate profits.

- Regulatory Differences: Global markets often operate under different regulatory standards, which can affect transparency and investor protection. For example, accounting standards and financial reporting may vary from country to country, making it challenging for investors to accurately assess the financial health of foreign companies. Investors need to conduct thorough due diligence or rely on trusted financial advisors when navigating these regulatory environments.

4. Market Liquidity and Volatility

- Liquidity Concerns: International markets, particularly in smaller or emerging economies, may have lower liquidity compared to domestic markets. This can make it more difficult to buy or sell investments without affecting the market price. Lower liquidity can lead to higher transaction costs and increased volatility, especially in times of market stress.
- Market Volatility: International markets can be more volatile than domestic markets, particularly in regions with political or economic instability. Emerging markets, while offering higher growth potential, are often more susceptible to large swings in market prices due to external shocks, such as commodity price fluctuations or global trade disruptions. This higher volatility can

lead to significant short-term losses, even for long-term investors.

5. Cultural and Information Barriers

   - Understanding Foreign Markets: International investments require an understanding of the cultural, economic, and business practices of foreign markets. Differences in corporate governance, accounting standards, and market practices can create barriers for investors unfamiliar with the region. Moreover, access to timely and accurate information about foreign companies and markets may be limited, making it more challenging to make informed investment decisions.
   - Language and Time Zone Differences: Communication barriers, including language and time zone differences, can further complicate international investing. Investors may face difficulties obtaining information or communicating with foreign companies or financial institutions in a timely manner.

Diversifying into international investments offers investors significant benefits, including access to high-growth markets, enhanced portfolio diversification, and the potential for improved returns. However, these advantages come with risks, such as currency fluctuations, political instability, regulatory challenges, and increased volatility. To navigate these risks, investors should conduct thorough research, consider professional guidance, and carefully assess their risk tolerance and investment objectives. By balancing the benefits and risks, international diversification can be a powerful tool for building a resilient and globally diversified portfolio that supports long-term wealth creation.

Navigating Geopolitical Risks

- How Global Political Events Impact Wealth: Trade Wars, Sanctions, and Policy Changes

In an increasingly interconnected world, global political events can have significant ripple effects on personal wealth, business strategies, and investment portfolios. Trade wars, sanctions, and policy changes are critical geopolitical events that can impact global markets and financial stability. Investors, businesses, and individuals must understand how these events influence economic landscapes and devise strategies to mitigate risks while capitalizing on emerging opportunities.

1. Trade Wars: Disrupting Supply Chains and Increasing Market Volatility

Definition and Overview: Trade wars occur when countries impose tariffs or other trade barriers to protect domestic industries, often triggering retaliatory measures from trading partners. Recent high-profile trade disputes, such as the U.S.-China trade war, illustrate how these conflicts can have far-reaching consequences.

Impact on Wealth:

- Market Volatility: Trade wars often lead to increased volatility in global stock and commodity markets. Businesses exposed to international supply chains may experience disruptions, increased costs, and reduced profitability, which can negatively affect their stock prices.
- Rising Costs for Consumers: Trade tariffs can increase the price of imported goods, leading to

inflationary pressures that reduce consumers' purchasing power. This erosion of disposable income can affect wealth-building efforts and savings rates.

- Corporate Profitability: Companies reliant on cross-border trade, particularly those in manufacturing and technology sectors, may experience a decline in profitability due to higher input costs, reduced access to global markets, and uncertainty in demand. Reduced profitability can lead to lower dividends and capital gains for investors.

Strategic Considerations:

- Sector Diversification: Investors can mitigate the risks of trade wars by diversifying their portfolios across sectors that are less reliant on international trade, such as healthcare, utilities, and consumer staples.
- Geographical Diversification: Investing in companies from regions or countries less affected by a particular trade conflict can provide insulation from market volatility and disruptions.
- Hedging Strategies: Businesses can employ hedging strategies, such as currency hedges and futures contracts, to minimize the impact of price fluctuations resulting from trade disputes.

2. Sanctions: Limiting Access to Global Markets and Investment Opportunities

Definition and Overview: Sanctions are economic and political measures imposed by one country or group of countries on another to achieve foreign policy objectives.

These measures can include asset freezes, trade embargoes, and restrictions on financial transactions.

Impact on Wealth:

- Restricted Access to Markets: Sanctions can restrict access to certain markets, industries, or financial systems. Investors holding assets or operating businesses in sanctioned regions may face significant challenges, including asset freezes, decreased liquidity, and loss of revenue.
- Devaluation of Assets: Assets in sanctioned countries or businesses directly impacted by sanctions may experience sharp declines in value. For example, in response to sanctions, affected currencies may depreciate rapidly, and local stock markets can experience sharp downturns, reducing the value of investments.
- Limited Investment Opportunities: Sanctions can reduce opportunities for investment in high-growth regions or industries. Investors may miss out on profitable ventures in sanctioned countries, especially in resource-rich or emerging markets.

Strategic Considerations:

- Compliance and Risk Management: Investors and businesses must carefully monitor sanctions lists and adhere to compliance regulations to avoid fines and legal complications. Consulting legal experts and staying informed about evolving sanctions regimes is essential.

- Regional Diversification: By diversifying investments across regions, investors can reduce the risk of concentrated exposure to sanctioned countries. This strategy provides more flexibility to reallocate capital in response to changing geopolitical dynamics.
- Opportunistic Investments: Investors can consider sectors that may benefit from sanctions, such as domestic industries poised to replace foreign suppliers or countries that may fill the void left by sanctioned entities in the global market.

3. Policy Changes: Tax Reforms, Trade Agreements, and Regulatory Shifts

Definition and Overview: Government policy changes, including tax reforms, trade agreements, and regulatory shifts, can significantly affect personal and corporate wealth. Changes in fiscal, monetary, or trade policy often reshape economic environments, creating both risks and opportunities for investors.

Impact on Wealth:

- Tax Reforms: Changes in corporate or personal tax rates can directly impact income and investment returns. Lower taxes generally increase disposable income and corporate profitability, while higher taxes reduce after-tax earnings, affecting both businesses and individuals.
- Regulatory Changes: Regulatory shifts, such as environmental or financial regulations, can create new costs or constraints for businesses. Stricter regulations may raise operational costs,

reduce profit margins, and decrease shareholder value, while deregulation can lead to greater profitability in certain industries.

- Trade Agreements: New trade agreements or changes to existing agreements can open up or restrict access to markets. Favorable trade policies may enhance global market access for businesses and boost exports, while protectionist measures can stifle growth and limit investment opportunities.

Strategic Considerations:

- Tax-Efficient Investment Strategies: Investors should stay informed about tax policy changes and consider strategies to optimize their portfolios for tax efficiency, such as tax-advantaged retirement accounts, municipal bonds, and capital gains deferral techniques.
- Sector-Specific Investing: Policy changes can create winners and losers among industries. Investors can capitalize on favorable policy shifts by investing in sectors poised to benefit, such as clean energy during periods of environmental regulation or technology during times of deregulation.
- Flexible Business Models: For businesses, building flexibility into supply chains, cost structures, and operational models is key to adapting to changing policies. Companies that can quickly pivot in response to policy changes are better positioned to maintain profitability and protect shareholder value.

4. Long-Term Implications for Global Wealth Distribution

Global political events, including trade wars, sanctions, and policy changes, not only affect immediate financial outcomes but also have long-term implications for wealth distribution across countries and regions. Emerging markets, for example, may see rapid growth as global supply chains shift due to trade wars or as sanctions realign political alliances. Conversely, long-standing global economic powerhouses may experience slower growth or diminished influence as they contend with evolving geopolitical challenges.

For investors and businesses seeking to build and protect wealth, understanding these political dynamics is essential. Geopolitical events shape the rules of engagement in global markets, and those who can anticipate and adapt to these shifts will be better equipped to navigate the complexities of the global economy.

Global political events like trade wars, sanctions, and policy changes play a pivotal role in shaping personal wealth, business outcomes, and investment strategies. Understanding how these events impact wealth creation and distribution allows investors and businesses to develop risk management strategies that protect their assets while taking advantage of emerging opportunities.

By employing strategies such as geographic and sector diversification, monitoring geopolitical trends, and adapting to policy changes, individuals and businesses can better navigate the challenges posed by global political events and maintain a robust wealth-building approach.

- Economic Cycles and Their Global Ripple Effects on Personal Wealth

Economic cycles are natural phases of expansion and contraction that occur in economies over time. These cycles, which include periods of growth (booms) and periods of decline (recessions or depressions), have profound effects on personal wealth, both locally and globally. Understanding how economic cycles work, and their ripple effects on wealth creation, preservation, and distribution, is crucial for effective financial planning, particularly in an era of increased global interconnectedness.

1. Understanding Economic Cycles: Phases and Dynamics

Economic cycles consist of four primary phases: expansion, peak, contraction, and trough. Each phase presents unique challenges and opportunities for personal wealth.

- Expansion: Characterized by rising GDP, employment, consumer spending, and corporate profits. During this phase, investments in stocks, real estate, and other assets typically appreciate in value, leading to wealth accumulation.
- Peak: The economy reaches its highest point of growth. Asset prices are often at their peak, and inflationary pressures may begin to rise. For individuals, this may present an opportunity to take profits from investments or reallocate portfolios to less volatile assets.
- Contraction: Also known as a recession, this phase sees a decline in economic activity, rising unemployment, and falling asset prices. For personal wealth, this period is marked by decreased investment returns, reduced consumer spending

power, and higher risks of job loss or business downturns.
- ❖ Trough: The economy hits its lowest point before recovery begins. Opportunities to invest in undervalued assets arise, setting the stage for wealth-building in the next expansion phase.

2. Global Ripple Effects of Economic Cycles on Personal Wealth

In today's interconnected global economy, economic cycles in one region can have far-reaching effects on personal wealth around the world. These ripple effects are amplified by cross-border trade, financial markets, and global investment flows.

- ❖ Stock Markets and Investment Portfolios: Global stock markets are highly interconnected, with volatility in one country often spilling over into others. For example, a recession in a major economy like the United States can trigger a global selloff in stocks, leading to declines in the value of portfolios held by investors worldwide. Diversifying investments across international markets can help mitigate this risk, but global economic downturns can still impact overall portfolio returns.
- ❖ Currency Fluctuations: Economic cycles affect currency values, which in turn impact personal wealth, particularly for individuals engaged in international trade, travel, or foreign investments. During periods of economic contraction, currencies may depreciate, reducing the value of overseas assets and increasing the cost of imported goods and services. Conversely, during

expansions, stronger currencies can enhance purchasing power abroad, benefiting those with international interests.

- ❖ Commodities and Inflation: Economic cycles can also impact global commodity prices, such as oil, gold, and agricultural products. During expansionary periods, increased demand for commodities can drive up prices, leading to inflation. Inflation erodes the purchasing power of money, reducing the real value of savings and investments. Conversely, during contractions, falling commodity prices can create deflationary pressures, affecting income and asset prices in commodity-dependent economies.
- ❖ Housing Markets: Real estate markets are closely tied to economic cycles. During expansions, rising employment and income levels increase demand for housing, driving up property values. This can be a boon for homeowners and real estate investors. However, during recessions, falling demand and rising defaults can cause property values to plummet, negatively impacting personal wealth tied to real estate assets.

3. How Global Recessions Affect Personal Wealth

Global recessions, such as the 2008 financial crisis or the economic fallout from the COVID-19 pandemic, provide clear examples of how economic cycles can have profound effects on personal wealth.

- ❖ Asset Depreciation: During a global recession, stock markets typically decline, leading to significant losses for investors. For example, the S&P 500 lost over 50% of its value during the 2008 financial crisis, resulting in massive wealth destruction for individuals with equity-heavy portfolios.

- Job Loss and Income Reduction: Global recessions often result in widespread layoffs, wage cuts, and reduced business revenues. This loss of income can force individuals to deplete their savings, sell off assets, or go into debt, leading to long-term financial setbacks. Diversifying income streams, including building passive income sources, can provide a buffer against income loss during economic downturns.
- Credit Tightening: During contractions, banks and financial institutions often tighten lending criteria, making it more difficult to access credit. For individuals relying on loans for home purchases, business expansion, or personal expenses, this can lead to delays or higher borrowing costs. On the other hand, those with strong credit and cash reserves may find opportunities to acquire assets at lower prices during these periods.

4. Opportunities for Wealth Building in Different Phases of the Economic Cycle

Despite the risks posed by economic cycles, each phase offers unique opportunities for wealth building:

- Expansion Phase:

    - Growth Investments: As corporate earnings rise and consumer spending increases, stocks, real estate, and other growth-oriented investments tend to perform well.

This is an ideal time to invest in equities, real estate, and other assets that benefit from economic growth.

- Entrepreneurship: The expansion phase is often the best time to start or grow a business, as consumer demand and access to capital are generally strong.

❖ Contraction Phase:

- Value Investing: During a contraction, many assets become undervalued. This creates opportunities for value investors to buy quality stocks, real estate, or businesses at discounted prices, setting the stage for future wealth accumulation once the economy recovers.
- Defensive Strategies: Investors may shift toward defensive assets like bonds, gold, and utilities, which tend to hold value or perform well during economic downturns.

❖ Trough Phase:

- Repositioning Portfolios: As the economy begins to recover, this is a key time to reposition investment portfolios to capture growth. Individuals who accumulated assets during the downturn can benefit from rising prices during the next expansion.

5. Strategies for Managing Personal Wealth through Economic Cycles

To navigate economic cycles and protect personal wealth, individuals must employ proactive financial strategies:

- Diversification: Spreading investments across asset classes, industries, and geographies helps reduce the impact of economic downturns. A diversified portfolio may include equities, bonds, real estate, commodities, and alternative investments, each reacting differently to economic conditions.
- Emergency Fund: Maintaining a robust emergency fund is essential for weathering periods of income loss or economic instability. An emergency fund provides liquidity without needing to sell long-term investments at a loss during a downturn.
- Rebalancing: Regularly rebalancing investment portfolios ensures that asset allocations align with risk tolerance and financial goals. During expansions, portfolios may become overweight in equities, necessitating a shift toward safer assets as a recession looms.
- Hedging: Investors can use hedging strategies, such as options or commodities, to protect against losses during periods of market volatility. Hedging allows individuals to mitigate risk while preserving opportunities for upside gains.

6. The Role of Government Policy in Mitigating Economic Cycles

Government interventions, such as monetary and fiscal policy, play a significant role in mitigating the extremes of economic cycles. Central banks, such as the U.S. Federal Reserve, can influence interest rates and money supply to smooth out booms and busts. Lowering interest rates during contractions encourages borrowing and investment, while raising rates during expansions helps curb inflation.

For individuals, understanding the likely direction of government policy can inform decisions about investments, loans, and spending. For example, low interest rates during a recession may present an opportunity to refinance debt or purchase a home at favorable rates.

Economic cycles are an inevitable aspect of financial markets and economies. By understanding their dynamics and global ripple effects, individuals can make informed decisions about managing and growing their personal wealth. Adopting strategies such as diversification, value investing during downturns, and repositioning portfolios during recoveries allows individuals to protect their wealth while capitalizing on opportunities that arise in different phases of the economic cycle.

CHAPTER FOUR

DIGITAL WEALTH AND FINANCIAL TECHNOLOGY (FINTECH)

In an increasingly digital world, technological advances are rapidly changing the landscape of wealth creation. This chapter explores how financial technology (FinTech) is democratizing access to wealth-building tools.

The Rise of FinTech in Wealth Management

- Overview of FinTech innovations: Robo-advisors, AI-driven investments, and algorithmic trading

FinTech (financial technology) innovations have radically transformed the wealth management landscape in recent years. New tools and platforms, powered by advancements in artificial intelligence (AI), data analytics, and algorithmic trading, are reshaping how investors manage their portfolios and make financial decisions. These innovations offer greater accessibility, efficiency, and personalization, allowing both individual and institutional investors to harness technology to optimize their wealth management strategies.

1. Robo-Advisors: Automating Investment Management

Robo-advisors are digital platforms that provide automated, algorithm-driven financial planning services with little to no human supervision. They typically require users to fill out an online questionnaire that gathers information about their financial goals, risk tolerance, and investment preferences. Based on this data, the robo-advisor uses algorithms to build and manage a customized investment portfolio.

Key Features and Benefits:

- Low-Cost Investment Management: Robo-advisors offer a more affordable alternative to traditional human financial advisors. By automating tasks such as portfolio construction, asset allocation, and rebalancing, they significantly reduce costs, with management fees often ranging from 0.2% to 0.5% per year.
- Accessibility: These platforms have democratized access to professional investment management. Investors with smaller portfolios, who might not have met the high minimums required by traditional advisors, can now benefit from sophisticated financial strategies.
- Diversification and Risk Management: Robo-advisors generally use Modern Portfolio Theory (MPT) to create diversified portfolios based on asset allocation models. They invest across asset classes such as stocks, bonds, and real estate to mitigate risk while aiming to achieve optimal returns.
- Automatic Rebalancing: One of the most significant advantages of robo-advisors is the automatic rebalancing of portfolios. As markets fluctuate, the platform adjusts the portfolio to maintain the desired asset allocation, ensuring the investor's strategy remains aligned with their financial goals.

Popular Platforms:

- Betterment: One of the earliest robo-advisors, Betterment offers goal-based investing and automated portfolio rebalancing.

- Wealthfront: Wealthfront provides a comprehensive suite of services, including tax-loss harvesting, portfolio rebalancing, and direct indexing for more personalized investment options.
- SoFi Invest: SoFi offers free robo-advisory services, making it one of the most affordable options for beginners.

2. AI-Driven Investments: Enhancing Decision-Making Through Machine Learning

Artificial Intelligence (AI) has introduced a new level of sophistication to wealth management. AI-driven investment tools leverage machine learning algorithms to analyze vast amounts of data, identify trends, and generate predictive models that enhance investment decisions. These innovations allow investors to gain insights beyond traditional analysis, helping them identify opportunities and manage risks more effectively.

Key Applications of AI in Investments:

- Predictive Analytics: AI-driven platforms can analyze market data, financial statements, news articles, and social media trends to forecast stock price movements, enabling more informed investment decisions.
- Sentiment Analysis: AI tools can process massive datasets, including news sentiment and social media posts, to gauge market sentiment about specific sectors or companies. This helps investors react to emerging trends and sentiments that might impact market movements.
- Personalization: AI can create highly personalized investment strategies tailored

to an investor's specific needs. By continuously learning from an investor's behavior and preferences, AI-powered systems can adjust portfolios dynamically, ensuring that they remain aligned with the investor's goals.

AI in Practice:

- BlackRock's Aladdin: BlackRock's Aladdin platform is one of the most advanced AI-driven tools in wealth management, used to analyze market risks, optimize portfolio performance, and generate investment strategies based on AI-driven insights.
- Kensho: Owned by S&P Global, Kensho utilizes AI to analyze vast datasets and provide predictive insights into financial markets. It helps institutional investors make informed decisions based on its deep data analytics.
- Numerai: Numerai is a hedge fund that uses AI models submitted by data scientists to manage its investment portfolio, blending machine learning with quantitative trading strategies.

3. Algorithmic Trading: Speed, Efficiency, and Data-Driven Execution

Algorithmic trading, or "algo trading," refers to the use of computer algorithms to automatically execute trades based on predefined criteria. These criteria can include timing, price, quantity, or a mathematical model. Algorithmic trading is widely used by institutional investors and hedge funds to execute large orders quickly and efficiently, minimizing the impact on the market and reducing transaction costs.

Key Advantages of Algorithmic Trading:

- Speed: Algorithms can execute trades at lightning speed, processing thousands of orders in seconds. This is critical in volatile markets where timing can make a significant difference in price execution.
- Reduced Costs: By automating the trading process, algorithmic trading reduces the need for human intervention, cutting down on the costs associated with manual trading and reducing the bid-ask spread by executing at optimal prices.
- Precision and Discipline: Algo trading eliminates the potential for human error or emotional decision-making, ensuring that trades are executed based on data and pre-set conditions. This leads to more disciplined trading and improved consistency in following strategies.

Strategies Employed in Algorithmic Trading:

- Trend Following: This strategy involves algorithms analyzing technical indicators such as moving averages to identify and follow trends. The algorithm will automatically execute trades when these trends are detected, without the need for predicting price movements.
- Arbitrage: Algorithms can identify price discrepancies between different markets or assets and execute trades to profit from these inefficiencies. For example, if a stock is priced lower on one exchange than on another, the algorithm will buy it at the lower price and sell it at the higher price, profiting from the spread.
- Market Making: This strategy involves continuously buying and selling securities to

provide liquidity to the market, earning profits from the bid-ask spread. Algorithms are programmed to rapidly quote and execute both buy and sell orders, ensuring liquidity and tight spreads.

Impact on Individual Investors:

Algorithmic trading was once limited to large financial institutions, but recent advances have made these strategies available to retail investors through online platforms and brokers. Platforms like QuantConnect and MetaTrader allow individual investors to develop, test, and deploy their own trading algorithms.

4. Risks and Challenges of FinTech Innovations in Wealth Management

While FinTech innovations have revolutionized wealth management, they are not without risks. Understanding these risks is essential for investors who are considering adopting these technologies.

- Over-Reliance on Algorithms: Automated systems, whether through robo-advisors or algorithmic trading, are only as effective as the algorithms they use. Market anomalies, black swan events, or unforeseen market conditions can cause these algorithms to malfunction or make poor investment decisions.
- Data Security and Privacy: With the growing reliance on digital platforms for investment management, data breaches and cybersecurity threats are increasing. Investors must ensure that they use secure platforms and understand the privacy policies of the services they engage with.

- Lack of Personalization for Complex Needs: While robo-advisors and AI-driven tools excel at managing simple, goal-based portfolios, they may not be able to address the complexities of high-net-worth individuals with unique tax situations, estate planning needs, or more sophisticated financial goals.

5. The Future of FinTech in Wealth Management

The future of FinTech in wealth management is poised for even greater innovation. Emerging technologies like blockchain, decentralized finance (DeFi), and enhanced AI models will further democratize access to financial tools and services.

Blockchain and Tokenization: Blockchain technology could revolutionize how assets are traded and managed by enabling secure, transparent, and decentralized financial transactions. Tokenization could allow for fractional ownership of assets, opening up new investment opportunities for retail investors.

- Decentralized Finance (DeFi): DeFi platforms, which operate on blockchain networks, offer peer-to-peer financial services without intermediaries. This could dramatically reduce costs and increase access to global investment opportunities.
- Enhanced AI: As AI models become more sophisticated, their ability to deliver personalized financial advice and manage portfolios with minimal human oversight will only improve, offering more tailored solutions for a broader range of investors.

6. Embracing FinTech for a Smarter Wealth Management Future

FinTech innovations such as robo-advisors, AI-driven investments, and algorithmic trading have significantly enhanced the efficiency, accessibility, and effectiveness of wealth management. These tools enable investors to make more informed decisions, minimize costs, and personalize their financial strategies. However, it is essential to balance the advantages with an understanding of the inherent risks, particularly in an environment that is increasingly reliant on technology. The rise of FinTech has democratized wealth management, but investors should remain vigilant, continually educate themselves on emerging technologies, and choose platforms that align with their financial goals and risk tolerance.

- How Technology is Reshaping Personal Finance and Wealth-Building Practices

The digital revolution has transformed nearly every aspect of modern life, and personal finance is no exception. The rise of financial technology (FinTech) has dramatically reshaped the way individuals manage money, save, invest, and build wealth. In the wealth management industry, the emergence of cutting-edge tools—ranging from robo-advisors and algorithmic trading to digital banking and blockchain—has democratized access to financial services, enhanced efficiency, and redefined the relationship between investors and their finances. Below is an in-depth look at how technology is reshaping personal finance and wealth-building practices as part of the rise of FinTech.

1. Automating Personal Finance and Investment Decisions

- One of the most significant advancements in FinTech is automation, particularly through robo-advisors and algorithmic tools. Robo-advisors are digital platforms that offer automated, algorithm-driven financial planning services with little to no human supervision. They typically collect information about a client's financial situation and goals through an online survey and then use data to offer advice or automatically invest client assets in a diversified portfolio.
- By lowering barriers to entry—such as requiring lower minimum balances and offering low-cost services—robo-advisors have made professional wealth management accessible to a broader demographic. What was once reserved for affluent individuals is now available to the masses. Additionally, automation removes human bias from investment decisions, allowing for more disciplined and efficient investment strategies.
- For instance, the use of algorithms to rebalance portfolios and optimize tax strategies ensures that investments are constantly working towards long-term goals without the need for frequent human intervention. This approach not only improves efficiency but also allows individuals to capitalize on real-time market changes, optimizing investment performance.

2. AI-Driven Wealth Management

- Artificial Intelligence (AI) is a game-changer in wealth management, providing predictive analytics and personalized recommendations based on vast amounts of data. AI-driven platforms analyze trends, user behavior, and market patterns to offer tailored advice and solutions that were previously only possible with human advisors.

- AI has the potential to help individuals make smarter financial decisions by providing insights that humans alone cannot. It can anticipate market shifts, suggest optimal times to invest, identify potential risks, and even recommend ways to diversify portfolios to minimize exposure. This data-driven decision-making leads to more informed financial strategies, which can enhance wealth accumulation.
- AI is also transforming customer service. Chatbots and virtual assistants provide 24/7 customer support, answering financial queries, assisting with budgeting, and even offering investment advice—without the need for human advisors.

3. Budgeting and Financial Planning Apps

- Financial technology has put sophisticated tools for budgeting, saving, and managing debt directly into consumers' hands. Mobile apps like Mint, You Need a Budget (YNAB), and Personal Capital help users track their income, expenses, and savings goals in real time. These apps often integrate with bank accounts, credit cards, and investment platforms, offering users a comprehensive view of their financial health.
- The accessibility of these tools enables individuals to create and monitor financial plans without the need for a financial advisor. For instance, automated notifications on overspending, bill payment reminders, and tools to track financial goals have empowered people to take control of their personal finances with minimal effort. This level of access and convenience helps users adopt better financial habits, accumulate savings, and ultimately build wealth over time.

4. The Power of Peer-to-Peer Lending and Crowdfunding

- FinTech has also revolutionized the way people borrow and invest through peer-to-peer (P2P) lending and crowdfunding platforms. These platforms eliminate traditional financial intermediaries like banks, connecting borrowers directly with investors. P2P lending allows individuals to secure personal or business loans at potentially lower interest rates than those offered by banks, while investors can earn returns by lending to vetted borrowers.
- Crowdfunding platforms like Kickstarter, GoFundMe, and Indiegogo provide opportunities for entrepreneurs to raise capital for innovative projects. Investors can participate in early-stage ventures, sometimes with the opportunity to profit from the success of these projects. This direct-access model to funding and investment opportunities has democratized wealth-building by opening up access to markets previously controlled by institutional investors.

5. Cryptocurrency and Blockchain in Wealth Management

Cryptocurrency and blockchain technology are rapidly changing the financial landscape. Digital currencies like Bitcoin and Ethereum offer new avenues for investment, while blockchain technology provides enhanced transparency, security, and efficiency in financial transactions.

- For investors, cryptocurrencies present an alternative asset class with high potential returns, although they are accompanied by considerable volatility and risk. Beyond cryptocurrencies, blockchain's distributed ledger technology (DLT) is transforming traditional finance by streamlining processes like cross-border payments, transaction settlements, and the execution of smart contracts. The decentralization and immutability of blockchain reduce transaction costs, increase security, and minimize the risk of fraud, thus playing a vital role in wealth preservation and management.

6. The Rise of Digital Banking

- FinTech has redefined traditional banking through digital banks, or "neobanks," which operate entirely online. These banks typically offer lower fees, higher interest rates on savings, and more flexible products than traditional banks. Digital banking platforms also incorporate features like real-time spending analytics, financial planning tools, and automated savings programs that round up purchases and deposit the difference into savings accounts.
- The convenience and user-friendly experience provided by digital banking platforms have prompted consumers to adopt them in greater numbers, empowering them to manage their finances more efficiently and make informed decisions that support long-term wealth-building.

7. Impact of Data Security and Privacy

- As technology continues to evolve, data security and privacy concerns have become paramount. The rise of digital platforms has increased the volume of personal and financial data that is shared online, making cybersecurity a top priority for FinTech companies. Wealth management platforms now incorporate state-of-the-art encryption, two-factor authentication, and biometric security measures to protect clients' financial information.

- For consumers, trusting these platforms with sensitive data is essential, and companies that prioritize transparency and security have a significant advantage in retaining clients. The ability to ensure data privacy and protect against cyber-attacks is crucial for the long-term success of FinTech in wealth management.

Technology has reshaped personal finance and wealth-building practices by making financial services more accessible, efficient, and personalized. From the rise of AI-driven investment strategies and robo-advisors to the democratization of banking and investment through P2P lending, FinTech is revolutionizing the way individuals manage their wealth. This transformation enables people to take control of their financial futures with tools that were once reserved for institutional investors. However, as the use of digital platforms grows, ensuring data security and ethical practices will be essential to building long-lasting trust in these systems. Ultimately, FinTech's innovations are empowering more individuals to grow, preserve, and manage their wealth on their own terms.

- The Democratization of Finance: Accessing Sophisticated Tools Previously Reserved for the Wealthy

The rise of FinTech (financial technology) has dramatically altered the financial landscape, creating an unprecedented level of accessibility to sophisticated financial tools. Previously, many of these services—such as professional-grade investment strategies, personalized financial advice, and advanced wealth management—were reserved for the wealthy or institutional investors. Today, FinTech platforms are democratizing finance, making it easier for people from all walks of life to access and leverage these tools to build and manage wealth.

1. Robo-Advisors: Lowering the Barrier to Entry

One of the most significant advancements in the democratization of finance has been the rise of robo-advisors. These platforms automate the investment process, offering low-cost portfolio management services that were once the domain of expensive financial advisors and wealth managers. Platforms such as **Betterment**, **Wealthfront**, and **Personal Capital** use algorithms to manage and rebalance portfolios based on individual goals and risk tolerance.

Key Features:

- Low-Cost Wealth Management: Traditional financial advisors typically charge around 1% of assets under management (AUM), a rate that is prohibitive for smaller investors. Robo-advisors, by contrast, charge a fraction of that, often as low as 0.25% to 0.50% of AUM.
- Automated Portfolio Rebalancing: Robo-advisors continuously monitor portfolios and make adjustments to maintain the desired asset allocation, a service that was once manual and reserved for high-net-worth clients.
- Accessible for Smaller Investors: Previously, individuals with less capital would have limited access to wealth management services. Robo-advisors remove this barrier by allowing people to begin investing with relatively small

amounts of money, democratizing access to professional-level investment strategies.

Impact on Wealth Building:

By lowering costs and enabling access to professional-grade wealth management, robo-advisors allow a broader range of individuals to grow their wealth. These platforms make it easier for people to start investing early, harnessing the power of compounding for long-term growth, even with modest initial investments.

2. Fractional Shares: Opening Up High-Priced Investments

The ability to purchase fractional shares has opened up access to expensive stocks and exchange-traded funds (ETFs) that were previously out of reach for many investors. Platforms like **Robinhood**, **M1 Finance**, and **Stash** allow investors to buy portions of high-priced stocks like Amazon or Tesla, even if they can't afford a full share.

Key Features:

- ❖ Investing with Smaller Sums: Instead of needing thousands of dollars to invest in high-priced stocks, fractional share platforms allow users to invest with amounts as low as $5. This democratization enables more people to diversify their portfolios, regardless of income level.
- ❖ Broader Access to Market Leaders: Traditionally, high-priced stocks acted as barriers for small investors. Fractional shares enable individuals to own shares in top-performing companies, helping them

build diversified portfolios with high-quality assets.

Impact on Wealth Building:

Fractional shares eliminate the need for large amounts of upfront capital, allowing small investors to access high-quality, high-priced assets. This opens the door to more diversified and balanced portfolios, reducing risk and increasing the potential for returns across a broader spectrum of investments.

3. Access to Sophisticated Trading Tools: Leveraging Data and Algorithms

Advancements in technology have also brought professional-level trading tools to the general public. Platforms like **TD Ameritrade**, **E*TRADE**, and **Interactive Brokers** offer retail investors access to tools such as real-time data analytics, algorithmic trading, and technical analysis. These features were once only available to institutional investors or high-net-worth individuals.

Key Features:

- Algorithmic Trading: Platforms like **QuantConnect** allow users to create and test algorithmic trading strategies, using complex algorithms to automate buying and selling decisions. Previously, algorithmic trading was limited to hedge funds and professional traders.
- Data-Driven Decision Making: Advanced charting tools and data analytics platforms are now widely available to individual investors. This gives everyday users access to the same market insights and

technical indicators that were once exclusive to professional traders.

Impact on Wealth Building:

The availability of sophisticated trading tools levels the playing field between retail and institutional investors. Individuals can now make data-driven investment decisions, increasing their ability to generate returns and build wealth more effectively. With access to real-time market insights, small investors can time their trades with more precision, increasing profitability.

4. Peer-to-Peer Lending and Crowd-funding: Access to Alternative Investment Opportunities

FinTech has also democratized access to alternative investments such as peer-to-peer (P2P) lending and crowdfunding. Platforms like **LendingClub**, **Prosper**, and **Fundrise** offer individuals the ability to invest in loans or real estate projects, providing opportunities that were previously reserved for institutional investors.

Key Features:

- Peer-to-Peer Lending: P2P lending platforms allow individuals to lend money to borrowers and earn interest, acting as an alternative to traditional bond investments. These platforms open the door to high-yield investment opportunities, especially for those seeking income-generating assets.
- Crowdfunding Real Estate: Platforms like **Fundrise** and **RealtyMogul** enable investors to pool funds to invest in real estate projects. This model lowers the capital requirements for real estate investment, making it possible for

individuals to diversify into property ownership with smaller amounts of money.

Impact on Wealth Building:

By providing access to alternative investment markets, these platforms allow small investors to diversify their portfolios beyond traditional stocks and bonds. This diversification reduces risk and opens up new avenues for wealth generation, such as real estate income or high-interest lending.

5. Blockchain and Cryptocurrency: Decentralizing Wealth (Discussed further below)

The rise of blockchain technology and cryptocurrency represents one of the most significant advancements in the democratization of finance. Platforms like **Coinbase** and **Binance** have opened up the ability for retail investors to participate in the cryptocurrency markets, which were previously dominated by early adopters and institutional players.

Key Features:

- ❖ Decentralization of Finance: Blockchain technology decentralizes financial systems, removing intermediaries like banks and making it easier for individuals to engage in global financial markets directly.
- ❖ Access to High-Risk, High-Reward Investments: Cryptocurrencies such as Bitcoin and Ethereum offer high-risk, high-reward investment opportunities. While volatile, they provide the potential for significant returns, and the barrier to entry has been lowered thanks to easy-to-use platforms.

Impact on Wealth Building:

Cryptocurrencies provide access to a new asset class, offering investors the opportunity to diversify into digital assets. While inherently riskier, the decentralized nature of blockchain technology and cryptocurrency also provides opportunities for wealth building that bypass traditional financial gatekeepers.

Cryptocurrency and Blockchain: Opportunities and Risks

- Introduction to Cryptocurrency: Bitcoin, Ethereum, and Emerging Digital Currencies

Cryptocurrency, a form of digital or virtual currency, has transformed global financial systems over the last decade. Built on decentralized blockchain technology, cryptocurrencies offer a new way to conduct transactions, store value, and invest in assets outside the traditional financial system. As the popularity of cryptocurrencies continues to grow, understanding their fundamentals, including major currencies like Bitcoin and Ethereum, is critical to navigating the opportunities and risks in this rapidly evolving landscape.

1. Bitcoin: The Pioneer of Cryptocurrency

Bitcoin (BTC) is the first and most widely recognized cryptocurrency. Launched in 2009 by an anonymous entity known as **Satoshi Nakamoto**, Bitcoin was created as a decentralized peer-to-peer digital currency that allows for secure and transparent transactions without the need for intermediaries such as banks or governments.

Key Features:

- ❖ Decentralization: Bitcoin operates on a blockchain, a distributed ledger technology (DLT) that records transactions across a network of computers, ensuring transparency and security. No central authority controls Bitcoin, making it resistant to censorship and government intervention.
- ❖ Scarcity: Bitcoin's supply is capped at 21 million coins, which adds a sense of scarcity and potentially drives its value over

time. This feature is often compared to gold, leading to Bitcoin being referred to as "digital gold."

- ❖ Store of Value: Over time, Bitcoin has increasingly been viewed as a store of value, similar to precious metals like gold, rather than just a medium of exchange. Many investors buy Bitcoin as a hedge against inflation and economic instability.

Investment Perspective:

Bitcoin's value has grown exponentially since its inception, making it a popular investment choice. However, its **extreme volatility** presents both significant profit opportunities and substantial risks. Investors in Bitcoin need to be prepared for rapid price swings, but those who understand its potential as a long-term store of value may view it as a key component of their diversified portfolio.

2. Ethereum: The Foundation of Decentralized Applications

While Bitcoin focuses primarily on being a decentralized digital currency, **Ethereum (ETH)** is a more versatile platform designed for smart contracts and decentralized applications (dApps). Launched in 2015 by **Vitalik Buterin**, Ethereum introduced a blockchain that supports complex code execution; enabling developers to build and run decentralized applications without relying on traditional servers.

Key Features:

- Smart Contracts: Ethereum's primary innovation is the use of smart contracts—self-executing contracts with the terms of the agreement directly written into code. These contracts can automatically enforce and execute agreements without the need for intermediaries, which opens up possibilities for a range of decentralized applications (dApps).
- Decentralized Finance (DeFi)**:** Ethereum has become the foundation of the rapidly growing **DeFi** ecosystem, which aims to replicate traditional financial services (lending, borrowing, trading) in a decentralized manner using blockchain technology. DeFi platforms built on Ethereum have created significant financial opportunities by offering higher returns and removing the need for intermediaries.
- Ethereum 2.0: Ethereum is undergoing a significant upgrade (Ethereum 2.0), transitioning from a **Proof of Work (PoW)** consensus mechanism to a **Proof of Stake**

(PoS) system. This change is expected to enhance scalability, reduce energy consumption, and improve security, making Ethereum more efficient and sustainable.

Investment Perspective:

Ethereum has gained widespread popularity not just as a currency but as a platform for building decentralized applications and financial systems. Its **utility** within the DeFi space and the planned Ethereum 2.0 upgrade have solidified Ethereum's position as one of the most valuable cryptocurrencies, second only to Bitcoin. Investors in Ethereum are often attracted to its broader potential within the blockchain ecosystem, beyond just currency use.

3. Emerging Digital Currencies

Beyond Bitcoin and Ethereum, there are thousands of other cryptocurrencies—commonly referred to as **altcoins**—that serve a variety of functions. Some altcoins seek to improve upon the features of Bitcoin or Ethereum, while others introduce entirely new use cases. A few notable emerging digital currencies include:

Binance Coin (BNB):

Originally launched as a utility token for the Binance cryptocurrency exchange, **BNB** has evolved into one of the largest cryptocurrencies by market capitalization. Binance Coin can be used for transaction fee discounts on the Binance platform and has expanded to power the **Binance Smart Chain**, a platform for decentralized applications and smart contracts.

Cardano (ADA):

Cardano is a third-generation blockchain platform that focuses on sustainability, scalability, and interoperability. It uses a Proof of Stake consensus mechanism called **Ouroboros**, which is more energy-efficient than Bitcoin's Proof of Work. Cardano's development is research-driven, and it aims to provide a robust platform for the deployment of decentralized applications.

Solana (SOL):

Solana is a high-performance blockchain designed to support decentralized applications and crypto projects on a massive scale. Known for its **low transaction fees** and **high-speed transactions**, Solana has attracted significant attention as a competitor to Ethereum in the dApp and DeFi space. It is particularly suited for applications that require high throughput, such as gaming and decentralized finance.

Polkadot (DOT):

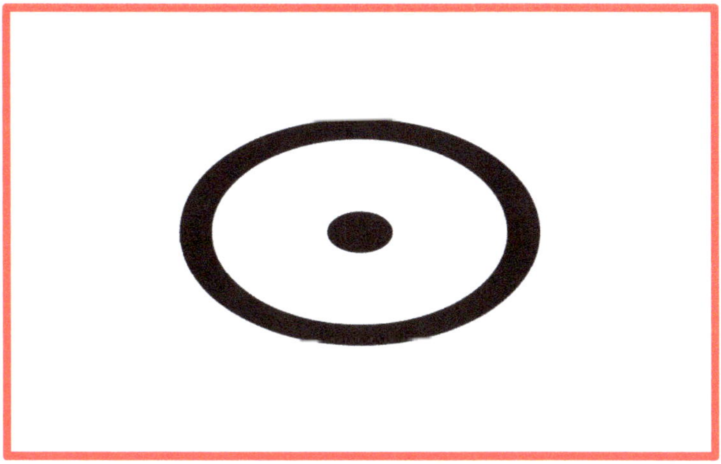

Polkadot focuses on enabling different blockchains to interoperate, solving one of the major challenges of early blockchain networks. By allowing various chains to share data and communicate seamlessly, Polkadot aims to create a more connected and scalable blockchain ecosystem. This multi-chain approach enhances flexibility and functionality for developers building on its platform.

Stablecoins:

Stablecoins, such as **Tether (USDT)** and **USD Coin (USDC)**, are cryptocurrencies designed to maintain a stable value by being pegged to traditional assets like the U.S. dollar. They are used as a bridge between traditional finance and crypto markets, providing liquidity and stability for transactions and investments in the volatile crypto space.

Investment Perspective:

Investing in emerging digital currencies presents both opportunities and risks. While many altcoins offer unique value propositions and the potential for rapid growth, they also come with **greater volatility** and **regulatory uncertainty**. Investors should conduct thorough research, understand the technology and utility behind each coin, and assess the potential risks before allocating capital to these assets.

4. Opportunities and Risks in the Cryptocurrency Market

The cryptocurrency market has opened up new financial opportunities for investors, but it is also fraught with risks. Understanding both the potential rewards and the challenges is essential for anyone looking to participate in this space.

Opportunities:

- High Returns: Cryptocurrencies have delivered staggering returns for early adopters. Despite periods of volatility, Bitcoin, Ethereum, and other coins have experienced significant price appreciation over the years.
- Decentralized Finance (DeFi)**:** The DeFi ecosystem built on Ethereum and other blockchains offers unique opportunities for yield generation, lending, and borrowing without relying on traditional financial institutions.
- Portfolio Diversification: Cryptocurrencies can offer portfolio diversification benefits, as their price movements may not be directly correlated with traditional assets like stocks and bonds.

Risks:

- Volatility: Cryptocurrency prices are notoriously volatile. Investors must be prepared for significant price fluctuations, which can result in both dramatic gains and losses.

- ❖ Regulatory Uncertainty: Governments around the world are still grappling with how to regulate cryptocurrencies. Sudden regulatory changes can have a significant impact on the market.
- ❖ Security Concerns: Although blockchain technology is inherently secure, the platforms and exchanges that manage cryptocurrencies can be vulnerable to hacks and fraud. Investors must take precautions, such as using secure wallets and enabling two-factor authentication.

Cryptocurrency represents a groundbreaking shift in how people transact, invest, and store wealth. Bitcoin and Ethereum, as the leading players in this space, have set the foundation for a growing ecosystem of digital currencies and decentralized applications. While cryptocurrencies offer significant financial opportunities, they also come with risks that investors must carefully consider. By staying informed and approaching the market with a strategic mindset, individuals can take advantage of the transformative potential of cryptocurrencies while managing the associated risks.

- Blockchain Technology's Role in Wealth Transfer, Security, and Transparency

Blockchain technology, the foundation of cryptocurrencies like Bitcoin and Ethereum, has far-reaching implications beyond digital currencies. Its decentralized, transparent, and immutable nature offers transformative benefits for wealth transfer, security, and transparency across various sectors. In wealth management, blockchain is increasingly being recognized for its ability to facilitate efficient transfers, enhance security, and ensure greater transparency in financial transactions. This detailed content explores how blockchain is reshaping these areas and creating opportunities for improved financial systems.

1. Blockchain and Wealth Transfer: Efficiency and Cost-Effectiveness

One of the most compelling applications of blockchain in wealth management is its role in facilitating more efficient and cost-effective wealth transfers. Traditional systems for transferring wealth, especially across borders, often involve intermediaries, high fees, and long processing times. Blockchain technology eliminates many of these barriers, offering several advantages:

- Faster Transactions: Blockchain allows for near-instantaneous transactions, especially when compared to traditional banking systems, which can take days or even weeks to settle cross-border transfers. Cryptocurrencies like Bitcoin or stablecoins (e.g., USDC, USDT) can be transferred from one user to another within minutes, no matter where they are located in the world.
- Lower Costs: Traditional wealth transfer methods often involve multiple intermediaries, such as banks, payment processors, and clearinghouses, each of which charges a fee. Blockchain technology reduces the need for intermediaries, significantly lowering transaction costs. This is particularly beneficial for high-value wealth transfers and remittances, where fees can be substantial.
- Cross-Border Capabilities: Blockchain technology eliminates the complexities and

costs associated with currency exchange and international transfers. For example, using stablecoins (cryptocurrencies pegged to traditional fiat currencies), individuals and businesses can transfer assets across borders without incurring foreign exchange fees or delays.

- ❖ Decentralization and Autonomy: With blockchain, individuals have direct control over their wealth without relying on third parties. This decentralization reduces the risk of third-party failures, such as bank insolvencies or freezes on accounts, providing greater autonomy and protection for high-net-worth individuals and businesses engaged in wealth transfers.

2. Blockchain and Security: Enhancing the Safety of Financial Transactions

Security is a primary concern in the management and transfer of wealth. Blockchain technology offers robust security features that significantly enhance the safety of financial transactions. Some of the key security advantages of blockchain include:

- ❖ Immutability: Once a transaction is recorded on the blockchain, it is extremely difficult to alter or delete. The immutability of blockchain records ensures that wealth transfers are tamper-proof, reducing the risk of fraud and ensuring that records remain accurate and trustworthy. This is particularly important for wealth transfers involving large sums or complex financial assets.
- ❖ Cryptographic Security: Blockchain networks rely on advanced cryptographic

techniques to secure transactions. Each transaction is verified by a network of nodes through a consensus mechanism (such as Proof of Work or Proof of Stake) and encrypted with public and private keys. This makes unauthorized access or manipulation of transaction data nearly impossible.

- Decentralized Validation: Unlike centralized systems, where a single point of failure (e.g., a compromised bank or financial institution) can lead to significant security breaches, blockchain uses a decentralized network of validators to confirm transactions. This reduces the risk of hacking, as an attacker would need to compromise the majority of the network's nodes, a feat that is both computationally and financially unfeasible in large, well-established blockchains.
- Smart Contracts for Automated Execution: Smart contracts—self-executing contracts where the terms are written directly into code—add another layer of security. These contracts ensure that wealth transfers and financial transactions are only executed when predefined conditions are met. For instance, an estate plan using a smart contract could automatically distribute assets to beneficiaries upon certain conditions, such as the passing of the estate holder, reducing the potential for disputes or delays.

3. Blockchain and Transparency: Increasing Trust in Financial Systems

Transparency is crucial in wealth management, as it ensures that all parties involved in a financial transaction can trust the process and the outcomes. Blockchain technology, with its inherent transparency, offers several benefits that increase trust and accountability in financial transactions:

- Public Ledger for Transparency: Blockchain operates as a distributed ledger that is visible to all participants in the network. Every transaction is recorded on the blockchain in a transparent manner, providing a verifiable history of asset transfers. This level of transparency is particularly beneficial in wealth management, where trust between parties (e.g., heirs, beneficiaries, investors) is critical.
- Auditability: Blockchain's transparent and immutable ledger provides a permanent and traceable record of all transactions. This makes audits far more efficient, as every transaction can be tracked and verified. For financial institutions, this reduces the complexity and cost of compliance with regulations such as Anti-Money Laundering (AML) and Know Your Customer (KYC) standards. In estate planning, blockchain could provide verifiable records of wealth transfer events, reducing legal disputes and enhancing the integrity of the process.
- Eliminating Fraud and Mismanagement: The transparency of blockchain reduces the risk of financial fraud or mismanagement of assets. Because all participants can independently verify the authenticity and accuracy of transactions, the potential for fraudulent manipulation of financial records is minimized. This is particularly useful in scenarios where multiple parties have a

vested interest in the outcome of a wealth transfer, such as in family estates or investment portfolios.

4. Blockchain in Estate Planning and Inheritance

Blockchain's role in estate planning and inheritance is gaining traction as an efficient and secure way to manage the transfer of wealth between generations. Some innovative uses of blockchain in this area include:

- Digital Wills and Trusts: Blockchain technology can be used to create and store **digital wills** and **smart contracts** that automatically execute when specific conditions are met. For example, a blockchain-based will could automatically transfer assets to beneficiaries upon the passing of the testator, ensuring an efficient and tamper-proof distribution of wealth.
- Tokenization of Assets: Blockchain allows for the tokenization of physical assets such as real estate, art, and intellectual property. Tokenized assets can be easily divided and transferred, making it simpler to distribute complex estates among multiple beneficiaries. This also provides a more liquid form of wealth transfer, as tokenized assets can be bought, sold, or transferred without the need for traditional intermediaries.
- Security and Privacy in Inheritance: Privacy is a critical concern in inheritance, particularly when it comes to safeguarding sensitive information about assets and beneficiaries. Blockchain's cryptographic nature ensures that only authorized parties can access and transfer wealth, providing

greater privacy and security for both the estate holder and beneficiaries.

5. Blockchain and Cross-Border Wealth Transfers

For individuals with global assets or those involved in cross-border wealth transfers, blockchain provides a unique solution to the challenges of transferring wealth internationally. Traditional cross-border transactions often involve lengthy processing times, high fees, and currency conversion complexities. Blockchain addresses these challenges by:

- Borderless Transactions: Blockchain enables the transfer of assets across borders without the need for intermediaries like banks or clearinghouses. This is particularly beneficial for high-net-worth individuals with assets in multiple countries or for global businesses that need to transfer wealth across jurisdictions.
- Currency Flexibility: Blockchain supports the use of stablecoins and cryptocurrencies, which can be easily converted into local currencies. This flexibility reduces the friction associated with currency exchange, making cross-border wealth transfers more efficient.
- Regulatory Compliance: While blockchain enables decentralized transactions, it can also support regulatory compliance through **programmable money** and **smart contracts**. For instance, wealth transfers can be programmed to comply with local tax laws and inheritance regulations, ensuring smooth transfers across different legal systems.

As blockchain technology continues to evolve, its applications in wealth management and financial systems are likely to expand, offering new opportunities for innovation and efficiency. However, like any emerging technology, blockchain also presents challenges that need to be addressed for it to fully realize its potential in this space. In this section, we explore both the future potential of blockchain in wealth management and the challenges that must be overcome.

1. Tokenization of Assets for Fractional Ownership

One of the most exciting future applications of blockchain in wealth management is the **tokenization of physical assets**, such as real estate, art, and intellectual property. Tokenization converts these assets into digital tokens on a blockchain, allowing for **fractional ownership**. This concept could revolutionize wealth creation and transfer in several ways:

- Increased Liquidity for Illiquid Assets: Traditionally, assets like real estate and fine art have been illiquid, meaning they cannot be easily sold or transferred without significant cost and time. By tokenizing these assets, fractional ownership can be sold in the form of digital tokens, allowing investors to buy, sell, or transfer ownership much more quickly and affordably.
- Access to Previously Inaccessible Markets: Tokenization democratizes access to high-value assets by allowing investors to purchase fractional shares. For example, a person might not have enough capital to purchase a luxury property, but they could buy a fraction of that property through tokenized ownership. This opens up new wealth-building opportunities for retail

investors who previously had limited access to these markets.

- ❖ Simplified Estate Transfers: For individuals with diverse or complex estates, tokenized assets simplify the transfer of ownership to heirs or beneficiaries. Instead of dividing physical assets like real estate, which can be cumbersome and involve legal disputes, tokenized assets can be distributed with precision and ease. Blockchain's transparency also ensures that all transactions are verifiable, reducing the potential for mismanagement or fraud during estate transfers.

2. Smart Contracts for Automated Wealth Management

Smart contracts are self-executing contracts where the terms are written directly into code. They enable automated wealth management processes, reducing the need for intermediaries and ensuring that transactions are executed exactly as planned. Some potential future uses of smart contracts in wealth management include:

- ❖ Automated Investment Portfolios: Smart contracts could manage automated investment portfolios based on pre-set rules defined by the investor. For instance, a smart contract could automatically rebalance a portfolio when certain conditions are met, such as a change in market conditions or the performance of specific assets. This would eliminate the need for manual intervention, optimizing efficiency and reducing management fees.
- ❖ Estate Planning and Trusts: Blockchain-based smart contracts could revolutionize estate planning by automatically executing

the distribution of assets upon the fulfillment of specific conditions. For example, a smart contract could release assets to beneficiaries when they reach a certain age, graduate from college, or meet other criteria outlined in the estate plan. This reduces the risk of disputes and delays, ensuring that wealth are transferred according to the deceased's wishes.

- Automated Tax Payments and Compliance: Smart contracts could also be programmed to automatically calculate and pay taxes when wealth transfers or investment gains occur. This could streamline the tax reporting process, reduce the risk of non-compliance, and save time for both individuals and businesses.

3. Challenges and Barriers to Blockchain Adoption in Wealth Management

While blockchain presents significant opportunities for wealth management, several challenges must be addressed to ensure widespread adoption and success:

- Regulatory Uncertainty: One of the biggest challenges facing blockchain technology is the lack of clear regulatory frameworks in many countries. As blockchain operates across borders and can involve multiple jurisdictions, it raises complex questions around compliance, taxation, and legal recognition. Governments and regulatory bodies are still in the process of developing laws to govern the use of blockchain, which creates uncertainty for investors and institutions looking to adopt this technology.

- Security Risks: While blockchain is highly secure, it is not immune to risks. Hacks, fraud, and theft can still occur, especially when users fail to properly secure their private keys (the cryptographic codes that give access to their blockchain assets). Additionally, while the blockchain itself is immutable, the platforms and exchanges that facilitate blockchain transactions can be vulnerable to cyberattacks. Ensuring robust cybersecurity measures is essential for widespread adoption.
- Scalability and Energy Consumption: Blockchain networks, particularly those that rely on Proof of Work (PoW) consensus mechanisms (such as Bitcoin), face issues related to scalability and energy consumption. As the number of transactions on a blockchain increases, so does the computational power required to process them. This can lead to slower transaction times and higher costs, making it less practical for large-scale applications. However, emerging technologies like Proof of Stake (PoS) and Layer 2 solutions are being developed to address these scalability concerns.
- Education and Understanding: Despite its potential, many investors and financial professionals still have limited understanding of how blockchain works and how it can be used in wealth management. A lack of education and awareness presents a barrier to adoption, as individuals may be hesitant to embrace new technologies they do not fully understand.

4. Blockchain and the Future of Global Wealth Transfers

The global nature of blockchain makes it an ideal tool for wealth transfers across borders. As globalization continues to shape the financial landscape, blockchain could become the backbone of international wealth management. Some future trends in global wealth transfers powered by blockchain include:

- Multi-Currency Wealth Management: Blockchain enables seamless transfers between different digital currencies and stablecoins, which are tied to traditional fiat currencies like the US dollar or the euro. This eliminates the need for expensive and time-consuming currency exchanges, making it easier for individuals to manage wealth across multiple countries.
- Decentralized Finance (DeFi): Decentralized finance, or DeFi, refers to the growing ecosystem of financial applications built on blockchain networks that operate without intermediaries like banks or brokerage firms. DeFi platforms allow users to borrow, lend, trade, and invest directly through smart contracts. As the DeFi sector grows, it could revolutionize global wealth management by offering more efficient and transparent financial services, especially for those in regions with underdeveloped financial systems.
- Cross-Border Estate Planning: Blockchain's decentralized and global nature makes it particularly useful for individuals with assets or beneficiaries in multiple countries. Traditional estate planning can be complicated by differing legal systems and inheritance laws across jurisdictions. Blockchain simplifies this process by

providing a universal platform for wealth transfer that transcends national borders, reducing the legal and logistical challenges of cross-border estate planning.

The Future of Blockchain in Wealth Management

Blockchain technology has the potential to revolutionize the way wealth is managed, transferred, and secured. Its decentralized, transparent, and efficient nature offers numerous benefits for individuals and institutions looking to optimize wealth management practices in an increasingly global and digital economy. From the tokenization of assets to automated smart contracts and cross-border wealth transfers, blockchain provides innovative solutions to some of the most pressing challenges in traditional financial systems.

However, realizing the full potential of blockchain in wealth management will require addressing several challenges, including regulatory uncertainty, security risks, and scalability issues. Education and awareness will also play a key role in driving adoption, as investors and financial professionals must fully understand the benefits and risks associated with blockchain technology.

As blockchain continues to evolve, its impact on wealth management is likely to grow, offering new opportunities for wealth creation, preservation, and transfer. For forward-thinking individuals and institutions, embracing blockchain represents a chance to stay ahead of the curve in a rapidly changing financial landscape.

- Risks and Rewards of Investing in Digital Assets: Volatility, Regulation, and Market Speculation

Investing in digital assets such as cryptocurrencies, NFTs (non-fungible tokens), and decentralized finance (DeFi) projects has grown exponentially in recent years. These assets, often underpinned by blockchain technology, offer high potential returns and innovative ways of generating wealth. However, they also come with substantial risks. In this section, we will explore the rewards and risks associated with digital assets, particularly focusing on their volatility, regulatory challenges, and the impact of market speculation.

1. Rewards of Investing in Digital Assets

a) High Growth Potential

Digital assets have shown incredible growth in a relatively short period. Cryptocurrencies like **Bitcoin** and **Ethereum** have generated significant returns for early investors. For example, Bitcoin, which was valued at less than $1 in its early days, soared to nearly $70,000 by 2021. This kind of exponential growth makes digital assets highly attractive to investors looking for high-risk, high-reward opportunities.

- Early Adopter Advantage: As digital assets are still evolving, early adopters who invest in promising technologies or projects can potentially experience outsized gains, akin to investing in early-stage tech companies like Google or Amazon.
- DeFi and Yield Farming: Beyond cryptocurrencies, decentralized finance (DeFi) platforms allow investors to earn interest, provide liquidity, or lend and borrow assets through blockchain networks without intermediaries. DeFi projects offer lucrative returns, often exceeding what traditional financial institutions can provide.

b) Diversification

Digital assets provide an alternative investment class that can diversify a portfolio. Since they often have low correlations with traditional asset classes like stocks and bonds, adding cryptocurrencies or other digital assets can help spread risk.

- Alternative to Traditional Markets: When traditional markets suffer due to economic downturns or geopolitical events, digital assets sometimes perform independently, providing a hedge against economic uncertainty.

c) Decentralization and Financial Inclusion

Blockchain technology allows for decentralized finance, bypassing traditional intermediaries like banks and brokers. This decentralization fosters **financial inclusion**, particularly in regions where banking infrastructure is underdeveloped. Individuals can participate in the global economy through digital assets with minimal barriers to entry.

- Global Access: Anyone with internet access can participate in digital asset markets, breaking down geographical and socio-economic barriers to investment.

2. Risks of Investing in Digital Assets

a) Volatility

One of the most significant risks associated with digital assets is their extreme price volatility. Cryptocurrencies, in particular, can experience rapid and dramatic price swings within short periods. For example, Bitcoin has seen multiple drops of more than 50% in value over just a few months, and other cryptocurrencies often exhibit even higher levels of volatility.

- ❖ Price Fluctuations: While high volatility offers the potential for significant gains, it also exposes investors to the risk of substantial losses. Price corrections, crashes, and extreme market fluctuations are common, driven by speculation, market sentiment, and external events such as regulatory announcements.
- ❖ Market Sentiment: Because digital assets are still relatively new and speculative, their prices can be heavily influenced by social media, public announcements, and changes in sentiment. For instance, a tweet from a prominent figure or a news report on regulatory crackdowns can trigger massive sell-offs or price surges.

b) Regulatory Uncertainty

The regulatory landscape surrounding digital assets is still evolving and varies widely across different countries. In some regions, cryptocurrencies are embraced and integrated into existing financial systems, while in others, they face severe restrictions or outright bans. This lack of consistent regulation creates uncertainty for investors.

- ❖ Government Crackdowns: In countries like China, regulators have cracked down on cryptocurrency mining and trading, significantly impacting global markets. Additionally, governments may impose stricter regulations or taxes, which can lower the profitability of digital asset investments.

- ❖ Legal Status of Digital Assets: The classification of digital assets as securities, commodities, or currencies is still under debate in many jurisdictions. Regulatory bodies such as the SEC (Securities and Exchange Commission) have taken action against some cryptocurrency projects, which could result in fines, shutdowns, or loss of value for investors in those assets.

c) Market Speculation and Manipulation

The digital asset market is highly speculative, and prices are often driven by hype, sentiment, and fear of missing out (FOMO), rather than underlying fundamentals. As a result, digital assets can experience price bubbles that eventually burst, leading to sharp declines in value.

- ❖ Pump-and-Dump Schemes: Some digital assets, particularly smaller or lesser-known cryptocurrencies, are subject to manipulation through "pump-and-dump" schemes, where the price is artificially inflated (pumped) by coordinated buying, only to be followed by mass selling (dumping) to unsuspecting investors.
- ❖ Illiquid Markets: Many digital assets, especially newer ones, may have relatively low liquidity, meaning that large buy or sell orders can significantly impact the price. This makes it difficult for investors to exit positions without causing a major price change, increasing risk during market downturns.

d) Security Risks

While blockchain technology itself is highly secure, digital assets are still vulnerable to hacking, fraud, and theft. **Cryptocurrency exchanges** and wallets have been frequent targets for cybercriminals, resulting in millions of dollars in losses for investors. In addition, private keys (the cryptographic keys that give access to digital assets) can be lost or stolen, leaving investors unable to access their funds.

- ❖ Exchange Vulnerabilities: Despite the security of blockchain, centralized exchanges where cryptocurrencies are traded have been hacked multiple times. If an exchange is compromised, users can lose their entire investment.
- ❖ Private Key Management: Mismanagement of private keys by users is another common risk. If an investor loses access to their private keys or stores them in an insecure manner, their funds can be permanently lost or stolen.

3. Balancing the Risks and Rewards

Investing in digital assets can be highly rewarding, but it requires a strong understanding of the unique risks involved. To balance the risks and rewards effectively, investors should consider the following strategies:

a) Portfolio Diversification

Diversification remains one of the most effective ways to mitigate the risks of digital asset investments. Instead of putting all funds into a single cryptocurrency or project, investors should consider spreading their investments across multiple assets, including traditional stocks and bonds.

- ❖ Balanced Approach: Digital assets can be part of a diversified portfolio but should not constitute an investor's entire strategy. Balancing digital assets with more stable, traditional investments helps reduce the overall risk profile.

b) Long-Term Investment Horizon

Due to their volatility, digital assets are best suited for investors with a long-term investment horizon. Short-term traders face high risks, as daily price swings can be unpredictable and driven by speculation. By holding assets for a longer period, investors can ride out market fluctuations and potentially capture significant gains over time.

- ❖ Avoiding Panic Selling: Investors should be prepared for extreme volatility and resist the temptation to panic-sell during market dips, as digital assets often experience strong recoveries after corrections.

c) Staying Informed on Regulations

Given the evolving regulatory environment, staying informed about legal changes is crucial. Investors should follow news and developments in the regulatory landscape in their country and globally to anticipate potential impacts on their holdings.

- ❖ Compliance with Local Laws: Ensuring compliance with local tax laws, securities regulations, and other legal requirements is essential for avoiding fines, penalties, or other legal consequences when investing in digital assets.

d) Security Best Practices

Investors in digital assets should take security seriously by using secure, trusted exchanges, hardware wallets, and two-factor authentication (2FA) to protect their holdings. They should also ensure proper private key management and consider using cold storage (offline wallets) for long-term holdings.

Weighing the Risks and Rewards

Digital assets present both significant opportunities and risks for investors. While the high growth potential, diversification benefits, and decentralized nature of blockchain-based assets can be rewarding, the extreme volatility, regulatory uncertainty, and susceptibility to market speculation and security breaches create unique challenges.

Investors should approach digital assets with caution, ensure proper diversification, and stay informed about regulatory and market developments. With a sound strategy that accounts for both the risks and rewards, digital assets can be a valuable component of a broader investment portfolio.

Using Financial Apps for Personal Wealth Management

- How to Leverage Personal Finance Apps for Budgeting, Investing, and Tracking Wealth

In today's digital age, personal finance apps have revolutionized the way individuals manage their finances.

These tools provide comprehensive solutions for budgeting, investing, and tracking wealth, enabling users to stay organized, make informed financial decisions, and achieve long-term financial goals. Whether you are working towards financial independence or simply looking to optimize daily money management, leveraging the right personal finance apps can be a game changer. This section explores how to effectively use these apps to manage various aspects of personal wealth.

1. Budgeting: The Foundation of Wealth Management

Budgeting is a crucial first step in personal wealth management, and personal finance apps simplify this process by providing tools for tracking income, expenses, and savings goals. A well-maintained budget gives individuals a clear picture of their cash flow, ensuring they can allocate resources effectively and avoid unnecessary debt. Personal finance apps like **Mint**, **YNAB (You Need A Budget)**, and **EveryDollar** automate the process of managing budgets, helping users stay on top of their spending.

a) Tracking Income and Expenses

Finance apps sync with bank accounts, credit cards, and other financial institutions, enabling real-time tracking of transactions. Users can categorize their spending into various segments (e.g., groceries, dining out, utilities) and monitor how closely their spending aligns with their budget.

- Automation: Apps automatically categorize expenses, reducing manual input and making it easier to identify spending patterns.
- Alerts and Notifications: Many apps send notifications when users approach or

exceed budget limits in particular categories, promoting financial discipline.

b) Setting Financial Goals

Personal finance apps allow users to set and track financial goals, such as saving for a house, vacation, or emergency fund. These apps break down long-term goals into manageable monthly savings targets, helping users stay on track.

- Visual Progress: Graphs and charts show progress toward goals, motivating users to maintain saving habits.
- Custom Budgets: Apps like **YNAB** emphasize the importance of assigning every dollar a job, encouraging users to prioritize spending in alignment with their goals.

c) Managing Debt

For those focused on paying off debt, personal finance apps offer tailored features. Apps like **Debt Payoff Planner** and **Tally** help users manage their debt repayment strategies, showing the best paths to pay down loans efficiently by prioritizing high-interest debts.

- Debt Tracking: These apps calculate how long it will take to pay off debt under different payment strategies, allowing users to understand the long-term impact of their choices.

2. Investing: Building Wealth through Smart Financial Decisions

Investing is one of the most critical steps to long-term wealth building, and many personal finance apps are designed to simplify this process for both novice and seasoned investors. Apps such as **Robinhood**, **Acorns**, **Wealthfront**, and **Betterment** have democratized investing by offering low-cost, user-friendly platforms for building and managing portfolios.

a) Automated Investing

Robo-advisors like **Wealthfront** and **Betterment** provide automated investment management based on users' risk tolerance and financial goals. These apps handle the complexities of asset allocation, diversification, and rebalancing without requiring active participation from the investor.

- Portfolio Customization: Robo-advisors allow users to create diversified portfolios using ETFs, index funds, and other investment vehicles that align with their long-term goals.
- Tax Optimization: Some platforms offer features like tax-loss harvesting, which minimizes taxable capital gains and maximizes after-tax returns.

b) Micro-Investing

Apps like **Acorns** make investing accessible by rounding up everyday purchases to the nearest dollar and investing the spare change. This micro-investing approach allows even those with limited capital to begin building wealth incrementally.

- ❖ Passive Growth: Small, automatic contributions accumulate over time, leveraging the power of compounding to grow wealth with minimal effort.
- ❖ Custom Portfolios: Acorns offers portfolios ranging from conservative to aggressive, allowing users to choose an investment strategy that fits their risk tolerance.

c) Direct Investing

For those who prefer a more hands-on approach, apps like **Robinhood** and **E*TRADE** provide commission-free trading for stocks, ETFs, options, and cryptocurrencies. These apps allow users to directly manage their investments, giving them control over buying and selling decisions.

- ❖ Market Insights: These platforms often provide tools like real-time data, news, and research reports to help investors make informed decisions.
- ❖ Fractional Shares: Apps like **Robinhood** enable users to buy fractional shares of expensive stocks, making high-priced securities accessible to investors with smaller budgets.

3. Tracking Wealth: Comprehensive Overview of Financial Health

As your investments grow and financial goals evolve, it's essential to have a clear overview of your entire financial picture. Wealth-tracking apps help users monitor net worth, track investments, and assess overall financial health. These apps consolidate financial accounts, assets, and liabilities, giving users a holistic view of their wealth. Popular apps like **Personal Capital** and **Quicken** offer sophisticated tracking features.

a) Net Worth Calculation

Wealth tracking apps aggregate all your financial information, including bank accounts, credit cards, loans, investments, and real estate. By compiling this data, they provide an accurate and up-to-date snapshot of your net worth.

- ❖ Asset and Liability Tracking: Users can track various asset classes, including stocks, bonds, real estate, and cash, while monitoring liabilities like mortgages, loans, and credit card debt.
- ❖ Wealth Growth Tracking: Many apps allow users to see how their net worth grows (or declines) over time, helping them adjust their financial strategy as needed.

b) Portfolio Tracking and Analysis

Apps like **Personal Capital** offer advanced portfolio tracking tools, allowing users to view asset allocation, investment performance, and potential for diversification. By linking all investment accounts, these apps provide insights into how different assets are performing in relation to one another.

- ❖ Investment Fees: Personal Capital's tools can also highlight hidden fees in mutual funds and other investments, helping users identify cost-saving opportunities.
- ❖ Retirement Planning: The app's retirement planning tools use projected returns, contribution rates, and retirement timelines to estimate future income and assess

whether users are on track to meet their retirement goals.

c) Cash Flow Analysis

By analyzing income and expenses, wealth-tracking apps help users identify patterns in their cash flow. This can be useful for budgeting, saving, and identifying opportunities for cost-cutting.

- Income Projections: These tools help forecast future income based on historical data and investment performance, allowing users to make better financial plans.
- Scenario Planning: Many apps offer tools to model different financial scenarios, such as the impact of major purchases, salary changes, or market downturns on future net worth.

4. Financial Apps for Holistic Wealth Management

a) Integrating Budgeting, Investing, and Wealth Tracking

Some apps combine all aspects of personal finance into a single platform, offering a comprehensive solution for managing wealth. **Personal Capital**, for example, not only tracks your net worth but also incorporates budgeting tools and investment tracking features. This integrated approach allows users to seamlessly manage their day-to-day finances while keeping an eye on long-term wealth accumulation.

b) AI and Data-Driven Insights

Many modern finance apps use AI to provide personalized insights and recommendations. For example, **Mint** analyzes spending habits to suggest areas where users can save money, while **Wealthfront** uses machine learning to adjust portfolio allocations based on changing market conditions. These AI-driven tools simplify wealth management by offering tailored advice based on real-time data.

- Smart Savings: AI-powered apps can help identify idle cash and suggest appropriate savings or investment options, maximizing the use of funds.
- Risk Management: Some apps assess a user's risk tolerance and recommend adjustments to their investment strategy based on their goals and the market environment.

5. Customizing Financial Apps for Personalized Wealth Management

While personal finance apps provide broad solutions, one of their greatest strengths is their ability to be tailored to individual financial situations. By customizing the features of these apps, users can focus on the aspects of wealth management that are most relevant to them, whether that's reducing debt, maximizing savings, or optimizing investments.

a) Personalized Financial Dashboards

Many apps offer customizable dashboards, allowing users to prioritize the financial metrics most important to them. For example, users focused on debt reduction might configure their dashboard to highlight outstanding balances, interest rates, and payment schedules, while investors might focus on portfolio performance and asset allocation.

- Flexible Views: Apps like **Personal Capital** allow users to create multiple views of their finances, from tracking net worth and cash flow to monitoring individual investment accounts.

- ❖ Goal-Specific Customization: Some apps let users customize goals, such as "debt-free by 2025" or "save $50,000 for a home down payment," allowing them to track progress toward specific objectives.

b) Tailored Alerts and Notifications

Apps offer alerts based on user preferences, notifying them of significant changes in their financial situation or upcoming deadlines. Custom alerts can be set for unusual spending, market conditions, or when a user's account balance falls below a certain threshold.

- ❖ Spending Alerts: These notifications help curb unnecessary expenditures by alerting users when they exceed their monthly spending limits in categories like dining, entertainment, or shopping.
- ❖ Investment Alerts: For active investors, personalized alerts can notify users of significant changes in stock prices, dividends, or market events.

c) Adaptive Financial Planning

Some apps use artificial intelligence (AI) to provide personalized recommendations based on the user's financial habits and long-term goals. For example, **Albert** analyzes spending patterns and offers smart recommendations for budgeting, while **Wealthfront** provides tailored investment strategies based on a user's risk profile and timeline for wealth goals.

- Real-Time Adjustments: If a user's income changes or expenses spike, AI-driven apps adjust financial plans in real-time, offering new strategies to stay on course.
- Comprehensive Insights: Personal finance apps can also provide insights on retirement savings, student loans, or credit card debt, ensuring that users are making well-rounded financial decisions.

6. Security and Privacy in Financial Apps

While the benefits of personal finance apps are extensive, users must also consider security and privacy issues when linking financial accounts. Fortunately, most reputable apps employ bank-level security features to safeguard personal and financial information.

a) Encryption and Two-Factor Authentication

Personal finance apps use end-to-end encryption to protect sensitive data, ensuring that user information remains secure during transmission. Additionally, most apps offer two-factor authentication (2FA) as an extra layer of security, requiring users to verify their identity before accessing their account.

- Biometric Authentication: Many apps now support biometric authentication methods like fingerprint and facial recognition, enhancing security while simplifying the login process.
- Multi-Device Access: Apps allow users to securely access their accounts across multiple devices (e.g., smartphone, tablet, desktop), ensuring that they can monitor and manage finances from anywhere without compromising security.

b) Account Monitoring and Fraud Detection

Several apps monitor user accounts for suspicious activity, such as unauthorized transactions or unusual spending patterns. If any irregularities are detected, users are immediately notified and can take action to protect their accounts.

- Instant Alerts: Apps like **Credit Karma** and **Experian** notify users when there are changes to their credit report, helping them stay on top of potential identity theft or fraudulent activity.
- Data Privacy: It's crucial to choose apps that prioritize user privacy, with clear policies on how data is stored, shared, and used. Most apps allow users to control the level of data access, ensuring that sensitive information is only shared with trusted parties.

In summary, personal finance apps are powerful tools that enable users to take control of their financial lives by simplifying complex tasks like budgeting, investing, and wealth tracking. From automating savings and debt payments to providing personalized investment advice, these apps streamline financial management and empower users to make more informed decisions. As technology continues to evolve, personal finance apps will offer even more innovative solutions, helping individuals achieve financial independence, grow their wealth, and ultimately, reach their long-term financial goals.

By leveraging these tools, you can establish a solid financial foundation, track your progress toward wealth-building objectives, and ensure that your financial strategies remain aligned with your life goals. Whether you are just starting on your financial journey or are well on your way to financial independence, the right personal finance apps can play a critical role in optimizing your path to wealth and security.

- Advantages of Mobile Banking, Peer-to-Peer Lending, and Digital Payment Systems

The rapid advancement of financial technology (FinTech) has reshaped the way individuals manage their money, invest, and conduct financial transactions. Mobile banking, peer-to-peer lending, and digital payment systems are at the forefront of these innovations, offering convenience, accessibility, and efficiency. This evolution has empowered people to take control of their finances and pursue wealth management strategies with ease. Below, we explore the advantages of these digital financial tools and how they can enhance personal wealth management.

1. Advantages of Mobile Banking in Wealth Management

Mobile banking is one of the most significant innovations in personal finance, offering users access to their bank accounts, investments, and financial services from their smartphones. It eliminates the need for physical bank visits and streamlines various financial processes.

a) Convenience and Accessibility

Mobile banking provides real-time access to your financial accounts, allowing you to manage your wealth anytime, anywhere. Whether you're checking account balances, transferring funds, or making payments, mobile banking platforms are designed to offer a seamless user experience on the go.

- ❖ 24/7 Account Management: You can access your banking information and manage transactions 24/7, without being restricted by banking hours. This is particularly valuable for busy professionals who may not have time to visit a bank during working hours.
- ❖ Mobile Alerts and Notifications: Mobile banking apps send instant alerts for account activity, bill payments, and even spending limits, helping users stay on top of their financial activities in real-time.

b) Efficient Money Management

Mobile banking apps offer tools to track spending, manage budgets, and set financial goals. These features give users greater control over their finances and help them stay disciplined in their wealth management efforts.

- ❖ Automated Budgeting: Apps like **Mint** integrate with your mobile banking platform to categorize expenses and track spending, giving you a clear view of where your money is going. This helps in identifying areas for saving and investing.
- ❖ Transaction History: Instant access to transaction history enables users to review and analyze past financial activities, helping them make better financial decisions based on their spending patterns.

c) Enhanced Security

Mobile banking platforms use advanced security measures, such as biometric login, two-factor authentication, and encryption, to safeguard users' financial data.

- ❖ Fraud Detection: Many apps offer fraud detection and alerts for suspicious activities, providing peace of mind and enhancing security.
- ❖ Remote Account Control: Users can remotely freeze or unfreeze debit or credit cards through mobile banking apps, reducing the risk of unauthorized use in case of loss or theft.

2. Advantages of Peer-to-Peer (P2P) Lending for Wealth Creation

Peer-to-peer lending platforms have revolutionized the way individuals borrow and lend money, bypassing traditional banks and offering a more direct way to access capital. These platforms have created new opportunities for wealth creation, both for borrowers seeking funding and investors looking for higher returns.

a) Higher Returns for Investors

For investors, P2P lending offers the potential for higher returns compared to traditional savings accounts or bonds. By lending directly to individuals or businesses, investors can earn interest on their loans, diversifying their investment portfolio and creating additional streams of income.

- ❖ Attractive Interest Rates: Investors on P2P platforms such as **LendingClub** or **Prosper** can earn competitive interest rates, depending on the risk profile of the borrowers. This makes it an appealing option for those seeking higher yields on their investments.
- ❖ Portfolio Diversification: P2P lending offers an alternative asset class that helps

investors diversify their portfolios beyond stocks and bonds, potentially lowering overall investment risk.

b) Accessibility to Capital for Borrowers

For borrowers, P2P lending provides easier access to funding, often with fewer restrictions than traditional banks. It's especially useful for entrepreneurs, small businesses, and individuals who may struggle to secure loans through conventional financial institutions.

- ❖ Lower Interest Rates: P2P lending platforms often offer lower interest rates than credit cards or traditional bank loans, making it a more affordable borrowing option for individuals and small businesses.
- ❖ Fast Approval Process: P2P lending typically has a streamlined application process with faster approval times than traditional banking channels, providing quick access to funds.

c) Flexible Loan Structures

P2P lending platforms offer flexibility in loan structures, including varying loan terms and repayment schedules. This adaptability is advantageous for both borrowers and lenders, allowing them to negotiate terms that best suit their financial goals.

- ❖ Customizable Loan Terms: Borrowers can choose loan terms that align with their cash flow needs, while lenders can select investments based on their risk tolerance and expected return.
- ❖ Loan Transparency: P2P platforms provide transparency in terms of credit risk, fees,

and borrower profiles, allowing lenders to make informed decisions.

3. Advantages of Digital Payment Systems for Personal Wealth Management

Digital payment systems, such as **PayPal**, **Venmo**, and **Apple Pay**, have drastically transformed the way we handle transactions. These systems provide a convenient and secure way to transfer money, make purchases, and manage expenses, all while enhancing personal wealth management.

a) Seamless Money Transfers

Digital payment systems enable users to transfer money instantly to friends, family, or businesses, making it easy to pay bills, split expenses, or send funds across borders. This level of convenience fosters better financial management by eliminating the need for cash or checks.

- Instant Payments: With just a few clicks, users can send and receive payments, saving time and effort compared to traditional banking methods.
- International Transfers: Many digital payment systems offer affordable international money transfers, making it easier for individuals to send funds abroad without incurring high fees.

b) Integration with Financial Management Tools

Digital payment platforms often integrate with personal finance apps, providing a holistic view of income and expenses. This integration streamlines financial tracking, allowing users to see their spending patterns in real-time and make informed decisions about budgeting and saving.

- Expense Tracking: Apps like **Venmo** and **PayPal** provide detailed transaction histories that users can review for better budgeting and expense tracking. These records can be easily synced with financial management apps to provide a complete financial picture.
- Bill Splitting: Apps such as **Venmo** allow users to easily split bills with others, making it convenient for group payments and expense management.

c) Enhanced Security and Fraud Prevention

Digital payment systems use encryption and secure authentication methods to protect transactions. Many platforms also offer buyer protection, reducing the risk of fraud for users making purchases or transferring money.

- Fraud Alerts: Users receive real-time notifications for any suspicious activities, allowing them to address potential issues immediately.
- Secure Payments: Features like tokenization ensure that sensitive financial information is never shared with merchants during transactions, reducing the risk of identity theft.

d) Cash-back and Rewards Programs

Many digital payment systems partner with retailers to offer cash back or rewards programs, providing additional incentives for users to manage their finances through these platforms. This feature helps users earn rewards while making everyday purchases, adding another layer of value to their wealth management strategy.

- ❖ Loyalty Programs: Some platforms, such as **Apple Pay**, offer loyalty programs that reward users with points, discounts, or cash-back for using their service at specific retailers.
- ❖ Savings on Purchases: Digital wallets and payment systems may offer exclusive deals or discounts, allowing users to save money while spending.

CHAPTER FIVE

FINANCIAL HABITS AND BEHAVIORAL ECONOMICS

This chapter dives into the psychology behind financial decision-making, focusing on how habits and behavioral economics influence the path to wealth and abundance.

The Science of Financial Habits

- How Habits Shape Financial Success or Failure

Financial habits are the building blocks of long-term wealth and security. While short-term financial decisions can influence immediate outcomes, it is the cumulative effect of daily habits that ultimately determines one's financial success or failure. Understanding the science of financial habits involves recognizing how behavior, psychology, and routine actions contribute to wealth-building or detracts from it. This content explores the role habits play in shaping financial outcomes and how cultivating positive financial habits can lead to sustained financial success.

1. The Role of Habits in Financial Behavior: Automaticity and Consistency

Financial habits are repetitive behaviors that become automatic over time. Just like in other areas of life, habits can either support or undermine long-term goals. The science of habits tells us that once behaviors are ingrained, they are performed with little conscious effort, which means both positive and negative financial behaviors can become automatic.

a) Automaticity of Habits

Automaticity refers to the process by which habits become unconscious and routine. In financial terms, automaticity means that actions like saving, spending, or investing can happen without deliberate decision-making. When positive financial habits are automated, they promote consistency and reduce the likelihood of emotional decision-making, which can often lead to poor financial outcomes.

- Positive Automatic Habits: Automatically transferring a portion of income into savings or investments each month can ensure steady progress toward financial goals without requiring constant effort.
- Negative Automatic Habits: Conversely, unchecked automatic habits like overspending on non-essential items or accumulating credit card debt can erode financial security over time.

b) Consistency is Key

Financial success is often the result of small, consistent actions repeated over a long period. Developing habits such as tracking expenses, paying bills on time, and regularly contributing to investment accounts allows individuals to build wealth incrementally.

- Regular Savings Contributions: Even modest savings, when contributed regularly, can grow significantly over time thanks to compound interest.
- On-Time Payments: Consistently paying bills on time builds a positive credit history, which can improve access to favorable loan terms and other financial opportunities.

2. The Psychology Behind Financial Habits: How Emotions and Cognition Shape Behavior

Understanding the psychology behind financial habits is essential for shaping positive financial behaviors. Our emotions, cognitive biases, and mental frameworks all influence how we manage money. Often, financial decisions are driven more by emotions than by rational analysis, which can lead to habits that either support or detract from financial well-being.

a) Emotional Triggers and Spending

Emotional spending is one of the most common negative financial habits. Stress, boredom, or social pressure can lead individuals to spend impulsively on unnecessary items, which can lead to financial strain.

- Emotional Triggers: Identifying emotional triggers for spending, such as shopping when feeling stressed or anxious, can help individuals adopt healthier financial habits.
- Mindful Spending: Practicing mindfulness and pausing before making a purchase can help individuals make more intentional financial decisions, aligning spending with long-term goals rather than short-term emotional gratification.

b) Cognitive Biases and Financial Decision-Making

Cognitive biases—mental shortcuts that often lead to irrational decisions—play a significant role in financial habits. Biases such as **loss aversion**, **present bias**, and **status quo bias** can hinder the development of positive financial habits.

- Present Bias: This bias leads individuals to prioritize immediate gratification over long-term benefits. For instance, spending money today rather than saving for the future can become an entrenched habit that undermines financial security.
- Overcoming Biases: Creating structured systems such as automatic savings plans can help mitigate the impact of these biases by removing the need for daily decision-making and encouraging long-term thinking.

3. The Impact of Positive Financial Habits on Wealth Building

Building positive financial habits is crucial for long-term wealth creation. These habits, once established, serve as a foundation for financial stability and growth. By focusing on intentional, proactive behaviors, individuals can develop habits that support their wealth-building goals.

a) Saving and Investing Regularly

One of the most effective wealth-building habits is consistently saving and investing. The habit of regularly setting aside money, whether for retirement, emergency funds, or other financial goals, is central to financial success. Automating savings and investment contributions ensures that individuals remain disciplined in their approach to wealth accumulation.

- Dollar-Cost Averaging: This investment habit involves contributing a fixed amount of money into investments at regular intervals, regardless of market conditions. Over time, this strategy can reduce the impact of market volatility and lead to steady portfolio growth.

- ❖ Emergency Fund Creation: Regularly contributing to an emergency fund builds financial resilience and reduces reliance on debt in times of crisis.

b) Living Below One's Means

A foundational habit of financial success is spending less than one earns. This habit not only enables savings and investments but also prevents debt accumulation and financial stress.

- ❖ Budgeting Tools: Using budgeting tools such as **YNAB** or **Mint** can help individuals track their spending habits and identify areas where they can cut costs and redirect funds toward savings or investments.
- ❖ Delayed Gratification: Developing the habit of delaying gratification—putting off non-essential purchases in favor of long-term goals—strengthens financial discipline and promotes wealth-building.

4. Breaking Negative Financial Habits: How to Overcome Poor Financial Behaviors

While positive financial habits are essential for success, breaking negative financial habits is just as important. Identifying and addressing poor behaviors like overspending, relying on credit for everyday expenses, or failing to save for emergencies can be challenging, but it is critical for long-term financial health.

a) Identifying Bad Financial Habits

The first step in overcoming negative financial habits is identifying which behaviors are holding you back. Common examples of negative financial habits include:

- ❖ Impulse Spending: Regularly making unplanned purchases that strain the budget and derail financial goals.
- ❖ Minimum Debt Payments: Only paying the minimum amount due on credit cards, this prolongs debt repayment and results in excessive interest charges.
- ❖ Lack of Budgeting: Failing to track spending or create a budget leads to overspending and prevents savings.

b) Replacing Negative Habits with Positive Ones

Breaking negative habits requires replacing them with positive alternatives. For example, setting a budget and sticking to it can curb impulse spending, while automating bill payments can prevent late fees and credit score damage.

- ❖ Habit Stacking: This technique involves pairing a new positive habit with an existing one. For instance, reviewing your budget every time you check your bank account balance can reinforce good financial management practices.
- ❖ Accountability Partners: Having a financial coach, mentor, or even a family member or friend hold you accountable can help reinforce positive habits and deter negative ones.

5. The Power of Small, Incremental Changes: The Compound Effect of Financial Habits

The **compound effect** is the principle that small, incremental changes, when repeated consistently, lead to significant long-term results. In the context of financial habits, this means that even modest savings, investments, or changes in spending can grow exponentially over time.

a) Small Savings Add Up

Even small contributions to savings accounts, investment portfolios, or retirement funds can have a substantial impact due to the power of compound interest. The earlier and more consistently these habits are developed, the greater the long-term benefits.

- Compounding Interest: Reinvesting dividends or capital gains allows savings and investments to grow exponentially, turning small contributions into significant wealth over time.
- Automatic Contributions: Setting up automatic transfers into savings or investment accounts helps individuals stay consistent without the need for ongoing manual effort.

b) Behavioral Compounding

In addition to financial compounding, habits themselves can compound. Developing positive financial habits builds momentum and creates a positive feedback loop. As individuals see the results of their efforts, they are more likely to continue and even enhance their good behaviors, leading to even greater financial success.

Financial habits are one of the most critical determinants of long-term wealth and security. By understanding how habits form, leveraging the power of automaticity, and applying positive behaviors consistently, individuals can build a strong foundation for financial success. The science of financial habits reveals that success is not the result of a single large action, but rather the cumulative effect of small, everyday decisions. Whether through automating savings, curbing impulse spending, or breaking negative cycles, cultivating the right habits is essential for achieving financial freedom and security.

- Overcoming Procrastination and Inconsistency in Financial Management

Procrastination and inconsistency are two of the most common barriers to effective financial management. Despite knowing the importance of saving, investing, budgeting, or paying down debt, many individuals struggle to take timely action or maintain consistency in their financial habits. Overcoming these challenges requires understanding the psychological and behavioral factors that lead to procrastination and inconsistency, and implementing strategies to develop stronger, more sustainable financial habits.

1. Understanding the Causes of Procrastination in Financial Management

Financial procrastination is often rooted in psychological factors such as fear, anxiety, overwhelm, or a lack of motivation. Many individuals find financial decisions intimidating, leading them to delay taking action, whether it's budgeting, investing, or addressing debt. Recognizing the reasons behind procrastination can be the first step in addressing the issue.

a) Fear of Making Mistakes

Fear of financial mistakes can paralyze individuals, especially when faced with decisions that involve risk, such as investing or taking out a loan. This fear of making the wrong choice often leads to inaction.

- ❖ Solution: Start small and educate yourself. Instead of diving into complex financial products, begin by learning the basics of budgeting, saving, or low-risk investments. This builds confidence over time, reducing the fear of error.

b) Overwhelm and Complexity

Financial management can feel overwhelming due to the perceived complexity of handling multiple accounts, financial products, and long-term goals. People often procrastinate because they don't know where to start or feel they don't have enough time to properly address their finances.

- ❖ Solution: Break tasks into smaller, manageable steps. Instead of trying to overhaul your entire financial system, focus on one aspect at a time. Start with creating a budget, setting up an emergency fund, or automating bill payments.

c) Lack of Immediate Consequences

The long-term nature of many financial goals means that the consequences of inaction aren't immediately apparent. This can lead to procrastination, as individuals may not feel the urgency to save or invest for retirement, or to pay off debt with higher interest rates.

- ❖ Solution: Create a sense of urgency by setting specific deadlines for financial tasks and visualizing the long-term impact of inaction. Using tools like retirement calculators or debt repayment schedules can show the future consequences of delaying financial action, making the need for immediate steps more tangible.

d) Perfectionism and Analysis Paralysis

The desire to make the "perfect" financial decision can lead to over-analysis, where individuals spend too much time researching options and fail to take action. This perfectionism often results in missed opportunities for investment, savings, or debt repayment.

- ❖ Solution: Adopt a "progress over perfection" mindset. Financial decisions don't need to be flawless; they just need to be made. Start with a reasonable action—such as setting up a basic investment account—and refine your strategy as you learn more over time.

2. Combatting Inconsistency in Financial Habits

Inconsistency in financial management is another common challenge, often stemming from a lack of routine, unclear goals, or fluctuating motivation. While many people start with good intentions, maintaining consistent financial habits—such as saving, investing, or budgeting—can be difficult over the long term. Addressing inconsistency requires building habits that are sustainable and aligned with long-term financial goals.

a) Creating a Financial Routine

One of the key strategies for overcoming inconsistency is establishing a routine that incorporates regular financial check-ins. When financial management becomes a regular part of your schedule, it is easier to stay on top of your goals and make continuous progress.

- ❖ Solution: Set specific times for financial tasks. Whether it's a weekly budget review or a monthly investment update, having a designated time for financial management ensures that you stay consistent. Use reminders or calendar appointments to make these tasks non-negotiable parts of your routine.

b) Leveraging Automation for Consistency

Automation is one of the most effective tools for overcoming inconsistency because it removes the need for active decision-making. By automating savings, investments, and bill payments, you ensure that important financial tasks are being completed regularly, even if you aren't actively managing them every day.

- ❖ Solution: Automate as much as possible. Set up automatic transfers to savings or investment accounts, and automate bill payments to avoid missed due dates. By removing the need for manual action, you make consistency easier to achieve.

c) Aligning Financial Goals with Personal Values

Inconsistency often arises when financial goals feel disconnected from personal values or aspirations. If your goals are too vague or not meaningful, it's harder to stay committed over time. Aligning your financial management with your deeper life goals creates a stronger sense of purpose and motivation.

- ❖ Solution: Revisit and clarify your financial goals. Make sure they are not only SMART (Specific, Measurable, Achievable, Relevant, Time-bound) but also aligned with your personal values. For example, if financial security for your family is important, frame your savings goals around that value to create a stronger emotional connection.

d) Tracking Progress and Celebrating Milestones

Without regular feedback on your progress, it's easy to lose motivation and fall into inconsistency. Tracking your financial achievements and celebrating milestones along the way helps reinforce positive behaviors and keeps you engaged with your financial goals.

- ❖ Solution: Use financial apps or spreadsheets to track your progress. Whether it's reducing debt, building savings, or growing your investment portfolio, seeing tangible progress reinforces the benefits of consistent action. Celebrate small wins—like paying off a credit card or reaching a savings goal—to stay motivated.

3. Developing a Mindset of Long-Term Discipline

Financial success requires a long-term perspective and the discipline to stick with good habits, even when progress is slow or obstacles arise. Building this mindset takes time, but it can be cultivated through intentional practice and psychological strategies.

a) Visualizing Long-Term Success

One reason for financial procrastination and inconsistency is that the rewards of good financial habits—such as retirement savings or wealth-building—are often far off in the future. By visualizing the long-term benefits of financial discipline, you can stay motivated to take action today.

- Solution: Create a financial vision board or write down your long-term financial goals, and revisit them regularly. Seeing your future financial security, freedom, or goals like homeownership or travel will provide daily motivation to take small steps toward those aspirations.

b) Implementing the "Two-Minute Rule"

The "Two-Minute Rule" is a productivity strategy that can be applied to financial management. The idea is to start any task that can be done in two minutes or less immediately, rather than putting it off. This strategy is especially useful for small but essential financial tasks, like checking bank balances, paying bills, or setting up a new savings account.

- Solution: Whenever faced with a small financial task, take action immediately. Even for larger tasks, commit to spending just two minutes on them—this often helps build momentum and reduces the mental barrier to getting started.

c) Building Financial Accountability

Accountability is a powerful tool for overcoming procrastination and inconsistency in financial management. Whether through a partner, financial advisor, or digital tools, having external or internal accountability helps ensure that you stay on track with your financial commitments.

- Solution: Partner with a friend or family member to regularly review financial goals and progress, or work with a financial coach or planner who can provide guidance and hold you accountable. Additionally, use financial apps that send notifications and reminders to keep you on track.

4. Tackling the Emotional Side of Financial Management

In many cases, procrastination and inconsistency in financial management are tied to emotional responses, such as anxiety, shame, or frustration about finances. Addressing these emotions directly can help alleviate the psychological burden that contributes to inaction.

a) Recognizing and Reducing Financial Anxiety

Financial anxiety can lead to avoidance and procrastination, especially when dealing with debt or complex financial situations. Learning to manage this anxiety is critical to taking consistent financial action.

- ❖ Solution: Break down overwhelming financial tasks into smaller, more manageable steps. Practice mindfulness and stress-reduction techniques, such as deep breathing or meditation, before tackling financial tasks. Seeking support from a financial advisor or coach can also help alleviate feelings of uncertainty.

b) Shifting the Narrative Around Money

Negative beliefs about money, such as associating it with stress, greed, or conflict, can lead to procrastination and inconsistency in financial habits. Shifting your mindset around money—viewing it as a tool for security, freedom, and opportunity—can help you engage more positively with financial tasks.

- Solution: Reframe financial management as a path to personal empowerment rather than a source of stress. Focus on the positive outcomes of financial discipline—such as freedom from debt or the ability to support your family—and remind yourself of these benefits when managing your finances.

Overcoming procrastination and inconsistency in financial management requires a combination of psychological awareness, practical strategies, and a long-term mindset. By addressing the root causes of procrastination, automating financial processes, aligning goals with personal values, and cultivating discipline, individuals can build sustainable habits that lead to lasting financial success. The key is to start small, remain consistent, and embrace a mindset of gradual progress rather than perfection, transforming procrastination into proactive and consistent financial management.

Behavioral Economics and Personal Finance

- An Introduction to Behavioral Economics: How Human Biases Affect Financial Decisions

Behavioral economics is a field that combines insights from psychology and economics to understand how individuals actually behave in financial situations, as opposed to how traditional economic theory predicts they should behave. While classical economics assumes that people are rational decision-makers who maximize their utility, behavioral economics recognizes that human decision-making is often influenced by cognitive biases, emotions, and social factors, leading to suboptimal financial choices.

Understanding how human biases affect financial decisions is essential for improving personal financial management. By becoming aware of these biases, individuals can make more informed, rational decisions that align with their long-term goals and avoid common financial pitfalls.

1. Cognitive Biases in Financial Decision-Making

Cognitive biases are systematic patterns of deviation from rational judgment. They arise because the human brain tends to rely on mental shortcuts, or heuristics, to process information quickly and efficiently. While these shortcuts can be useful in everyday decision-making, they often lead to errors in complex or uncertain financial situations. Some of the most common cognitive biases that affect financial decisions include:

a) Loss Aversion

Loss aversion refers to the tendency for individuals to feel the pain of losses more acutely than the pleasure of equivalent gains. This bias can lead to risk-averse behavior, where people avoid taking necessary financial risks, such as investing in the stock market, because they fear losses more than they value potential gains.

- Impact on Personal Finance: Loss aversion can cause individuals to hold onto poor-performing investments for too long, fearing the realization of a loss, or to avoid higher-risk, higher-return investments like stocks, resulting in missed opportunities for wealth growth.
- Overcoming the Bias: Diversifying investments and focusing on long-term financial goals can help counteract the emotional pull of short-term losses.

b) Anchoring

Anchoring occurs when individuals rely too heavily on the first piece of information they encounter when making decisions. In financial contexts, this might involve focusing on an initial price or number—such as the price at which a stock was purchased—when deciding whether to buy or sell, even if market conditions have changed.

- Impact on Personal Finance: Anchoring can lead to poor decision-making in negotiations, budgeting, or investments, where individuals are "anchored" to an arbitrary figure rather than considering the current situation.
- Overcoming the Bias: To counter anchoring, it's important to reassess decisions based on updated, objective data rather than sticking to initial impressions or past figures.

c) Overconfidence Bias

Overconfidence bias is the tendency for individuals to overestimate their knowledge, abilities, or the accuracy of their predictions. In financial contexts, this can manifest as overestimating one's ability to pick winning stocks, time the market, or predict economic trends.

- Impact on Personal Finance: Overconfidence can lead to excessive risk-taking, frequent trading, and ignoring expert advice, which may result in financial losses.
- Overcoming the Bias: Seeking the advice of financial professionals, regularly reviewing financial performance, and avoiding overactive trading can help mitigate the impact of overconfidence.

d) Status Quo Bias

Status quo bias refers to the preference for maintaining the current situation, even when change would be beneficial. This can cause inertia in financial decision-making, where individuals stick with their current financial products or strategies, even when better alternatives are available.

- ❖ Impact on Personal Finance: Status quo bias may lead to staying in a high-fee savings account, keeping outdated investment portfolios, or neglecting to update wills or insurance policies.
- ❖ Overcoming the Bias: Regularly reviewing and updating financial plans, investments, and other financial products can help ensure that individuals are making decisions that align with their evolving financial goals.

e) Herd Mentality

Herd mentality describes the tendency for individuals to follow the actions of a larger group, often without independently evaluating the situation. In financial markets, this can lead to irrational behaviors, such as panic selling during a market downturn or over-investing in a popular asset bubble.

- ❖ Impact on Personal Finance: Herd behavior can lead to poor timing in buying or selling investments, as individuals are influenced by market trends rather than sound financial analysis.
- ❖ Overcoming the Bias: Developing a well-researched, long-term investment strategy and sticking to it—regardless of market

trends—can help prevent decisions driven by herd mentality.

2. Emotional Biases and Financial Decision-Making

While cognitive biases arise from how our brains process information, emotional biases stem from the emotions we experience when making decisions. Emotions like fear, greed, excitement, and regret can cloud judgment and lead to irrational financial choices.

a) Fear and Panic

During times of economic uncertainty or market volatility, fear can cause individuals to make hasty decisions, such as selling investments during a downturn. This reaction is often based on short-term emotions rather than long-term financial strategies.

- Impact on Personal Finance: Fear-based decisions can lock in losses and derail long-term financial goals, especially when individuals sell assets during temporary market corrections.
- Overcoming the Bias: Maintaining a diversified portfolio and focusing on long-term goals can help mitigate fear during short-term market fluctuations.

b) Greed and Over-Exuberance

On the flip side, greed can drive individuals to take excessive risks, chasing high returns without properly evaluating the risks involved. This bias is often seen during asset bubbles, where individuals invest heavily in overvalued markets or products.

- Impact on Personal Finance: Greed can lead to speculative investments, such as investing in a booming stock without understanding the fundamentals, or taking on excessive debt to fuel high-risk investments.
- Overcoming the Bias: Setting clear financial goals and adhering to a risk tolerance plan can prevent decisions driven by greed or short-term excitement.

c) Regret Aversion

Regret aversion occurs when individuals avoid making decisions because they fear the regret of making the wrong choice. In financial contexts, this might mean delaying investment decisions or avoiding action altogether, leading to missed opportunities.

- Impact on Personal Finance: Regret aversion can cause paralysis in financial decision-making, preventing individuals from taking necessary steps like investing for retirement or making estate planning decisions.
- Overcoming the Bias: Accepting that mistakes are a natural part of financial management and focusing on long-term goals can reduce the fear of regret.

3. Behavioral Economics and Personal Financial Management

Behavioral economics has practical applications in personal financial management by providing insights into how people can design better systems for themselves. By understanding and accounting for biases, individuals can take proactive steps to improve their financial habits and decision-making processes.

a) Using Nudges to Improve Financial Behavior

A "nudge" is a subtle intervention that encourages individuals to make better choices without restricting their freedom of choice. For example, many companies automatically enroll employees in retirement savings plans, relying on inertia to increase participation rates—this is an application of behavioral economics.

- Impact on Personal Finance: Automating savings, debt payments, or investments can help overcome biases like procrastination and status quo bias, encouraging consistent progress toward financial goals.

b) Setting Mental Accounting Rules

Mental accounting refers to the tendency to categorize money differently depending on its source or intended use, which can lead to suboptimal financial decisions. For example, individuals may treat a tax refund as "extra money" and spend it on luxury items, even if they have outstanding debt.

- Impact on Personal Finance: Establishing clear financial rules—such as directing any windfalls toward savings or debt reduction—can help counteract the irrational use of money driven by mental accounting.

c) Framing Decisions in Terms of Losses and Gains

How financial choices are framed can greatly influence decisions. For example, framing an investment as having a "90% success rate" versus a "10% failure rate" can lead to different outcomes, even though the two statements are mathematically identical.

- ❖ Impact on Personal Finance: Being aware of how financial products or opportunities are framed, and reframing them in neutral terms, can help individuals make more objective decisions.

4. Overcoming Behavioral Biases for Better Financial Outcomes

Awareness of behavioral biases is the first step to overcoming them, but individuals also need practical strategies to minimize their effects. Some key approaches include:

a) Education and Self-Awareness

Understanding how common biases influence decision-making can help individuals recognize when they are falling into these patterns. Regular financial education and self-awareness can reduce the impact of biases over time.

b) Decision-Making Frameworks

Creating structured financial decision-making frameworks—such as having a clear investment strategy or a set of rules for saving and spending—can reduce the influence of emotions and cognitive biases on financial choices.

c) Seeking Professional Advice

Financial advisors and planners can provide objective, data-driven advice, helping individuals avoid decisions driven by biases like overconfidence, herd mentality, or loss aversion.

5. Practical Applications of Behavioral Economics in Personal Finance

Understanding behavioral economics isn't just about identifying biases—it's about creating systems and habits that help individuals make better financial choices. Here are some practical applications of behavioral economics principles to improve personal financial management:

a) Automating Financial Decisions

Automation is one of the most powerful tools for overcoming procrastination and poor decision-making. By automating regular savings, debt payments, and investment contributions, individuals can bypass the emotional and cognitive biases that might lead to inaction or suboptimal choices.

- Savings Automation: Setting up automatic transfers to a savings account each payday ensures that individuals save consistently, even if they're tempted to spend.
- Investment Automation: Automated contributions to retirement accounts or investment portfolios ensure that individuals invest regularly, avoiding market timing and emotional decisions.
- Debt Repayment Automation: Automatic payments for loans and credit cards prevent missed payments and help individuals stay on track with debt reduction goals.

Automation reduces the need for ongoing decision-making and removes the temptation to spend money that should be allocated toward long-term goals.

b) Pre-Commitment Strategies

Pre-commitment involves making decisions in advance that limit future options, thereby reducing the influence of short-term emotions. This concept, grounded in behavioral economics, can be applied to financial planning.

- Commitment to Saving: Setting up a savings plan with automatic increases in contributions over time (often offered by retirement accounts) can ensure individuals save more as their income grows.
- Budgeting: Pre-committing to a budget and allocating money into specific categories (e.g., savings, bills, discretionary spending) can prevent overspending and ensure that financial goals are prioritized.
- Pre-Setting Investment Strategies: Creating a clear investment strategy that outlines when to buy, sell, or rebalance can prevent individuals from making emotional decisions during market volatility.

c) Using Default Options

Behavioral economics research shows that people are more likely to stick with default options than actively change them. This is why setting default options that align with long-term financial goals can significantly impact personal wealth.

- Defaulting into Retirement Plans: Many employers use automatic enrollment in retirement savings plans (like 401(k)s), which significantly increases participation rates. Opting for a higher default savings rate can accelerate retirement savings without requiring constant decision-making.

- ❖ Default Investment Choices: Setting low-cost index funds or diversified portfolios as default investment options can help avoid emotional market timing and reduce fees that erode long-term returns.

d) Leveraging “Nudges” for Better Financial Behavior

Nudges are subtle changes to the way choices are presented that encourage better decisions without restricting freedom of choice. Behavioral economists advocate for nudges in personal finance because they make positive actions easier.

- ❖ Text and Email Reminders: Banks, investment apps, and financial planners often use reminders to nudge individuals to take action, such as reviewing budgets, making payments, or increasing savings contributions.
- ❖ Visualization Tools: Financial apps that show individuals the future benefits of current actions (such as retirement calculators) can nudge them to save more by making the long-term payoff feel more immediate.

e) Mental Accounting and Categorization

Mental accounting refers to the practice of assigning different values to money depending on its source or intended use. Although it can sometimes lead to poor financial decisions, it can also be used strategically.

- ❖ Purpose-Driven Accounts: Setting up separate bank accounts for specific purposes—such as emergency savings, vacation funds, or home purchases—can help individuals allocate money more effectively and avoid dipping into long-term savings for short-term needs.

- Reward Accounts: Using mental accounting to treat discretionary or "fun" spending separately from essential bills ensures that indulgences don't interfere with financial stability. Allocating a specific amount for rewards and non-essential purchases can reduce guilt and maintain balance.

f) Social Proof and Accountability

Social influences play a significant role in decision-making, as seen with herd mentality. However, leveraging social proof and accountability can also encourage positive financial behaviors.

- Financial Accountability Partners: Sharing financial goals with a friend, family member, or financial advisor creates accountability and makes it more likely that individuals will follow through with their commitments.
- Public Commitments: Announcing financial goals—such as paying off debt or saving for a down payment—through social media or within a group can create external pressure to stay on track.

g) Reframing Financial Decisions

How individuals perceive financial decisions can significantly influence their behavior. Behavioral economics emphasizes that framing decisions in terms of losses versus gains can lead to different choices.

- Loss Aversion in Savings: Reframing a missed savings contribution as a "loss" can encourage people to prioritize saving. For example, thinking about the potential growth lost by not contributing to a retirement fund can nudge individuals to save more.
- Framing Investment Returns: Instead of focusing on short-term market volatility, reframing investment success in terms of long-term average returns can help investors stay calm during market fluctuations and avoid emotional reactions.

6. Long-Term Behavioral Change for Financial Success

To achieve lasting financial success, individuals must develop habits that align with long-term wealth-building goals. Behavioral economics provides valuable insights into creating these habits and sustaining them over time.

a) Developing Consistency through Small Wins

One of the key principles of behavioral economics is that small, consistent actions lead to long-term success. Setting achievable financial goals and celebrating small victories (like paying off a credit card or hitting a savings milestone) reinforces positive behavior.

- Snowball Effect in Debt Repayment: The "snowball method" of debt repayment, where individuals focus on paying off the smallest debt first, creates quick wins that build momentum and encourage continued progress.

b) Adopting a Growth Mindset

A growth mindset emphasizes the belief that financial success is the result of learning, effort, and adaptation. This contrasts with a fixed mindset, which views financial success as predetermined or unchangeable.

- Learning from Financial Mistakes: Viewing mistakes as opportunities for growth (rather than as failures) helps individuals learn from past decisions and adjust strategies moving forward.
- Continuous Education: Staying informed about financial strategies, investment opportunities, and behavioral biases ensures that individuals are better equipped to make informed, rational decisions.

c) Incorporating Feedback Loops

Feedback loops involve receiving regular, timely information on progress, which helps individuals stay on track and adjust as needed.

- Regular Financial Check-Ins: Reviewing budgets, net worth, and investment performance on a regular basis ensures that individuals are aware of their financial health and can make adjustments when necessary.
- Tracking Spending and Savings: Financial apps that track spending and categorize purchases provide real-time feedback, helping individuals identify where they can cut back or improve their saving habits.

Behavioral economics provides a powerful framework for understanding why individuals make suboptimal financial decisions and how they can improve their financial outcomes by recognizing and mitigating these biases. By automating good financial behaviors, using nudges, setting default options, and being mindful of how choices are framed, individuals can build habits that support long-term wealth accumulation.

Moreover, the insights from behavioral economics emphasize that the path to financial success isn't just about knowledge—it's about creating environments, systems, and habits that align with human psychology and encourage positive financial behaviors. Through self-awareness, pre-commitment strategies, and consistent feedback, individuals can overcome the cognitive and emotional biases that often lead to poor financial outcomes, enabling them to make decisions that are aligned with their long-term financial well-being.

- Leveraging Behavioral Economics to Make Smarter Financial Choices

In the context of personal finance, leveraging behavioral economics means becoming aware of the common psychological traps people fall into and developing strategies to avoid them. This approach can lead to better savings habits, more informed investment decisions, and overall improved financial well-being.

Key Behavioral Economics Concepts in Personal Finance

1. Loss Aversion

   Loss aversion refers to the tendency for people to prefer avoiding losses rather than acquiring equivalent gains. For example, losing $100 feels more painful than the pleasure of gaining $100. In financial contexts, loss aversion can cause investors to hold on to losing investments longer than they should, hoping to avoid realizing a loss, or avoid riskier but potentially rewarding investments due to fear of losses.

How to Overcome Loss Aversion:

One way to overcome loss aversion is by reframing financial decisions. Instead of focusing on the potential loss, investors should evaluate the overall long-term benefits and consider diversification as a way to reduce risks without avoiding opportunities altogether. Automation in investing, such as using robo-advisors, can also help by removing the emotional attachment to individual investments.

2. Anchoring

Anchoring occurs when individuals rely too heavily on the first piece of information they encounter when making financial decisions. For example, if a person sees a stock that has dropped from $200 to $150, they may assume $200 is the "correct" price, leading them to think the stock is undervalued, even though the market may have adjusted due to new information.

How to Overcome Anchoring:

To avoid anchoring bias, always conduct thorough research and focus on broader market trends and fundamentals rather than arbitrary price points. Make decisions based on data-driven insights, and compare investments across different criteria, such as performance metrics, industry trends, and historical returns.

3. Herding Behavior

   Herding refers to the phenomenon where individuals follow the crowd, assuming that the collective knowledge of the group must be correct. This behavior is common in financial markets, where investors may buy stocks simply because others are doing the same, without understanding the underlying value of the asset.

   How to Overcome Herding Behavior:

   To avoid herding behavior, develop a clear, personalized financial plan that aligns with your goals and risk tolerance. Stick to your strategy even when market trends suggest otherwise, and take time to assess the fundamental value of investments rather than simply following market hype.

4. Overconfidence Bias

   Overconfidence bias leads individuals to overestimate their financial knowledge or ability to predict market trends. This can result in risky behaviors, such as over-trading or underestimating the need for diversification.

   How to Overcome Overconfidence:

   To counter overconfidence bias, practice humility in financial decision-making by continuously learning and acknowledging what you don't know. Seek advice from financial professionals when needed, and ensure your portfolio is diversified to hedge against unpredictable risks. Conduct regular reviews of your financial decisions to objectively assess their performance and learn from any mistakes.

5. Present Bias (Hyperbolic Discounting)

   Present bias refers to the tendency for people to prioritize immediate gratification over long-term financial gains. This often manifests in under-saving for retirement or making impulse purchases rather than investing.

   How to Overcome Present Bias:

   One way to mitigate present bias is to automate savings and investments. Setting up automatic transfers to savings accounts or retirement funds ensures that money is set aside before it can be spent. Creating short-term milestones that tie into long-term goals can also help sustain motivation by providing a sense of accomplishment along the way.

6. Mental Accounting

   Mental accounting is the cognitive process by which people categorize money into different "accounts," often irrationally. For instance, someone may treat a tax refund as "free money" and spend it impulsively, even though it could be better used for paying down debt or investing.

   How to Overcome Mental Accounting:

   To combat mental accounting, adopt a holistic view of your finances. Treat all income, whether from salary, bonuses, or windfalls, as part of a single pool of resources that can be allocated toward your financial goals. Prioritize paying off high-interest debt and contributing to long-term investments before discretionary spending.

Applying Behavioral Economics to Specific Financial Decisions

1. Saving for Retirement

   Many people fail to save adequately for retirement because of biases such as present bias and loss aversion. Behavioral economics suggests automating retirement contributions through employer-sponsored 401(k) plans or individual retirement accounts (IRAs) to ensure consistent saving. Additionally, framing retirement saving as a non-negotiable expense can help individuals prioritize it.

2. Investment Strategies

   Investors are often influenced by herding behavior, loss aversion, and overconfidence when making investment decisions. Behavioral economics suggests sticking to a long-term strategy, focusing on diversification, and using tools like robo-advisors to reduce emotional decision-making. Dollar-cost averaging is another technique that can mitigate the impact of market volatility by regularly investing a fixed amount regardless of market conditions.

3. Debt Management

   Behavioral economics can help individuals make better decisions about debt management by framing debt reduction in terms of incremental goals. The “snowball” method of paying off smaller debts first, even if the interest rates are higher on other debts, leverages the psychological boost of small victories to encourage continued progress.

Leveraging Behavioral Insights in Financial Technology (FinTech)

The rise of financial technology (FinTech) has incorporated behavioral economics principles to help individuals make better financial choices. Many apps and platforms are designed to nudge users toward smarter behaviors by making saving, investing, and budgeting easier and more automated.

- Micro-savings apps, like Acorns, round up users' purchases to the nearest dollar and invest the difference, capitalizing on present bias to help people save painlessly.
- Budgeting apps, such as YNAB (You Need A Budget), use psychological triggers to promote saving and careful spending by encouraging users to assign every dollar a job and create accountability for financial decisions.
- Robo-advisors leverage data and automation to remove emotional biases from investment decisions, offering users diversified portfolios and managing risk without requiring active involvement.

By understanding and leveraging the principles of behavioral economics, individuals can take more control over their financial decisions and avoid common pitfalls that hinder wealth accumulation. Whether through automating savings, reframing losses, or avoiding herding behavior, integrating behavioral insights into personal finance leads to more rational, informed, and ultimately successful financial strategies.

CHAPTER SIX

SUSTAINABLE AND ETHICAL WEALTH

This chapter addresses the growing movement toward sustainable and ethical wealth building, aligning financial goals with personal values.

The Case for Sustainable Investing

- Introduction to ESG Investing: The Case for Sustainable Investing

Environmental, Social, and Governance (ESG) investing, also known as sustainable or responsible investing, integrates environmental, social, and governance factors into investment decision-making. ESG investing is based on the belief that businesses that operate ethically, responsibly, and sustainably can deliver long-term financial returns while also addressing global challenges such as climate change, social inequality, and corporate governance issues. As investors increasingly recognize the importance of aligning financial goals with personal values, ESG investing has grown into a significant trend in the world of finance.

1. What is ESG Investing?

ESG investing focuses on three primary pillars:

- ❖ Environmental: This pillar evaluates a company's impact on the environment, including its carbon footprint, waste management practices, renewable energy use, and pollution control. Companies that demonstrate responsible environmental practices can reduce regulatory risks, improve efficiency, and appeal to environmentally conscious consumers.

- Social: The social aspect assesses how a company manages relationships with employees, customers, suppliers, and the communities where it operates. Key factors include labor practices, diversity and inclusion, product safety, human rights, and corporate social responsibility. Companies with strong social practices foster brand loyalty, reduce turnover, and contribute to social well-being.
- Governance: Governance evaluates a company's leadership, board structure, executive pay, transparency, and shareholder rights. Strong governance ensures accountability, mitigates risks such as corruption or financial mismanagement, and promotes long-term value creation for investors.

Incorporating ESG factors into investment strategies allows investors to identify companies that are not only financially sound but also committed to sustainability, ethical practices, and sound governance.

2. The Growth of ESG Investing

Over the past decade, ESG investing has evolved from a niche strategy into a mainstream approach embraced by institutional and individual investors alike. Several factors have contributed to the rise of ESG investing:

- Increasing Awareness of Global Challenges: As concerns about climate change, social inequality, and corporate responsibility grow, more investors are demanding that their investments reflect these values. ESG investing offers a way to align financial portfolios with sustainability goals.

- Performance and Risk Mitigation: Research has shown that companies with strong ESG practices tend to outperform their peers in the long term, as they are better equipped to manage risks such as regulatory changes, environmental disasters, and social unrest. ESG investments can also be less volatile, as sustainable businesses are often better at managing risks and responding to stakeholder demands.
- Regulatory and Policy Changes: Governments and regulatory bodies worldwide are increasingly emphasizing sustainability and ESG disclosures. Policies such as the European Union's Sustainable Finance Disclosure Regulation (SFDR) and the Task Force on Climate-related Financial Disclosures (TCFD) have encouraged companies to provide more transparency on ESG issues, further driving investor interest.
- Millennial and Gen Z Investors: Younger generations are particularly focused on investing with purpose. As they inherit wealth and become a larger share of the investor base, demand for ESG investments is expected to rise. Millennials and Gen Z investors are more likely to prioritize environmental sustainability, social justice, and corporate ethics when making investment decisions.

3. Key Benefits of ESG Investing

ESG investing offers a range of financial and non-financial benefits, making it an attractive strategy for investors seeking both returns and impact.

- Enhanced Long-Term Performance: Companies that focus on ESG factors are more likely to have long-term, sustainable business models. By mitigating environmental risks, fostering social good, and ensuring strong governance, these companies are often more resilient to market volatility and regulatory changes, leading to better financial performance over time.
- Risk Management: ESG investing helps investors identify companies that may face future risks related to environmental damage, social unrest, or governance failures. For instance, companies with high carbon emissions or poor labor practices may face lawsuits, regulatory fines, or reputational damage, negatively impacting their stock prices. ESG factors can serve as red flags, helping investors avoid companies with potential risks.
- Alignment with Personal Values: For many investors, ESG investing is about more than financial returns—it's about making a positive impact on the world. ESG investments allow individuals and institutions to align their portfolios with their values, supporting businesses that are committed to ethical practices, sustainability, and social responsibility.
- Increased Market Demand: The growing demand for ESG investments has led to a proliferation of ESG-focused funds, exchange-traded funds (ETFs), and other financial products. As the market for ESG products continues to expand, investors have more options for building diversified portfolios that prioritize sustainability.

4. Challenges and Criticisms of ESG Investing

Despite its growing popularity, ESG investing faces several challenges and criticisms:

- ❖ Lack of Standardization: One of the biggest challenges in ESG investing is the lack of consistent standards and metrics for measuring ESG performance. Different rating agencies and investment firms use varying criteria to evaluate ESG factors, leading to confusion and inconsistency in ESG scores. This makes it difficult for investors to compare companies or funds based on ESG criteria.
- ❖ Green washing: Green washing refers to the practice of companies or investment products falsely claiming to be environmentally friendly or socially responsible in order to attract ESG-focused investors. Investors must conduct thorough due diligence to ensure that their investments truly align with ESG principles and are not simply marketing gimmicks.
- ❖ Short-Term vs. Long-Term Focus: Some critics argue that ESG investing may sacrifice short-term financial performance for long-term sustainability goals. While ESG-focused companies may outperform in the long run, there may be instances where prioritizing sustainability leads to lower returns in the short term, particularly in industries like fossil fuels or mining.
- ❖ ESG Data Availability: Many companies, especially smaller or emerging market firms, may not provide comprehensive ESG data. This lack of transparency can make it challenging for investors to assess the true

ESG impact of their investments, potentially leading to misinformed decisions.

5. ESG Investment Strategies

There are several approaches investors can take when incorporating ESG factors into their portfolios, depending on their goals and risk tolerance:

- Negative Screening: This strategy involves excluding companies or industries that do not meet specific ESG criteria. For example, investors may avoid investing in sectors like tobacco, fossil fuels, or weapons manufacturing. Negative screening is one of the most common ESG strategies and allows investors to align their portfolios with ethical values.
- Positive Screening: Positive screening involves selecting companies that excel in specific ESG areas, such as environmental sustainability or social responsibility. Investors using this approach actively seek out companies that demonstrate leadership in ESG practices.
- Thematic Investing: Thematic investing focuses on specific ESG-related themes, such as renewable energy, clean technology, gender equality, or healthcare access. This approach allows investors to target particular areas of social or environmental impact while seeking returns from high-growth sectors.
- Impact Investing: Impact investing goes beyond traditional ESG strategies by directly targeting investments that aim to generate measurable positive social or environmental outcomes, alongside

financial returns. For instance, impact investors may focus on companies or projects that provide clean energy to underserved communities or finance affordable housing initiatives.

6. The Future of ESG Investing

As ESG investing continues to grow, it is likely to become an integral part of mainstream investment strategies. Several trends are expected to shape the future of ESG investing:

- Greater Standardization: As demand for ESG products increases, there will be a push for greater standardization and transparency in ESG metrics and reporting. Regulatory bodies and rating agencies will likely develop more consistent frameworks for measuring ESG performance, making it easier for investors to evaluate companies.
- Technological Advancements: Advances in data analytics, artificial intelligence, and block-chain technology could enhance the transparency and accuracy of ESG reporting. These tools will help investors track and verify the impact of their investments, reducing the risk of green washing.
- Corporate Accountability: Companies will face increasing pressure from stakeholders—including investors, consumers, and regulators—to improve their ESG practices. Those that fail to prioritize sustainability, social responsibility, and governance may find it harder to attract capital and maintain long-term competitiveness.

The Case for Sustainable Investing

ESG investing represents a powerful shift in the way investors think about their portfolios. It combines financial performance with positive environmental and social impact, making it an attractive option for those seeking to align their investments with their values. While challenges such as standardization and green washing remain, the growing demand for ESG investments and the potential for long-term financial benefits make sustainable investing a compelling strategy for the future. As global challenges like climate change and social inequality continue to evolve, ESG investing will play a key role in shaping the future of wealth creation and responsible corporate behavior.

- How Sustainable Investments Can Drive Long-Term Wealth While Contributing to Positive Global Outcomes

Sustainable investing, also known as Environmental, Social, and Governance (ESG) investing, has become a vital strategy for those seeking to align their financial goals with responsible and impactful practices. Beyond just being a trend, it has shown that investors do not need to compromise financial returns to make a difference in the world. By incorporating sustainability principles into investment decisions, sustainable investments not only contribute to long-term wealth accumulation but also foster positive global change in areas like environmental preservation, social equality, and improved governance.

1. The Dual Benefit of Sustainable Investing: Wealth and Impact

Sustainable investing offers the unique advantage of generating financial returns while addressing critical global challenges. Investors are increasingly recognizing that companies with strong ESG practices can reduce risk, create competitive advantages, and generate superior long-term value. The benefits include:

- Mitigation of Risks: Companies that prioritize environmental stewardship, social responsibility, and robust governance are often more resilient to market disruptions, regulatory changes, and reputational risks. They tend to avoid costly liabilities such as fines for environmental damage, labor strikes, or governance scandals.
- Enhanced Long-Term Returns: Numerous studies have shown that companies with strong ESG ratings often outperform their peers. They are better positioned to capture opportunities in emerging industries like renewable energy, technology-driven health solutions, and sustainable agriculture. These companies tend to have forward-thinking management, strong customer loyalty, and innovative approaches to solving global issues.
- Tapping into Consumer and Investor Demand: As consumers and stakeholders become more conscientious, businesses that prioritize sustainability are favored in the marketplace. Likewise, financial institutions are launching more ESG-focused products, which are attracting capital from institutional investors, pension funds, and individuals alike.

By investing in sustainable businesses, individuals can build wealth while ensuring their capital supports initiatives that aim to create a better future.

2. Long-Term Wealth Creation through Sustainable Investing

Sustainable investing can drive long-term wealth growth through several key mechanisms:

- ❖ Access to High-Growth Sectors: Sustainability-related industries—such as renewable energy, electric vehicles, waste management, and sustainable agriculture—are poised for rapid growth as governments, corporations, and individuals focus on reducing carbon footprints and promoting green economies. These industries are beneficiaries of global trends like climate change mitigation and technological advancements in clean energy, offering attractive opportunities for investors.
- ❖ Innovation and Efficiency: Companies focused on sustainability often invest heavily in innovation, particularly in areas like energy efficiency, resource management, and waste reduction. This can lead to operational efficiencies that improve profitability and reduce costs over time. Moreover, such innovations open the door to new markets and revenue streams, enhancing the long-term growth prospects of these businesses.
- ❖ Reduced Volatility: Sustainable companies tend to exhibit lower volatility, as they are less exposed to risks that can disrupt traditional business models. For example, companies with sustainable practices are less likely to be impacted by fluctuations in fossil fuel prices, legal challenges related to environmental harm, or social unrest caused by poor labor practices. Lower

volatility can translate into more stable, long-term returns for investors.

- ❖ Sustainability as a Driver of Corporate Longevity: Companies that prioritize ESG factors are more likely to adapt to changing regulatory landscapes and shifting consumer demands, ensuring their longevity. As governments around the world introduce stricter environmental regulations and incentivize green technologies, businesses that have already embraced sustainability will be better positioned to thrive in the evolving global economy.

3. Contributing to Positive Global Outcomes

Sustainable investments do more than generate financial returns—they actively contribute to solving global challenges. Here's how sustainable investing can drive positive global outcomes:

- ❖ Climate Change Mitigation: By investing in renewable energy, clean technology, and carbon-neutral businesses, investors can support the transition to a low-carbon economy. This helps mitigate the impact of climate change by reducing greenhouse gas emissions and promoting environmentally friendly business practices.
- ❖ Social Impact: ESG investing also promotes social justice, diversity, and community engagement. Companies that adhere to strong social practices—such as fair labor conditions, human rights protections, and gender equality—contribute to a more equitable and inclusive global economy. By investing in such companies, individuals can play a role in promoting social welfare

while benefiting from the economic success of ethical businesses.

- Improved Corporate Governance: Companies with strong governance structures are less prone to corruption, mismanagement, and unethical behavior. Through sustainable investing, investors can encourage transparency, accountability, and responsible leadership in the business world. This helps create a more stable and trustworthy global financial system, which benefits both investors and society as a whole.
- Sustainable Development Goals (SDGs): The United Nations has outlined 17 Sustainable Development Goals (SDGs) aimed at addressing global issues like poverty, hunger, clean water, education, and climate action. Many ESG-focused investment funds align their portfolios with these goals, directing capital toward businesses and projects that directly contribute to achieving the SDGs. Investors in these funds are not only pursuing returns but also supporting initiatives that can transform lives and communities around the world.

4. Challenges to Consider in Sustainable Investing

While sustainable investing holds significant potential for both wealth creation and positive impact, it is not without its challenges:

- Green-washing: Some companies may falsely claim to be environmentally or socially responsible in order to attract investors. Known as green-washing, this practice can mislead investors into supporting companies that are not genuinely committed to sustainability. Thorough due diligence and third-party ESG ratings can help investors avoid green-washed investments.

- Lack of Standardization: The absence of uniform standards for measuring ESG factors can make it difficult for investors to evaluate the true sustainability of a company. However, initiatives like the Task Force on Climate-related Financial Disclosures (TCFD) and the Sustainability Accounting Standards Board (SASB) are working to create standardized reporting frameworks.
- Short-Term Volatility: While sustainable investments tend to perform well over the long term, they can be affected by short-term volatility. For example, renewable energy companies may experience fluctuations in stock prices due to changes in government policies, technological advancements, or competition. Investors should maintain a long-term perspective when investing in sustainable assets.

5. Steps for Building a Sustainable Investment Portfolio

To fully benefit from the wealth-building potential of sustainable investing while contributing to positive global outcomes, investors should follow these steps:

- Educate Yourself: Start by understanding the core principles of ESG investing and how different companies and industries align with sustainability goals. Explore funds, ETFs, and individual stocks that incorporate ESG criteria and align with your values.

- Diversify Across Sustainable Sectors: Don't limit your portfolio to just one sector—spread your investments across various ESG-focused industries, including renewable energy, clean technology, healthcare, and social enterprises. This diversification not only helps manage risk but also allows you to participate in different sustainable growth opportunities.
- Use ESG Ratings and Third-Party Tools: Many financial institutions and rating agencies provide ESG scores for companies. Utilize these resources to ensure you're investing in genuinely sustainable businesses. Third-party tools such as Sustainalytics, MSCI ESG Ratings, and Morningstar's Sustainability Rating offer valuable insights into the sustainability practices of companies and funds.
- Engage in Shareholder Advocacy: One of the most powerful ways to drive positive change is through shareholder advocacy. As an investor, you can use your voting power to influence company decisions on issues related to the environment, social responsibility, and governance. Many sustainable funds actively participate in shareholder activism to push companies toward better ESG practices.

6. The Future of Sustainable Investing: Trends and Innovations

Sustainable investing is not a static field—it is constantly evolving as new trends and innovations shape the landscape. Investors who stay ahead of these developments can capture unique opportunities and make an even greater impact on global challenges. Here are some of the emerging trends and innovations in sustainable investing:

a. ESG Integration in Traditional Investment Strategies

Many mainstream investment funds are increasingly integrating ESG criteria into their traditional investment strategies. This shift reflects growing awareness that strong ESG performance is linked to long-term financial success.

A Win-Win for Investors and the Planet

Sustainable investing offers a win-win opportunity: it allows investors to grow their wealth while making a tangible impact on the world. Companies that embrace environmental, social, and governance principles are better positioned for long-term success, resilience, and innovation. Moreover, sustainable investments support global efforts to address urgent issues such as climate change, social inequality, and poor corporate governance. By incorporating sustainable investments into their portfolios, individuals can achieve financial success and contribute to a brighter, more sustainable future for generations to come.

In the coming years, sustainable investing is likely to continue growing in importance, not only as a responsible approach to investing but as a key driver of financial and global transformation.

- Balancing Profitability and Impact in Investment Decisions

In sustainable investing, balancing profitability with positive environmental, social, and governance (ESG) impact is a key challenge. Investors no longer need to choose between financial returns and ethical values. The rise of sustainable investing demonstrates that both goals can coexist, driving long-term wealth creation while contributing to global well-being.

1. Aligning Profit with Purpose

Sustainable investors focus on aligning their financial goals with their values. This involves selecting investments that not only offer strong returns but also contribute to positive social and environmental outcomes. Companies that embrace ESG principles often demonstrate resilience in market downturns, build consumer trust, and foster innovation. This alignment positions investors for long-term success while supporting global sustainability goals.

2. The Profitability of ESG Investments

Contrary to the belief that ESG-focused investments underperform, studies show that companies with strong ESG practices can outperform their peers in several ways:

- Reduced Risk: Companies with solid governance and environmental practices are often better equipped to manage regulatory changes, avoid lawsuits, and respond to consumer demand for sustainability.
- Enhanced Innovation: Firms that prioritize sustainable business practices tend to be more forward-thinking, often leading the market in innovations that can create new revenue streams and business models.
- Long-Term Growth: Sustainable companies that invest in the well-being of their workers and the environment tend to have more

stable, long-term growth as they attract investors, customers, and talent who align with their values.

3. Measuring Impact and Profitability

Balancing impact and profitability requires careful measurement. Investors must use frameworks that assess both financial returns and the social or environmental impact of their portfolios. Some tools for measuring ESG impact include:

- ESG Ratings: Several agencies, such as MSCI and Sustainalytics, provide ESG scores for companies, helping investors gauge the impact of potential investments.
- Impact Reporting: Impact-focused funds often provide regular reports on how their investments contribute to social, environmental, and governance goals, offering transparency alongside financial performance data.

4. Strategies for Balancing Impact and Profit

Achieving a balance between profit and impact involves employing various investment strategies:

- Thematic Investing: This approach focuses on investing in companies or industries that directly address sustainability challenges, such as renewable energy, clean water, or healthcare access, while still delivering financial returns.
- Best-in-Class Investing: Investors choose top-performing companies within each sector based on ESG criteria. This strategy

ensures investments in profitable industries while supporting leaders in sustainability.

- Active Ownership: Investors use their influence as shareholders to push companies toward better ESG practices, promoting sustainability while still benefiting from corporate profitability.

5. Managing Trade-Offs

Not every investment offers a perfect balance of profit and impact. Some investments may deliver strong returns but fall short in ESG impact, while others may excel in sustainability but offer lower financial returns. Investors can manage these trades-offs by:

- Portfolio Diversification: Allocating a portion of the portfolio to high-impact, lower-return investments and balancing it with more traditional, profit-driven assets.
- Blended Finance: Combining public, philanthropic, and private capital to invest in projects that have both high impact and financial returns.
- Long-Term Perspective: Sustainable investments may not always deliver immediate financial gains but tend to provide better long-term performance, thanks to their alignment with evolving consumer preferences and regulatory frameworks.

6. Case Study: The Rise of Renewable Energy Investments

Renewable energy is a prime example of balancing profitability and impact. Once considered a niche market, renewable energy investments have seen explosive growth as the world transitions to cleaner energy sources. These investments offer both strong financial returns and a positive environmental impact, reducing carbon emissions and combating climate change. Investors in this sector benefit from government incentives, increasing consumer demand, and advancing technologies that lower costs, making it a win-win for profit and impact.

Achieving a Sustainable Balance

Balancing profitability and impact is not only possible but increasingly necessary in today's investing landscape. Investors who adopt sustainable investing practices can achieve competitive financial returns while contributing to a better future. By aligning investment decisions with ESG goals, using impact measurement tools, and employing diversified strategies, investors can harness the power of sustainable investing to create long-term wealth and meaningful change.

Impact Investing: Aligning Wealth with Values

- The Rise of Impact Investing: Funding Projects with Measurable Social and Environmental Benefits

Impact investing has emerged as a powerful strategy for aligning wealth with personal values, offering investors a way to generate financial returns while driving measurable social and environmental progress. Unlike traditional philanthropy or conventional investing, impact investing seeks a dual return: monetary gain and positive change. As the world faces growing challenges such as climate change, income inequality, and global health crises, impact investing is gaining traction as a critical tool for sustainable development.

1. Defining Impact Investing: Beyond Financial Returns

Impact investing focuses on directing capital toward companies, organizations, or projects that generate positive social or environmental outcomes. The primary goal is to address global challenges while achieving a financial return. Unlike corporate social responsibility (CSR) initiatives, which may focus on minimizing negative impacts, impact investing actively seeks opportunities to create measurable and meaningful benefits.

Key features of impact investing include:

- Intentionality: The explicit intention to generate positive social or environmental impact, alongside financial returns.
- Measurability: The ability to track, assess, and report on the social and environmental impact of investments.
- Financial Returns: A spectrum of financial goals, ranging from market-rate returns to more concessionary returns, depending on the investor's priorities.

2. Growth of the Impact Investing Market

Impact investing is no longer a niche strategy reserved for a few socially conscious investors. According to the Global Impact Investing Network (GIIN), the global impact investing market reached an estimated $1.16 trillion in assets under management in 2022, underscoring the growing interest in investments that make a difference.

Several factors have driven the rise of impact investing:

- ❖ Increased Demand for Ethical Investments: Modern investors, especially millennials and Gen Z, prioritize ethical considerations when making financial decisions. They seek investments that reflect their values, leading to a surge in demand for impact-focused financial products.
- ❖ Corporate Responsibility and ESG Trends: Many companies are now recognizing the importance of sustainability and governance in their long-term success, aligning with broader ESG (Environmental, Social, and Governance) principles. Impact investing takes this a step further by focusing on positive outcomes, not just responsible business practices.
- ❖ Government and Regulatory Support: Policies aimed at encouraging sustainable development, such as carbon pricing or tax incentives for renewable energy projects, have fueled opportunities for impact investors.

3. Key Sectors for Impact Investing

Impact investors typically focus on sectors that offer the greatest potential for positive change. Some of the most common areas include:

- ❖ Clean Energy: Renewable energy projects, such as solar and wind farms, contribute to the transition to a low-carbon economy while offering attractive returns as the global demand for clean energy rises.
- ❖ Healthcare and Biotechnology: Investments in healthcare innovation, including affordable medicines and technologies for

underserved populations, create life-saving solutions while generating high returns.

- Sustainable Agriculture: Impact investors support sustainable farming practices, food security initiatives, and innovations that reduce environmental harm while enhancing food production systems.
- Affordable Housing: Addressing the global housing crisis, impact investments in affordable housing provide essential shelter for underserved communities while delivering steady income streams.
- Education and Financial Inclusion: Projects that expand access to education and financial services, especially in underserved regions, create long-term economic benefits and contribute to poverty reduction.

4. Measuring Impact: Accountability and Transparency

One of the defining characteristics of impact investing is the emphasis on measurability. Investors require robust frameworks to assess both the financial and non-financial outcomes of their investments. Tools such as the **Global Impact Investing Rating System (GIIRS)** and the **Impact Reporting and Investment Standards (IRIS)** have been developed to standardize impact measurement and ensure transparency.

Key impact metrics may include:-

- Environmental Impact: Reduction in carbon emissions, water conservation, or increased use of renewable energy.
- Social Impact: Improved health outcomes, increased access to education, job creation, or community development.

- Governance Impact: Improved corporate governance practices, diversity in leadership, or ethical labor practices.

5. Financial Performance of Impact Investments

While some may assume that impact investing sacrifices financial returns, evidence suggests otherwise. Many impact investments offer competitive, market-rate returns, particularly in sectors like renewable energy and healthcare, where strong growth opportunities exist. In fact, according to GIIN, the majority of impact investors reported that their financial performance met or exceeded expectations.

Performance drivers include:

- Alignment with Long-Term Trends: Impact investments often focus on sectors that are growing due to long-term macroeconomic trends, such as renewable energy or healthcare innovation, making them attractive for long-term investors.
- Risk Mitigation: Companies and projects that address ESG factors are often more resilient in the face of environmental or social risks, reducing exposure to regulatory, reputational, and operational risks.
- Access to Untapped Markets: Many impact investments target underserved or emerging markets, offering investors' access to new revenue streams that may not be available in more traditional investments.

6. Case Study: Renewable Energy Investments

Renewable energy projects exemplify the synergy between impact and financial returns. With the global push toward clean energy, renewable energy companies and projects have attracted significant investment. For example:

- Solar Energy Projects: Solar power companies provide clean energy to communities while delivering consistent financial returns through long-term power purchase agreements (PPAs).
- Energy Access in Developing Countries: Impact investors support off-grid solar companies in developing nations, helping bring affordable electricity to rural areas while tapping into a growing market for clean energy.

7. The Future of Impact Investing

As the world faces ever more urgent challenges, from climate change to social inequality, impact investing is poised to play a crucial role in addressing these issues. The global shift toward sustainability, responsible capitalism, and ethical finance will continue to drive the growth of impact investing as both institutional and individual investors seek to align their wealth with their values.

Moreover, advances in technology, data analytics, and AI will make it easier to track and measure the social and environmental impact of investments, enabling more transparency and accountability in the impact investing space.

Investing with Purpose

Impact investing represents a new paradigm in wealth management—one that allows investors to align their financial goals with their ethical beliefs. By funding projects that generate measurable social and environmental benefits, investors can play a role in shaping a more sustainable, equitable world while still achieving financial success. As impact investing continues to grow, it offers a unique opportunity for both seasoned investors and newcomers to

- How to Assess Impact Investments and Measure Both Financial and Non-Financial Returns drive change.

Impact investing, which seeks to generate positive social or environmental outcomes alongside financial returns, has gained significant traction as a way for individuals and institutions to align their wealth with their values. However, assessing and measuring both financial and non-financial returns presents unique challenges, given the dual objectives involved. To successfully navigate impact investing, investors must adopt a rigorous evaluation process that includes both traditional financial metrics and specialized impact measurement frameworks.

Here are detailed approach to assessing impact investments and measuring their success in delivering both financial and non-financial returns.

1. Defining the Dual Objectives of Impact Investments

Before delving into assessment, it is crucial to clearly define the dual objectives of impact investing:

- ❖ Financial Returns: These vary based on the investment strategy, ranging from market-rate returns to concessionary returns (lower financial returns in exchange for greater social or environmental impact).

- ❖ Non-Financial Returns: These include measurable improvements in social, environmental, or governance-related outcomes. Investors may seek to impact areas such as education, poverty alleviation, renewable energy adoption, healthcare access, or gender equality.

An effective assessment must balance these two components, ensuring that both are factored into decision-making and performance evaluation.

2. Steps to Assess Impact Investments

a. Establish Clear Impact Goals

Investors must start by defining their **impact thesis**—a clear articulation of the social or environmental issues they wish to address and the outcomes they aim to achieve. For example, an investor might seek to reduce carbon emissions by investing in renewable energy, or to enhance education access by supporting edtech platforms.

Key questions to consider when setting impact goals:

- ❖ What specific issue is being addressed?
- ❖ What are the target outcomes or metrics (e.g., number of people educated, reduction in emissions)?
- ❖ What is the timeline for achieving these outcomes?

b. Due Diligence on Potential Investments

Impact investing requires the same level of financial diligence as traditional investments, along with an added layer of impact-related evaluation. Investors should thoroughly vet potential opportunities, focusing on both financial performance and their capacity to deliver measurable impact.

Financial Due Diligence:

- Review company financials, revenue models, and growth potential.
- Assess the risk factors, including market conditions and industry trends.
- Analyze the management team's track record and operational efficiency.

Impact Due Diligence:

- Evaluate the mission alignment between the investment and the investor's impact goals.
- Understand the company or project's operational model for delivering social or environmental impact.
- Review the credibility and track record of the company's impact initiatives.

Example: When considering an investment in a clean energy company, an investor would assess the company's financial viability (revenue, costs, scalability) alongside its potential to reduce carbon emissions (measured in tons of CO2 avoided).

c. Align Investment with Recognized Frameworks

To streamline assessment, many investors turn to **impact measurement frameworks** that provide standard criteria for evaluating non-financial outcomes. Some widely recognized frameworks include:

- Global Impact Investing Rating System (GIIRS): Provides third-party ratings of companies and funds based on their social and environmental impact.
- Impact Reporting and Investment Standards (IRIS): A set of standardized metrics used to measure and manage the social, environmental, and financial performance of impact investments.
- Sustainable Development Goals **(SDGs)**: Investors can align their impact goals with the United Nations' SDGs, which provide globally accepted benchmarks for social and environmental progress.

Using these frameworks ensures that impact investments are evaluated consistently and according to industry best practices.

d. Financial Performance Analysis

Just as in any investment, the financial aspect of impact investments must be rigorously assessed. Investors should consider:

- Expected Return on Investment (ROI): Depending on their risk appetite, investors should determine whether they expect market-rate returns or are willing to accept concessionary returns in exchange for greater impact.
- Liquidity and Exit Strategy: Investors need to understand the liquidity of the investment, potential exit options (e.g., sale to other investors or IPO), and the timeline for financial returns.
- Risk Profile: Assess the potential risks associated with the investment, including

market volatility, geopolitical factors, and industry-specific risks.

3. Measuring Non-Financial Returns: Impact Metrics and Reporting

a. Selecting Key Impact Indicators

The non-financial returns in impact investing are often complex to measure, as they go beyond profit to capture social and environmental outcomes. Investors should select **key performance indicators (KPIs)** that are specific, measurable, and relevant to their impact goals.

For example:

- Environmental Metrics: Tons of CO2 emissions avoided, megawatts of clean energy generated, or water saved.
- Social Metrics: Number of jobs created, improved educational outcomes (e.g., higher graduation rates), or increased access to healthcare services.
- Governance Metrics: Improved corporate governance practices, increased diversity on boards, or greater transparency in business operations.

b. Continuous Monitoring and Reporting

After making an impact investment, continuous monitoring is essential to track progress toward both financial and impact goals. Impact measurement is often conducted on an ongoing basis, with regular updates provided by the company or fund manager. Investors can use third-party impact assessment tools, such as the **B Impact Assessment**, or require portfolio companies to provide detailed impact reports.

Effective impact reporting should include:

- Quantitative Data: Specific numbers that reflect the impact (e.g., 10,000 people given access to clean drinking water).
- Qualitative Data: Narratives or case studies that illustrate the real-world effect of the investment (e.g., stories of improved quality of life due to clean energy access).
- Comparison to Benchmarks: How the impact compares to industry averages or targets set at the beginning of the investment.

c. Impact Auditing and Validation

To ensure accountability and transparency, impact investments may undergo **third-party audits** to verify the social or environmental outcomes. Impact validation ensures that the reported outcomes are accurate, trustworthy, and aligned with the stated goals. This is especially important for institutional investors and high-net-worth individuals who are looking for accountability and credibility in their investments.

4. Blending Financial and Non-Financial Performance

Once both financial and non-financial returns are measured, investors must assess whether the investment is delivering the desired outcomes. This involves a holistic review of the dual returns and an understanding of trade-offs:

- Balancing Profit and Impact: While some impact investments may deliver high financial returns along with social impact, others may require investors to accept lower financial gains in exchange for greater social benefits. Investors should clearly define their priorities and decide what trade-offs, if any, they are willing to make.

- ❖ Adjusting Strategy: Based on performance, investors may need to adjust their strategy, including shifting capital to projects or companies that are better aligned with their goals or altering the focus of their portfolio.

5. Case Study: Impact Investing in Affordable Housing

Consider an impact investment in affordable housing development. The financial goal may be to achieve steady returns from rental income, while the non-financial goal is to provide housing for low-income families.

Impact Metrics:

- ❖ Number of housing units made available to low-income families.
- ❖ Percentage of tenants who receive rental assistance or government subsidies.
- ❖ Reduction in homelessness or housing insecurity in the local community.

Financial Metrics:

- ❖ Cash flow from rental income.
- ❖ Occupancy rates and tenant retention.
- ❖ Property appreciation over time.

By combining these metrics, the investor can evaluate whether the investment is meeting both financial and social goals.

- Creating a values-based investment portfolio

Creating a values-based investment portfolio involves aligning your investment choices with your personal beliefs, ethics, and values, while aiming to achieve financial returns. This approach not only seeks to generate profits but also focuses on promoting social good, environmental sustainability, and responsible governance. Here's how you can create a values-based investment portfolio that reflects your principles and financial goals.

1. Define Your Values and Impact Goals

- Identify Core Values: Start by articulating your core values. These might include environmental sustainability, social justice, community development, gender equality, or corporate responsibility.
- Set Specific Goals: Establish what you hope to achieve through your investments. This could range from supporting renewable energy initiatives to promoting diversity in corporate leadership.

2. Conduct Research on Investment Options

- Screen Investments: Use positive and negative screening techniques to filter investments. Positive screening involves actively selecting companies or funds that align with your values, while negative screening involves excluding those that do not meet your ethical criteria (e.g., fossil fuels, tobacco, or companies with poor labor practices).
- Explore ESG Ratings: Investigate Environmental, Social, and Governance (ESG) ratings provided by various rating agencies. These ratings evaluate

companies based on their practices and impact in these three categories, helping you to identify suitable investment opportunities.

3. Choose Appropriate Investment Vehicles

- ❖ Impact Funds and ETFs: Consider investing in mutual funds or exchange-traded funds (ETFs) that focus on impact investing. These funds often have a diverse portfolio of companies that meet specific sustainability and social criteria.
- ❖ Direct Investments: If you're comfortable with higher risk and a more hands-on approach, consider directly investing in startups or companies that align with your values, particularly in sectors like clean energy or social enterprises.
- ❖ Community Investments: Explore options for community investments, such as community development financial institutions (CDFIs) that lend to underserved communities.

4. Diversify Your Portfolio

- ❖ Balance Risk and Return: While it's crucial to adhere to your values, ensure your portfolio is diversified across various asset classes and sectors. This can help manage risk while still adhering to your investment principles.
- ❖ Global Reach: Consider global investment opportunities that align with your values, as some markets may have stronger offerings in sustainable and responsible investments.

5. Set Metrics for Measuring Impact

- Define Impact Metrics: Establish clear metrics to evaluate the social and environmental impact of your investments. This could include measuring the number of jobs created, carbon emissions reduced, or improvements in community health.
- Financial Performance Monitoring: In addition to assessing impact, regularly monitor the financial performance of your portfolio to ensure that it meets your financial objectives.

6. Engage with Companies

- Active Ownership: If you hold shares in companies, consider exercising your rights as a shareholder to engage with management on ESG issues. This can involve voting on shareholder resolutions or participating in dialogues to advocate for positive change.
- Stay Informed: Keep abreast of developments in the companies you invest in, and be proactive about understanding their impact practices and reporting.

7. Review and Adjust Your Portfolio

- Regular Assessment: Periodically review your portfolio to assess both its financial performance and its alignment with your values. Be prepared to make adjustments based on changing market conditions or evolving personal values.
- Rebalance as Necessary: Depending on market performance and your impact goals,

rebalance your portfolio to maintain alignment with your values and financial objectives.

Creating a values-based investment portfolio is a powerful way to harness your financial resources in alignment with your principles. By carefully selecting investments that reflect your values and goals, you can contribute to positive social and environmental outcomes while working towards financial growth. As impact investing continues to grow, your portfolio can be a testament to the idea that investing with purpose can lead to meaningful change.

Ethical Wealth-Building Practices

- Understanding ethical concerns in business and finance

Ethical concerns in business and finance play a crucial role in shaping sustainable, responsible, and transparent practices in the global economy. Ethical wealth-building involves not only adhering to legal standards but also upholding values like fairness, integrity, and accountability, both in investment decisions and corporate governance. This ensures long-term profitability without compromising moral principles or social responsibility. Here are detailed exploration of key ethical concerns in business and finance and how they relate to ethical wealth-building practices.

1. Corporate Governance and Accountability

- ❖ Ethical Leadership: Companies should have leadership that promotes a culture of transparency, ethical behavior, and accountability. This involves making decisions that protect shareholder interests, support employee well-being, and adhere to regulatory compliance. Ethical leaders ensure that the pursuit of profit doesn't come at the expense of the environment or social justice.

- Board Oversight: Ethical concerns arise when corporate boards fail to provide effective oversight of executive actions. A responsible board holds management accountable, ensuring that business practices align with ethical standards, especially in areas such as environmental sustainability and human rights.

2. Fair Treatment of Employees

- Labor Rights and Fair Wages: One of the most prominent ethical concerns is the treatment of employees. Ethical businesses must ensure that their workers are paid fair wages, have safe working conditions, and are free from exploitation. Companies that engage in unethical labor practices, such as child labor or gender discrimination, face not only legal repercussions but also reputational damage.
- Diversity and Inclusion: Ethical wealth-building involves fostering a diverse and inclusive workforce. Businesses must provide equal opportunities regardless of gender, race, or socioeconomic background. Ethical concerns arise when companies fail to promote diversity or address systemic inequalities in hiring, promotion and pay equity.

3. Environmental Sustainability

- Sustainable Resource Use: Ethical businesses are mindful of their environmental impact. They prioritize sustainability in their operations, using resources in ways that minimize harm to the planet. Companies that exploit natural resources irresponsibly contribute to environmental degradation, which can lead to long-term ecological harm and ethical violations.
- Corporate Responsibility to Climate Change: Addressing climate change is a growing ethical concern. Investors and consumers are increasingly holding businesses accountable for their carbon footprints and demanding transparency in sustainability efforts. Ethical wealth-building emphasizes investment in companies that prioritize environmental responsibility and align their practices with global sustainability goals, such as reducing greenhouse gas emissions.

4. Consumer Protection

- Transparency in Marketing and Advertising: Ethical concerns arise when businesses use deceptive advertising, hiding critical information about their products or services. Ethical wealth-building practices involve supporting companies that provide clear, honest, and transparent communication to consumers, ensuring that products and services meet ethical and safety standards.
- Data Privacy and Security: In an increasingly digital world, businesses face

ethical responsibilities to protect consumer data. Mishandling or exploiting personal data for profit without consumer consent is a violation of ethical standards. Companies that prioritize cybersecurity and data privacy uphold ethical principles and build trust with their stakeholders.

5. Ethical Investment Practices

- Responsible Investment Screening: Ethical investing involves avoiding investments in companies that engage in harmful or unethical practices. This could include industries such as tobacco, arms manufacturing, or fossil fuels. Ethical investors often use screening methods to exclude businesses that conflict with their moral or ethical values while prioritizing investments in companies with positive social and environmental impacts.
- Support for ESG (Environmental, Social, and Governance) Practices: ESG criteria help investors evaluate businesses based on their ethical practices. Ethical wealth-building emphasizes investing in companies with strong ESG ratings, which not only provide competitive financial returns but also contribute to social and environmental progress.

6. Corporate Social Responsibility (CSR)

- Community Engagement and Social Impact: Ethical companies invest in their communities and contribute to social good through corporate social responsibility (CSR) initiatives. These initiatives range from charitable donations to direct involvement in local development projects. Businesses that ignore their social responsibilities risk reputational damage and loss of consumer trust.

- ❖ Ethical Supply Chains: CSR also extends to ensuring that supply chains are free from unethical practices, such as forced labor, unsafe working conditions, or environmentally harmful activities. Ethical wealth-building requires businesses and investors to carefully assess and manage their supply chains to avoid unethical practices.

7. Bribery, Corruption, and Financial Misconduct

- ❖ Combatting Corruption: Corruption undermines the fairness and integrity of financial markets. Ethical concerns arise when businesses engage in bribery or other forms of corruption to gain an unfair advantage. Wealth-building practices that promote transparency and regulatory compliance help prevent financial misconduct and contribute to fair competition.
- ❖ Financial Mismanagement and Fraud: Ethical concerns are especially prevalent in financial markets where mismanagement or fraudulent behavior can lead to economic instability and loss of investor trust. Ethical investors and companies adhere to financial regulations, engage in transparent reporting, and avoid fraudulent practices, such as insider trading or market manipulation.

8. Tax Evasion and Avoidance

- Fair Tax Practices: Ethical concerns also extend to corporate tax strategies. While tax avoidance may be legally permissible, it raises ethical questions about whether companies are contributing their fair share to the economies in which they operate. Ethical businesses and investors prioritize paying taxes responsibly and supporting the economic systems that enable wealth creation.

9. Ethical Issues in Technology and Finance

- Artificial Intelligence (AI) and Automation: As AI and automation increasingly drive business operations, ethical concerns arise around the potential displacement of workers and the fairness of algorithmic decision-making. Ethical businesses use technology in ways that complement human workforces and address the societal impact of technological advancements.
- FinTech and Data Ethics: The rise of FinTech raises ethical concerns regarding financial access, data privacy, and algorithmic bias. Businesses in this sector must prioritize ethical practices to ensure that technology improves financial inclusion without compromising consumer rights or data security.

Understanding and addressing ethical concerns in business and finance is critical for building wealth responsibly and sustainably. Ethical wealth-building goes beyond financial performance to encompass transparency, fairness, environmental stewardship, and social responsibility. By promoting ethical practices, businesses and investors can contribute to long-term wealth creation that benefits both individuals and society, ensuring that financial success is achieved without compromising moral principles.

- Strategies for Building Wealth Responsibly: Fair Trade, Socially Responsible Investing, and Green Finance

In today's world, wealth-building practices are increasingly shifting from a focus on mere profit maximization to more responsible and ethical strategies. Individuals and institutions are becoming more conscious of the broader impact their financial decisions have on society, the environment, and future generations. Ethical wealth-building is about ensuring that the pursuit of financial success aligns with values of fairness, sustainability, and positive social impact. Three key areas that embody these principles are fair trade, socially responsible investing (SRI), and green finance.

1. Fair Trade: Promoting Ethical Business Practices

Fair trade is an economic model that prioritizes fairness, transparency, and equitable relationships between producers in developing countries and consumers in more affluent regions. It ensures that farmers, artisans, and workers are paid fair wages, work under decent conditions, and operate in a way that is sustainable for their communities and the environment.

Key Principles of Fair Trade:

- ❖ Fair Compensation: Fair trade ensures that producers receive fair compensation for their goods and services, which helps lift them out of poverty and promotes economic independence.

- ❖ Decent Working Conditions: Fair trade supports the creation of safe, healthy working environments, free from exploitation and abusive labor practices.
- ❖ Environmental Sustainability: Fair trade practices often promote organic farming, reduced carbon footprints, and sustainable agriculture, aligning with broader goals of environmental preservation.
- ❖ Community Development: A portion of fair trade premiums is reinvested in local communities to improve infrastructure, healthcare, and education, contributing to long-term social and economic growth.

Building Wealth Responsibly through Fair Trade:

As a consumer or investor, supporting fair trade can contribute to building wealth responsibly by investing in businesses and products that promote social good. Purchasing fair trade goods, or investing in companies with fair trade certifications, allow individuals to generate returns while ensuring their money supports sustainable and ethical business practices. Moreover, consumers are increasingly willing to pay a premium for fair trade products, recognizing the value of supporting responsible supply chains, making it a growing and viable market.

2. Socially Responsible Investing (SRI): Aligning Investments with Values

Socially Responsible Investing (SRI) integrates ethical, environmental, and social considerations into investment decisions, in addition to traditional financial factors. SRI aims to generate both financial return and positive social impact, allowing investors to align their financial portfolios with their personal values. This approach appeals to individuals who wish to avoid investing in companies that contribute to social harm—such as those involved in tobacco, weapons, or environmental degradation—and prioritize companies that foster positive change.

Key Principles of SRI:

- Environmental, Social, and Governance (ESG) Criteria: SRI focuses on companies that score well on ESG criteria, such as reducing carbon emissions, promoting fair labor practices, and having transparent governance structures.
- Positive and Negative Screening: Investors can choose to include (positive screening) or exclude (negative screening) specific companies or sectors from their portfolios based on ethical considerations. For example, they may avoid investing in fossil fuel companies (negative screening) while focusing on renewable energy companies (positive screening).
- Impact Investing: This subset of SRI focuses on investing in companies or projects with measurable social or environmental benefits, such as affordable housing, clean energy, or healthcare initiatives.

Building Wealth Responsibly through SRI:

Investing in SRI funds or directly in companies with strong ESG practices offers individuals the opportunity to build wealth while fostering positive social outcomes. Studies have shown that companies with strong ESG performance often have lower risk profiles and are better positioned for long-term financial success. By adopting an SRI strategy, investors can contribute to positive global outcomes while still achieving competitive returns, creating a win-win scenario for wealth-building and ethical responsibility.

3. Green Finance: Financing the Transition to a Sustainable Economy

Green finance refers to financial activities that are designed to support environmentally sustainable projects, products, and industries. This includes investments in renewable energy, sustainable agriculture, green buildings, and other eco-friendly initiatives that aim to mitigate climate change and protect natural resources. The green finance movement is gaining traction globally as governments, corporations, and individual investors seek ways to contribute to environmental sustainability while generating financial returns.

Key Principles of Green Finance:

- Renewable Energy Investment: Investing in wind, solar, hydro, and other renewable energy sources helps reduce reliance on fossil fuels and promotes the transition to a cleaner, more sustainable energy infrastructure.
- Green Bonds: These are fixed-income instruments designed to raise capital for climate-related or environmentally beneficial projects. Investors who purchase green bonds support sustainability initiatives while earning a fixed return.
- Sustainable Infrastructure: Green finance supports the development of energy-efficient buildings, smart cities, and transportation systems that reduce carbon footprints and enhance sustainability.
- Circular Economy: Green finance can also fund business models that prioritize reducing waste, recycling, and reusing materials, which is central to the circular economy approach.

Building Wealth Responsibly through Green Finance:

Green finance offers significant opportunities for wealth-building by tapping into the growing demand for sustainable products and services. Investors can support the global transition to a low-carbon economy by investing in green bonds, renewable energy projects, and other environmentally focused ventures. This not only aligns with the goal of protecting the planet but also positions investors to benefit from the increasing profitability of green industries, particularly as governments and consumers push for more sustainable alternatives.

Combining Strategies: The Holistic Approach to Ethical Wealth-Building

To build wealth responsibly, individuals can integrate fair trade, socially responsible investing, and green finance into a holistic wealth strategy. By combining these approaches, investors can maximize their positive impact across various aspects of social and environmental responsibility.

For example:-

- Diversify Your Portfolio with SRI and Green Investments**:** Consider incorporating SRI and green finance into your investment portfolio. Look for mutual funds, ETFs, or individual companies that prioritize ethical practices, ESG performance, and sustainability.
- Support Fair Trade in Consumer Spending**:** When making purchases, prioritize products that carry fair trade certifications, ensuring that your consumer dollars contribute to ethical business practices.

- Measure Financial and Social Returns: Ethical wealth-building means balancing financial gains with social and environmental impact. Tools such as ESG ratings, impact reports, and sustainability indices can help investors track their progress on both fronts.

CHAPTER SEVEN

FINANCIAL INDEPENDENCE RETIRE EARLY (FIRE) MOVEMENT

This chapter explores the principles of the FIRE movement, a growing trend focused on achieving financial independence early in life to retire and pursue personal passions.

The Fundamentals of FIRE

- Understanding the core principles of the FIRE movement: Aggressive saving, investing, and minimalism

The FIRE movement (Financial Independence, Retire Early) has gained widespread popularity as a financial strategy designed to enable individuals to achieve financial independence at a younger age by focusing on aggressive saving, investing, and living a minimalist lifestyle. Rooted in the desire for freedom from traditional employment and financial constraints, FIRE adherents seek to optimize their income and lifestyle to retire well before the traditional retirement age, giving them more time to pursue personal interests, passions, or alternative career paths.

To fully understand how the FIRE movement operates, it's essential to explore its three core principles: aggressive saving, strategic investing, and minimalism. Each of these pillars works together to accelerate wealth-building, allowing individuals to achieve financial independence faster than conventional methods.

1. Aggressive Saving: Maximizing Income Retention

Aggressive saving is at the heart of the FIRE movement, where participants aim to save and invest as much of their income as possible—often 50-70% or more of their earnings. These focuses on high savings rates helps individuals accumulate wealth quickly, laying the foundation for early financial independence.

- Prioritizing High Savings Rates: The primary goal of FIRE enthusiasts is to save a significant portion of their income each month, which requires careful budgeting and disciplined spending. By minimizing discretionary expenses and focusing on essentials, individuals can free up more capital for saving and investing.
- Maximizing Income: Increasing one's earning potential is another key element in aggressive saving. Many in the FIRE community pursue additional income streams, side hustles, or high-paying career paths to boost their savings rate. Higher incomes combined with disciplined saving lead to a faster accumulation of wealth.
- Frugality and Expense Optimization: Frugality plays a vital role in aggressive saving. FIRE adherents practice expense optimization by identifying areas of their budget where they can cut costs, such as housing, transportation, and entertainment. This often involves making significant lifestyle choices, such as downsizing homes, minimizing car usage, or reducing luxury spending.
- Emergency Fund and Debt Management: Building an emergency fund and paying off high-interest debt are essential steps in the aggressive saving process. These financial safeguards prevent unexpected expenses or debt from derailing one's savings plan. By eliminating debt early and building a

safety net, individuals can focus more heavily on wealth accumulation.

2. Investing: Building Long-Term Wealth for Financial Independence

While saving aggressively is important, investing is what truly accelerates wealth growth within the FIRE framework. Strategic investing allows individuals to grow their wealth over time through compound interest, capital gains, and passive income, which is essential for achieving financial independence and sustaining early retirement.

- Leveraging Compound Interest: Compound interest is the key to long-term wealth-building in the FIRE movement. The earlier individuals start investing, the longer their money has to grow. By investing in vehicles like index funds, mutual funds, and other long-term assets, FIRE adherents can maximize the compounding effect, accelerating their path to financial independence.
- Diversified Investment Portfolio: A well-diversified investment portfolio is crucial to managing risk and ensuring steady growth. Many FIRE followers opt for a **low-cost index fund** strategy, which spreads investments across a wide range of stocks, reducing volatility while still benefiting from overall market growth. Others diversify further by including bonds, real estate, or alternative investments.
- Tax-Advantaged Accounts: FIRE adherents often take full advantage of tax-advantaged investment accounts, such as 401(k)s, IRAs, and Roth IRAs, to maximize their

savings and reduce tax liabilities. These accounts allow for tax-deferred or tax-free growth, increasing the efficiency of their investment strategies.

- Dividend Investing and Passive Income: Generating passive income streams through dividends, rental properties, or other investment vehicles is a critical part of the FIRE strategy. This income helps support early retirees without needing to liquidate their principal investments, allowing their wealth to continue growing during retirement.
- Investment Discipline: Sticking to an investment strategy, especially during periods of market volatility, is essential for FIRE enthusiasts. Since financial independence often hinges on the growth of long-term investments, maintaining discipline in both contributions and market participation is vital.

3. Minimalism: Redefining Lifestyle Choices for Financial Freedom

Minimalism is a lifestyle philosophy that aligns closely with the goals of the FIRE movement. By reducing unnecessary consumption and focusing on simplicity, minimalism helps FIRE participants reduce their living expenses and free up more resources for saving and investing. It also fosters a mindset of contentment with less, which makes it easier to transition into early retirement.

- Living Below Your Means: Minimalism encourages individuals to live a lifestyle that is well below their financial means. This could involve forgoing expensive habits, such as regular dining out, luxury travel, or high-end consumer goods, and instead prioritizing financial freedom over material possessions.

- ❖ Mindful Spending: Minimalism promotes mindful spending, where individuals focus on purchasing only what brings them true value or joy. This conscious approach to spending ensures that money is spent intentionally, rather than impulsively, leading to significant savings over time.
- ❖ Downsizing and Simplicity: In line with the FIRE principle of reducing expenses, many followers of the movement embrace smaller, more affordable housing options, minimal wardrobes, and fewer belongings. Downsizing to a smaller home or moving to a lower-cost area can significantly cut housing expenses, which often represent the largest cost for most people.
- ❖ Sustainable Living: Minimalism often overlaps with sustainability, where individuals prioritize practices that reduce waste and environmental impact. This can include embracing renewable energy, using public transportation, or adopting second-hand buying habits. These sustainable choices not only save money but also reflect a values-driven approach to financial independence.

4. Calculating the FIRE Number: How Much is Enough?

At the core of the FIRE movement is the idea of achieving a level of wealth that allows individuals to retire early and live comfortably off their investments. This figure is often referred to as the **FIRE number**—the amount of money needed to reach financial independence. This number is typically calculated by determining annual living expenses and applying a withdrawal rate.

- The 4% Rule: The most common method for calculating the FIRE number is the **4% Rule**, which suggests that individuals can withdraw 4% of their investment portfolio annually in retirement without running out of money. To calculate the FIRE number, individuals multiply their annual living expenses by 25. For example, if someone's yearly expenses amount to $40,000, their FIRE number would be $1 million ($40,000 x 25).
- Adjusting for Inflation and Market Conditions: While the 4% Rule is a widely accepted guideline, it may need to be adjusted based on factors such as inflation, investment performance, and personal financial goals. Some FIRE enthusiasts adopt a more conservative withdrawal rate (e.g., 3-3.5%) to ensure their portfolio lasts through market downturns and longer lifespans.

5. Variations of the FIRE Movement

The FIRE movement has evolved into several variations, allowing individuals to tailor their approach based on their financial goals, risk tolerance, and desired lifestyle.

- Lean FIRE: Lean FIRE involves living an extremely frugal lifestyle to achieve financial independence faster, often with a lower overall savings goal. Followers of Lean FIRE focus on minimal living expenses and may embrace a more austere lifestyle both before and after reaching financial independence.
- Fat FIRE: Fat FIRE, on the other hand, allows for a more comfortable and luxurious

lifestyle in retirement. Individuals pursuing Fat FIRE save and invest more aggressively to support a higher standard of living in early retirement. This path often appeals to those who do not want to compromise on their lifestyle but still aim to retire early.

- Barista FIRE: Barista FIRE is a middle ground where individuals achieve partial financial independence and supplement their investment income with part-time work or passion projects. This allows them to enjoy the flexibility of early retirement without fully giving up paid work, often in low-stress or enjoyable roles.

Achieving FIRE and Its Long-Term Impacts

Once the core principles of the **FIRE movement** are integrated into daily life—through aggressive saving, strategic investing and minimalism—the journey towards financial independence begins to take shape. However, it's not just about reaching a financial milestone; it's about ensuring sustainability and purpose in the post-FIRE phase. Here's a deeper look at how individuals maintain financial independence and adapt to early retirement, alongside the broader impacts on lifestyle and mental well-being.

6. Maintaining Financial Independence Post-FIRE

Reaching financial independence is only part of the equation. To ensure long-term sustainability, early retirees must carefully manage their portfolios, maintain lifestyle choices aligned with their values, and be prepared for economic uncertainties. Here are the critical areas to consider:

- Portfolio Management After FIRE: Once individuals have reached their FIRE number, continued portfolio management is crucial. This includes rebalancing investments periodically, adjusting for risk tolerance as one ages, and keeping track of withdrawal rates. It’s important to revisit financial plans regularly, especially in response to significant market shifts or life changes.
- Adjusting Withdrawal Rates: Even though the 4% Rule serves as a guideline, it's essential to monitor and adjust withdrawal rates based on portfolio performance and inflation. During periods of economic downturns or bear markets, some FIRE followers reduce their withdrawal rate temporarily to preserve their investment principal.
- Healthcare and Insurance Costs: Retiring early means losing access to employer-sponsored healthcare, which can be a significant expense. Individuals pursuing FIRE need to carefully plan for healthcare costs, including insurance, long-term care, and unexpected medical emergencies. Proactive financial planning, such as health savings accounts (HSAs), can help cover medical costs in retirement.
- Flexibility in Lifestyle: Achieving FIRE requires not just a large nest egg but also the flexibility to adjust one's lifestyle based on external factors. This might mean returning to work part-time, picking up freelance gigs, or exploring new income streams when needed. Maintaining financial independence requires an adaptable mindset, especially when faced with economic or personal challenges.

- ❖ Emergency Funds and Liquidity: While most of the focus in FIRE is on long-term investments, maintaining an emergency fund or liquid assets for unexpected expenses is crucial. Keeping six to 12 months of living expenses in a highly liquid and safe account ensures that unforeseen costs don't force individuals to dip into their long-term investments prematurely.

7. The Psychological and Emotional Adjustment to Early Retirement

Transitioning to early retirement is not just a financial change—it's a significant lifestyle shift that requires careful psychological preparation. Early retirees often experience a shift in identity, time management, and purpose, which must be addressed to avoid post-FIRE burnout or dissatisfaction.

- ❖ Finding Purpose Post-Retirement: Many people derive a sense of purpose and identity from their careers. After achieving FIRE, it's essential to fill the gap left by full-time work with fulfilling activities or passions. Whether it's starting a passion project, volunteering, or exploring hobbies, having a sense of purpose is critical to emotional well-being in early retirement.
- ❖ Maintaining Social Connections: Work often provides social interaction and networking opportunities that early retirees may miss. Maintaining a social network, joining groups, or finding new communities to engage with ensures that one's social needs are met, which is crucial for long-term happiness.

- Time Management and Structure: Retirement means having much more time, and that freedom can feel overwhelming without structure. Early retirees benefit from planning their days with a mix of leisure, learning, personal growth, and, if desired, part-time work or entrepreneurship. Having goals and a routine, even in retirement, fosters a sense of accomplishment and balance.
- Avoiding Burnout in FIRE: The pursuit of FIRE can sometimes lead to burnout, especially for those who focus too heavily on frugality and saving without finding balance. While financial independence offers freedom, it's important not to lose sight of personal well-being and happiness along the journey. Living frugally should not come at the expense of mental health or personal fulfillment.

8. Adapting FIRE for Different Lifestyles and Family Needs

FIRE is not a one-size-fits-all approach. Depending on life stage, family structure, and personal goals, individuals can adapt the principles of FIRE to fit their unique circumstances. Whether pursuing FIRE as a single individual, with a family, or later in life, the movement offers flexibility for achieving financial independence.

- FIRE with a Family: For individuals with families, achieving FIRE requires thoughtful planning around larger expenses like housing, education, healthcare, and childcare. Families pursuing FIRE often prioritize financial education for children and instill values of saving and minimalism. Additionally, family FIRE plans may involve purchasing rental properties or engaging in family-run businesses to generate additional income streams.

- Pursuing FIRE Later in Life: While most people associate FIRE with younger individuals, many decide to pursue financial independence later in life. For these individuals, aggressive saving and investing become even more critical, though retirement timelines may be shorter. Older FIRE enthusiasts may also place more emphasis on healthcare planning and passive income generation.
- Legacy Planning for FIRE Enthusiasts: Many people who achieve FIRE focus on ensuring their wealth is used purposefully beyond their retirement. This includes **estate planning**, **philanthropy**, and ensuring their wealth continues to grow for the benefit of their family or society. Creating a sustainable financial legacy is a long-term goal for many who achieve FIRE.

9. The Broader Impact of the FIRE Movement on Society

The FIRE movement has sparked debates on work, lifestyle, and consumption patterns in modern society. Its popularity highlights shifting attitudes towards traditional career paths and consumerism, offering alternatives to the “work until retirement” model. As FIRE gains momentum, it influences discussions on:

- Changing Work Expectations: FIRE challenges the notion of working until age 65, encouraging people to rethink their relationship with work. It promotes the idea that work should not define one's entire life, but rather be a means to achieve financial independence and freedom. As more people pursue FIRE, workplaces may see greater demand for **flexible work arrangements** and **remote work** opportunities.

- ❖ Consumerism and Sustainability: The minimalist lifestyle associated with FIRE promotes mindful consumption and challenges traditional consumerism. By prioritizing financial independence over material possessions, the movement aligns with environmental sustainability and more conscious living. This shift in values could have long-term effects on consumer behavior and global demand patterns.
- ❖ Financial Education and Empowerment: The FIRE movement has contributed to a broader interest in personal finance and investing. As more individuals explore FIRE, financial literacy becomes a priority, leading to greater awareness about **investment strategies**, **savings tools**, and **tax optimization**. The spread of these ideas can empower individuals across various income levels to take control of their financial futures.

The Evolution of FIRE

The FIRE movement continues to evolve, driven by changing economic conditions, technological advances, and the diverse needs of those pursuing financial independence. As the movement grows, it offers individuals a pathway to redefine their relationship with money, work, and time. Whether through aggressive saving, investing, or adopting minimalist practices, FIRE provides a roadmap for individuals seeking financial freedom and autonomy over their lives.

Achieving FIRE isn't just about financial independence—it's about creating a lifestyle centered on purpose, freedom, and long-term fulfillment. By adapting FIRE principles to their unique circumstances, individuals can enjoy a life that is rich not only in financial stability but also in personal satisfaction and holistic well-being.

- Calculating Your FIRE Number: The Amount Needed to Retire Early

In the Financial Independence, Retire Early (FIRE) movement, your FIRE number represents the total amount of savings or investments required to sustain your lifestyle without the need for active income. Calculating your FIRE number is a critical step in planning your path to early retirement, as it defines the financial goal you need to reach before you can confidently leave the workforce. This process requires a careful assessment of your living expenses, investment strategy, and assumptions about future returns and inflation.

1. Understanding the Basic Formula

The most common way to calculate your FIRE number is based on the **4% Rule**, which is a widely used guideline in retirement planning. The 4% Rule suggests that if you withdraw 4% of your total investment portfolio each year, your savings should last for 30 years or more, assuming average market returns and inflation adjustments. This rule translates into a straightforward formula for calculating your FIRE number:

FIRE Number = Annual Expenses/0.04

In simpler terms, your FIRE number is 25 times your annual expenses.

For example:

- ❖ If you expect to live on $50,000 per year in retirement, your FIRE number would be: **50,000×25=1,250,000**

This means you would need $1.25 million in investments to retire early and sustain that $50,000 per year through withdrawals.

2. Estimating Your Annual Expenses

To calculate your FIRE number accurately, you need a clear understanding of your annual living expenses during retirement. This includes both your current expenses and any anticipated changes that might occur after you retire.

- ❖ Housing: Will your mortgage be paid off by the time you retire? Consider future rent or property taxes.
- ❖ Healthcare: Healthcare costs often increase with age, so it's important to plan for medical insurance or out-of-pocket expenses.
- ❖ Lifestyle: Think about the lifestyle you want in retirement—whether it's travel, hobbies, or downsizing your living space.
- ❖ Taxes: Account for any taxes on withdrawals from retirement accounts or capital gains from investments.

Creating a detailed retirement budget can help you estimate your future living costs. This estimate serves as the foundation for calculating how much you'll need to withdraw each year from your savings.

3. Adjusting for Inflation and Market Conditions

While the 4% Rule is a good starting point, it's based on historical averages and may not account for individual circumstances, such as higher inflation, lower market returns, or longer life expectancy.

- Inflation Adjustments: Over a long retirement, inflation can erode the purchasing power of your money. To account for inflation, you may need to adjust your annual withdrawal rate or increase your target savings. For example, if you expect 2% inflation, you might need to increase your FIRE number accordingly.
- Conservative Withdrawal Rates: Some FIRE followers opt for more conservative withdrawal rates, such as 3% or 3.5%, to account for market volatility or unexpected expenses. A lower withdrawal rate requires a higher FIRE number. For instance, with a 3.5% withdrawal rate, you would need to multiply your annual expenses by 28.6 instead of 25.

4. Different Types of FIRE and Their Implications for Your FIRE Number

Your lifestyle goals and financial ambitions will also affect how you calculate your FIRE number. There are several variations of FIRE, each with its own financial requirements:

- Lean FIRE: This approach involves living a **frugal lifestyle** and cutting expenses as much as possible. For Lean FIRE, your FIRE number might be lower because you expect to live on less. For example, if you plan to live on $30,000 a year, your FIRE number would be $750,000.

- Fat FIRE: For those who want to maintain or even increase their current standard of living in retirement, Fat FIRE is the goal. This requires a higher FIRE number, as you'll be planning for a more comfortable or luxurious retirement. If you plan to spend $100,000 per year in retirement, your FIRE number would be $2.5 million.
- Coast FIRE: With Coast FIRE, the idea is to build up enough early on so that your investments grow on their own without needing further contributions. This approach allows you to coast into full FIRE by reducing your work hours or retiring part-time before reaching full financial independence.

5. Investment Strategy and Growth Assumptions

Your investment strategy plays a key role in determining how long it will take to reach your FIRE number and how sustainable your withdrawals will be over time. Stock market returns, bond yields, and real estate performance all influence the growth of your portfolio.

- Asset Allocation: A typical FIRE portfolio might consist of stocks, bonds, and real estate. Stocks offer higher returns but come with more risk, while bonds and real estate provide stability and income. The balance between these assets should reflect your risk tolerance and time horizon.

- Expected Market Returns: Historically, the stock market has returned around 7-8% annually (adjusted for inflation). However, more conservative estimates might assume a 5-6% return to account for market volatility or economic downturns.
- Rebalancing and Withdrawal Strategy: Once you reach your FIRE number and begin withdrawing, it's important to maintain a balanced portfolio. Regular rebalancing ensures that you don't take on too much risk or miss out on growth opportunities.

6. Factoring in Social Security, Pensions, and Other Income Sources

While many FIRE adherents focus on building a large investment portfolio, you may also have other sources of retirement income that affect your FIRE number:

- Social Security: If you plan to retire early, you may not be able to access Social Security benefits for several years. However, you should still factor it in as part of your long-term income strategy.
- Pensions: If you have a pension from a government job or employer, this could reduce the amount of savings needed to reach your FIRE number.
- Part-Time Work or Side Income: Some people in the FIRE community continue to work part-time or run side businesses in retirement. This additional income could allow for a lower FIRE number since it supplements your investment withdrawals.

7. Tracking and Adjusting Your FIRE Plan

The process of reaching your FIRE number is dynamic. Life events, market conditions, and personal goals may change over time, requiring adjustments to your savings rate, investment strategy, or target FIRE number.

- Annual Progress Reviews: Review your savings, investments, and expenses regularly to ensure you're on track. Make adjustments to your plan as needed, based on your financial progress or changing circumstances.
- Flexibility and Contingency Planning: Build flexibility into your FIRE plan to account for unexpected events, such as medical emergencies, market crashes, or major lifestyle changes. Having a contingency plan can help you stay on track, even when life throws surprises your way.

Achieving Financial Independence: Fine-Tuning Your FIRE Strategy

Once you've calculated your FIRE number and set your sights on financial independence, the next step involves creating a detailed and strategic plan to reach that goal as efficiently as possible. This involves maximizing savings, choosing the right investments, and minimizing financial risks along the way.

8. Maximizing Your Savings Rate

The foundation of the FIRE movement is aggressive saving. The higher your savings rate, the faster you can reach your FIRE number. While the conventional advice is to save around 10-20% of your income for retirement,

FIRE enthusiasts often aim for much higher savings rates—**50% or more of their income**.

Here are how to achieve a high savings rate:

- ❖ Cutting Expenses: Analyze your budget and identify areas where you can reduce spending. This might include downsizing your home, driving a more affordable car, or cutting back on dining out and entertainment. Every dollar you save can be redirected toward investments that bring you closer to your FIRE goal.
- ❖ Increase Income: In addition to cutting costs, consider ways to increase your income. This could be through asking for a raise, changing careers, building a side hustle, or investing in skills that increase your earning potential.
- ❖ Optimize Tax Efficiency: Take advantage of tax-advantaged retirement accounts, such as 401(k)s, IRAs, or HSAs. These accounts allow you to invest pre-tax dollars or benefit from tax-free growth, which can significantly boost your savings rate.
- ❖ Frugality vs. Minimalism: Embrace a mindset of intentional spending. This doesn't necessarily mean depriving yourself of joy, but rather focusing on spending money on things that bring lasting value. Minimalism encourages people to spend less on material possessions and more on experiences or long-term goals.

9. Choosing the Right Investment Strategy

Maximizing your savings rate is essential, but equally important is how you invest those savings. Your investment choices will determine how quickly your wealth grows and how secure your finances will be in retirement.

- Index Funds and ETFs: For most FIRE followers, low-cost index funds or exchange-traded funds (ETFs) are the core of their investment strategy. These funds provide broad market exposure, minimize fees, and typically outperform actively managed funds over time.
- Real Estate: Real estate can be a powerful tool in the FIRE toolkit. Whether through rental properties or real estate investment trusts (REITs), real estate provides diversification, cash flow, and potential for appreciation. Rental income can serve as a **passive income stream**, helping you cover living expenses during retirement.
- Dividend Stocks: Dividend-paying stocks offer a reliable stream of income that can supplement your investment withdrawals. Many FIRE adherents include high-quality dividend stocks in their portfolio to benefit from both income and long-term capital appreciation.
- Bonds for Stability: While stocks tend to dominate FIRE portfolios due to their higher long-term returns, bonds provide stability. As you approach your FIRE date, gradually shifting a portion of your portfolio into bonds can reduce volatility and safeguard your wealth.

10. Tracking Your Progress Toward FIRE

Tracking your financial progress is critical to staying motivated and making adjustments along the way. There are several tools and strategies you can use to monitor your journey toward financial independence:

- Net Worth Tracking: Regularly track your net worth, which is the total value of your assets minus your liabilities. Watching your net worth grow over time can provide motivation and help you stay focused on your FIRE goals.
- Expense Tracking: Keeping a close eye on your monthly expenses ensures that you're staying within your budget and that your savings rate remains high. Many personal finance apps can automate this process, making it easier to see where your money is going.
- Investment Growth: Monitor the performance of your investments regularly. While it's essential to take a long-term view, periodic check-ins will help you ensure that your portfolio is aligned with your risk tolerance and FIRE timeline.
- Milestones and Mini-Goals: Breaking your journey into smaller financial milestones can make the process more manageable. For example, celebrate when you save your first $100,000, then $250,000, and so on. Each milestone represents progress toward the ultimate goal of financial independence.

11. Mitigating Financial Risks on the Path to FIRE

No financial plan is without risks, and it's important to manage and mitigate potential pitfalls that could delay your FIRE timeline. Here are some key risks to consider:

- Market Volatility: The stock market can be unpredictable, with periods of sharp declines that can test your resolve. By maintaining a diversified portfolio, rebalancing regularly, and staying the course during downturns, you can mitigate the impact of market volatility.

- ❖ Sequence of Returns Risk: This risk refers to the order in which you experience investment returns. If you encounter poor returns early in your retirement, it can negatively affect your withdrawal strategy. Having a well-balanced portfolio and a flexible withdrawal rate can help mitigate this risk.
- ❖ Health Insurance: For early retirees, healthcare is one of the largest potential expenses, particularly if you retire before becoming eligible for Medicare. Planning for health insurance costs, whether through private insurance, health-sharing plans, or an HSA, is crucial to protecting your savings.
- ❖ Emergency Fund: Ensure you have an adequate emergency fund in place to cover unexpected expenses, such as home repairs or medical bills. An emergency fund prevents you from having to dip into your investment portfolio prematurely.

12. The Psychological and Emotional Aspects of Reaching FIRE

The journey to FIRE is as much about mindset as it is about finances. The psychological and emotional shifts that come with planning for and achieving early retirement can be profound:

- ❖ Delayed Gratification: Achieving FIRE requires a commitment to delayed gratification. This can mean making sacrifices in the short term—such as skipping luxury vacations or expensive gadgets—in favor of long-term financial security.

- The Freedom of Choice: One of the most powerful aspects of FIRE is the freedom it grants. You may not want to stop working entirely, but FIRE gives you the freedom to choose how you spend your time, whether that's pursuing passion projects, traveling, or dedicating time to family.
- Post-FIRE Purpose: Many FIRE followers emphasize the importance of having a sense of purpose after reaching financial independence. The transition from a traditional career to early retirement can be disorienting if you don't have a clear plan for how to spend your time. Some people pursue new hobbies, volunteer, or start a second career in a field they're passionate about.

13. Building a Sustainable Withdrawal Plan

Once you've achieved your FIRE number, the final piece of the puzzle is designing a sustainable withdrawal plan that ensures your investments last throughout your retirement.

- Safe Withdrawal Rate: The 4% Rule serves as a guideline, but some retirees adjust this rate based on market conditions or personal preferences. During economic downturns, you might lower your withdrawal rate to preserve capital, then increase it during better times.
- Dynamic Withdrawals: Instead of sticking rigidly to a 4% withdrawal, consider a dynamic withdrawal strategy. This involves adjusting your annual withdrawals based on the performance of your portfolio, ensuring you don't deplete your savings during market downturns.

- Alternative Income Sources: Even after reaching FIRE, many early retirees continue to generate some form of passive income through side businesses, part-time work, or investments. This additional income reduces the strain on your portfolio and offers a buffer during periods of economic uncertainty.

Achieving FIRE is about more than just hitting a financial target—it's about designing a lifestyle that reflects your values, goals, and priorities. By carefully calculating your FIRE number, maximizing savings, building an appropriate investment portfolio, and planning for financial risks, you can create a sustainable path to early retirement. Whether your goal is to travel the world, pursue passion projects, or simply enjoy more time with family, FIRE offers the financial freedom to live life on your own terms.

Saving and Frugality Strategies

- How to cut expenses and maximize savings to accelerate wealth accumulation

In the journey toward financial independence and wealth accumulation, cutting unnecessary expenses and maximizing savings are pivotal. The combination of reducing expenditures and strategically directing savings toward investments can accelerate the accumulation of wealth. Below is a professional guide on how to effectively cut expenses and maximize savings while maintaining a balance between frugality and living a fulfilling life.

1. Budgeting as a Foundation for Cutting Expenses

Creating and adhering to a detailed budget is essential for understanding where your money is going and identifying areas where you can cut back. A well-structured budget provides clarity and control over your finances, allowing you to allocate resources to essential expenses while minimizing unnecessary spending.

- Zero-based budgeting: This method involves allocating every dollar of your income toward specific categories, including savings and investments, so that at the end of the month, you've accounted for every dollar. It forces a thorough review of your income and spending habits, making it easier to pinpoint wasteful spending.
- 50/30/20 rule: If you prefer a simplified approach, the 50/30/20 rule divides your after-tax income into three categories—50% for necessities, 30% for discretionary spending, and 20% for savings and debt repayment. By applying this rule, you can systematically control discretionary spending while ensuring that savings are prioritized.

2. Cutting Fixed and Variable Expenses

Both fixed and variable expenses present opportunities for savings. Reviewing recurring payments for necessity, cost-efficiency, and alternatives can help free up significant amounts of money for savings.

- Refinance Loans and Mortgages: With historically low interest rates in some economic environments, refinancing your mortgage or student loans can lead to lower monthly payments, freeing up cash flow for other priorities.
- Downsizing Housing Costs: Housing is often the largest expense for most households. Downsizing your home, moving to a less expensive area, or renting instead of owning

are ways to reduce this significant fixed cost. Alternatively, if you have extra space, renting out a room can help generate additional income.

- ❖ Negotiate Utility Bills: Call service providers for utilities such as electricity, water, or cable and internet to negotiate better rates. Switching to energy-efficient appliances and adopting energy-saving habits can also significantly reduce monthly utility costs.
- ❖ Subscription Audits: Many people subscribe to services they rarely use, whether for entertainment, streaming, apps, or software. Conduct a **subscription audit** to identify and cancel services you no longer need. Use free or lower-cost alternatives when possible.

3. Adopting a Frugal Mindset Without Compromising Quality of Life

Frugality doesn't mean deprivation; rather, it's about spending intentionally on things that truly matter to you and cutting back on areas that don't. Adopting a frugal mindset requires a shift in priorities and awareness of the value of each dollar spent.

- ❖ Embrace Minimalism: Minimalism encourages you to focus on the essentials and eliminate excess. Instead of buying more, invest in fewer, higher-quality items that last longer, whether it's clothing, household goods, or technology. This reduces long-term replacement costs and avoids the accumulation of clutter.
- ❖ Cook at Home: Dining out can quickly add up. Cooking at home is not only cheaper but also healthier. Meal planning and cooking in bulk allow you to save on groceries while reducing

food waste. Apps that offer meal planning tips or discounted grocery items can further reduce costs.

- Avoid Lifestyle Inflation: As your income grows, it can be tempting to upgrade your lifestyle. However, if you maintain your current standard of living and direct salary increases toward investments, you can accelerate wealth accumulation without sacrificing your long-term goals.
- Value-Based Spending: Focus your spending on experiences and purchases that bring long-term fulfillment. If an expense doesn't align with your values or contribute to your happiness, consider eliminating or reducing it. Redirecting unnecessary spending toward wealth-building activities can help achieve financial independence faster.

4. Automating Savings for Maximum Impact

Automating savings ensures that a portion of your income is consistently directed toward your financial goals without the temptation to spend it first. By setting up automatic transfers from your checking account to a dedicated savings or investment account, you can build wealth on autopilot.

- Pay Yourself First: Before you pay any other bills or expenses, allocate a portion of your income to your savings and investments. This concept, known as **paying yourself first**, helps ensure that your savings goals take priority over discretionary spending.
- Automate Retirement Contributions: If your employer offers a 401(k) or similar retirement plan, set up automatic contributions. Consider maximizing any employer matching programs,

as this represents free money for your future. If you're self-employed, automate contributions to an IRA or other tax-advantaged accounts.

- High-Yield Savings Accounts: Ensure your savings are earning the highest possible return by using a high-yield savings account or money market account. This can help your emergency fund and short-term savings grow faster while maintaining easy access to funds.

5. Smart Debt Management

Eliminating high-interest debt is one of the most powerful ways to accelerate wealth accumulation. Interest payments on debt can erode your ability to save and invest, so prioritizing debt repayment is crucial.

- Debt Avalanche vs. Debt Snowball: Two popular debt repayment strategies are the **debt avalanche** (where you pay off the highest-interest debts first) and the **debt snowball** (where you pay off the smallest balances first for quick wins). Choose the method that aligns with your financial psychology and goals, then stick to it to eliminate debt as quickly as possible.
- Avoid New Debt: Practice discipline with credit cards and avoid taking on new debt unless it's absolutely necessary. If you must use credit cards, ensure you pay off the balance in full each month to avoid interest charges.
- Consider Balance Transfers or Debt Consolidation: If you're struggling with high-interest debt, consider a balance transfer credit card with a 0% introductory APR or a debt consolidation loan with a lower interest rate. These options can help reduce the total

amount of interest you pay, freeing up more money for savings.

6. Leveraging Tax-Efficiency to Maximize Savings

Taxes can take a significant portion of your income, so incorporating tax-efficient strategies can help you retain more money to save and invest.

- Max Out Tax-Advantaged Accounts: Contribute the maximum allowed to tax-advantaged retirement accounts like 401(k)s, IRAs, or Health Savings Accounts (HSAs). These accounts either offer **tax-free growth** or **tax-deferred contributions**, reducing your taxable income and allowing your investments to grow more efficiently.
- Tax-Loss Harvesting: If you have taxable investment accounts, consider tax-loss harvesting strategies, which involve selling investments at a loss to offset gains in other parts of your portfolio. This can help minimize your capital gains taxes and maximize the growth of your wealth over time.
- Charitable Giving and Deductions: If charitable giving is part of your financial plan, ensure that you're taking full advantage of any deductions it offers. This can help reduce your taxable income while supporting causes that align with your values.

7. Investing the Savings to Build Wealth

Cutting expenses and saving aggressively is just the first step; to accelerate wealth accumulation, it's crucial to invest those savings for growth.

- ❖ Invest in the Stock Market: Long-term investing in the stock market, particularly through low-cost index funds or ETFs, allows your savings to grow over time. Take advantage of **compound interest**, where your returns generate additional earnings, leading to exponential growth.
- ❖ Real Estate: If you have substantial savings, consider investing in real estate for rental income and property appreciation. Real estate can offer passive income and serve as a hedge against inflation.
- ❖ Reinvest Dividends: Reinvesting dividends and capital gains from your investments instead of cashing them out allows your portfolio to grow faster. By reinvesting, you are compounding your returns over time, accelerating your wealth-building journey.

8. Regularly Review and Adjust

As your financial situation evolves, it's essential to review and adjust your expense-cutting and savings strategies regularly. Life changes such as a new job, a move, or an unexpected expense might require you to modify your budget or increase your savings rate. Consistently evaluating your progress ensures that you stay on track toward your financial goals.

By focusing on cutting unnecessary expenses and maximizing savings, you can significantly accelerate the accumulation of wealth. A disciplined approach to budgeting, reducing fixed and variable costs, automating savings, managing debt, and leveraging tax-efficient strategies ensures that you make the most of every dollar earned. These methods, when combined with smart investing, will help you build financial security and independence more quickly, putting you on the path to long-term wealth.

- Case Studies of Individuals Who Successfully Achieved FIRE

The Financial Independence, Retire Early (FIRE) movement has grown in popularity, with many individuals striving to break free from the traditional work model by aggressively saving, cutting expenses, and investing wisely to achieve financial independence. Below are detailed case studies of individuals who successfully implemented FIRE principles and the strategies they employed to reach their goals. Each case highlights different approaches, challenges, and key takeaways that can inspire others on their journey toward financial independence.

Case Study 1: Mr. Money Mustache (Pete Adeney)

Background:
Pete Adeney, also known by his pseudonym "Mr. Money Mustache," is one of the most well-known figures in the FIRE community. He retired at age 30 after working for only nine years as a software engineer. Adeney achieved financial independence by embracing extreme frugality, living well below his means, and focusing on aggressive saving and investing.

Strategies:

- ❖ Frugal Living: Adeney and his wife adopted a minimalist lifestyle, focusing on reducing unnecessary expenses. They lived in a modest home, used bicycles instead of cars, and avoided most forms of consumerism. Their expenses were kept to around $25,000 a year, even with a child.

- Aggressive Saving: By saving more than 50% of their income, Adeney and his wife were able to build a significant investment portfolio quickly. Their high savings rate allowed them to accumulate enough capital to generate passive income from investments.
- Index Fund Investing: Adeney focused on low-cost index funds for long-term growth. This investment strategy allowed their savings to grow steadily, fueled by the power of compound interest.
- DIY Mentality: Adeney embraced the DIY (do-it-yourself) approach to home repairs, gardening, and general maintenance. This further reduced living costs and enhanced their savings capacity.

Outcome:-
By maintaining an exceptionally high savings rate and living a frugal, value-based lifestyle, Adeney was able to retire by 30 and has since used his time to promote financial independence through his blog. He continues to live a fulfilling life, focused on family, community, and personal hobbies, without the need for a traditional job.

Key Takeaways:

- Extreme frugality can dramatically accelerate the path to FIRE.
- Cutting major expenses like housing, transportation, and consumer spending can significantly increase your savings rate.
- Low-cost index fund investing, combined with a high savings rate, is an effective strategy for achieving financial independence.

Case Study 2: The Frugal woods (Elizabeth Willard Thames and Nate Thames)

Background:
Elizabeth and Nate Thames, known for their blog "Frugalwoods," achieved financial independence in their early 30s. Both had careers in urban areas but decided to embrace a simpler, rural lifestyle as part of their path to FIRE. They now live on a homestead in Vermont, where they focus on sustainability and intentional living.

Strategies:

- Extreme Frugality: Similar to Mr. Money Mustache, the Frugalwoods embraced a highly frugal lifestyle. They drastically reduced their spending by cutting out luxury goods, expensive social outings, and even minor convenience purchases like coffee. They used price-conscious grocery shopping and cut unnecessary services such as cable and memberships.
- DIY and Sustainability: The couple focused on sustainability by growing their own food, performing home repairs, and practicing homesteading. This approach allowed them to save on both living and grocery costs while aligning with their personal values.
- Minimalism: Rather than accumulating more possessions, the Thames family focused on buying only what they needed and what added real value to their lives. They also avoided debt, with the exception of a mortgage for their homestead.
- Side Hustles and Income Diversification: While working traditional jobs, the couple also earned extra income through blogging and writing.

This additional income stream allowed them to accelerate their savings.

- ❖ Moving to a Lower-Cost Area: One of the key decisions was relocating from the city to a rural area with a much lower cost of living. This move dramatically reduced their housing expenses and allowed them to pursue a simpler, less expensive lifestyle.

Outcome:-
By their early 30s, Elizabeth and Nate had saved enough to leave their traditional careers behind and live a life focused on family, community, and sustainable living. Their homestead lifestyle allows them to live with fewer expenses, yet they find fulfillment in non-materialistic pursuits.

Key Takeaways:

- ❖ A shift in lifestyle to a lower-cost area can significantly reduce expenses, enabling faster financial independence.
- ❖ Minimalism and sustainability can reduce financial stress and align with personal values, allowing for a fulfilling, yet frugal life.
- ❖ Multiple income streams can provide additional security and speed up the journey to financial freedom.

Case Study 3*: *Grant Sabatier (Millennial Money)

Background:
Grant Sabatier, founder of Millennial Money, went from having just $2.26 in his bank account at 24 to accumulating over $1 million and achieving financial independence by age 30. Sabatier's story is a testament to how anyone, even those starting with very little, can reach financial independence with the right strategies.

Strategies:

- Aggressive Income Growth: While many in the FIRE community focus on cutting expenses, Sabatier took a different approach by aggressively increasing his income. He worked in digital marketing, which allowed him to command higher salaries and freelance rates. He also developed a variety of side hustles, including website flipping and consulting.
- High Savings Rate: Despite his rapidly growing income, Sabatier kept his lifestyle relatively modest and saved 60-70% of his income. He avoided lifestyle inflation and continued to prioritize saving and investing.
- Real Estate Investment: In addition to traditional investments in index funds, Sabatier also invested in real estate, using rental income to further diversify his income streams and build passive income.
- Smart Investing: Sabatier used a combination of index fund investing, stock investments, and real estate to grow his wealth. He also took advantage of the stock market's Bull Run from 2010 to 2017, which contributed to the rapid growth of his portfolio.
- Financial Optimization: He optimized every aspect of his finances, from credit card rewards to low-fee investment accounts. By making sure every dollar worked as hard as possible, he was able to accelerate his journey to FIRE.

Outcome:
By age 30, Sabatier had amassed enough wealth to retire early, although he chose to continue working on projects that align with his passion. Today, he spends his time traveling, writing, and teaching others how to achieve financial independence.

Key Takeaways:

- Increasing income through side hustles and career growth can be as effective as cutting expenses for achieving FIRE.
- Maintaining a high savings rate, even as income increases, prevents lifestyle inflation and accelerates wealth accumulation.
- Diversification across investments, including real estate and stocks, can create multiple streams of income, offering both security and growth.

Case Study 4: The Mad Fientist (Brandon)

Background:
Brandon, known as the "Mad Fientist," retired early at age 34 after optimizing his financial life to achieve FIRE. As a software engineer, he focused on maximizing tax efficiency, hacking his savings strategy, and embracing the principles of FIRE.

Strategies:

- Tax Efficiency: One of Brandon's key strategies was using tax-advantaged accounts to maximize savings and reduce tax liability. He contributed heavily to his 401(k) and Roth IRA, ensuring that his investments grew with minimal tax burden.
- Geoarbitrage: The Mad Fientist embraced **geoarbitrage**, a concept where you earn money in a high-income area but live or retire in a lower-cost region. By taking advantage of the cost-of-living differences between cities or even countries, he stretched his savings much further.

- Optimizing Travel Rewards: Like many in the FIRE community, Brandon used travel rewards and credit card points to reduce the cost of travel significantly. This allowed him to continue enjoying travel while maintaining a frugal budget.
- Low-Cost Index Fund Investing: Like many FIRE adherents, Brandon invested in low-cost index funds, allowing his investments to grow passively over time. By keeping investment costs low, he maximized his returns and reduced fees.
- Simple Living: Although he had a high income, Brandon kept his lifestyle simple and focused on what mattered most to him. This allowed him to save a significant portion of his income and retire early.

Outcome:
Brandon retired at 34, well before the traditional retirement age, and has been living a fulfilling life focused on passion projects, travel, and family. His detailed analysis and breakdown of tax strategies and financial hacks have inspired many others to follow in his footsteps.

Key Takeaways:

- Tax optimization strategies, such as using tax-advantaged accounts and maximizing deductions, can significantly speed up the path to FIRE.
- Geoarbitrage can be a powerful tool for reducing living costs while maintaining a higher standard of living in lower-cost areas.
- Simple, low-cost investing strategies like index funds, combined with frugality and smart

financial decisions, can lead to early financial independence.

These case studies highlight the diverse strategies that individuals can use to achieve FIRE. While the path may vary—whether through extreme frugality, increasing income, leveraging investments, or optimizing taxes—key principles such as saving aggressively, living below your means, and investing wisely remain central to achieving financial independence. Each individual's journey is unique, but the consistent themes of discipline, intentionality, and financial optimization provide a roadmap for those seeking to achieve FIRE.

- The Potential Challenges of Early Retirement: Maintaining Financial Discipline and Adaptability

The allure of early retirement, a core goal of the Financial Independence, Retire Early (FIRE) movement, offers the promise of freedom from the conventional work-life grind. While the prospect of achieving financial independence in your 30s or 40s can be deeply motivating, it comes with significant challenges that demand ongoing discipline and adaptability. Early retirees must plan for extended periods of financial independence, navigate unpredictable markets, and adjust to life without traditional work structures. Below are the key challenges and strategies to maintain both financial discipline and adaptability throughout an early retirement journey.

1. Longevity Risk: Planning for an Extended Retirement Period

One of the greatest challenges early retirees face is the need to plan for a much longer retirement period than conventional retirees. If someone retires in their 30s or 40s, they may need to sustain their financial resources for 40 to 50 years or more. This extended time frame introduces several risks, including market volatility, inflation, and healthcare costs, all of which can erode wealth over time.

Strategies to Address Longevity Risk:

- Build a Larger Safety Net: Early retirees need to ensure that their investment portfolios are large enough to account for unforeseen circumstances. Many within the FIRE community recommend a withdrawal rate of 3-4%, but early retirees should consider a more conservative rate, or aim to accumulate 25-30 times their annual expenses to better safeguard against longevity risk.
- Consider Part-Time Work: To alleviate the pressure on retirement savings, some early retirees choose to continue part-time work or freelance projects. This not only generates additional income but can also provide social engagement and intellectual stimulation, extending the sustainability of their financial resources.
- Multiple Income Streams: Diversifying income streams through real estate, dividend-paying stocks, or royalties can reduce reliance on portfolio withdrawals and provide more flexibility in adapting to changing financial circumstances.

2. Market Volatility and Sequence of Returns Risk

Early retirees are more exposed to market volatility and what's known as **sequence of returns risk**. This refers to the risk that market downturns in the early years of retirement could significantly diminish a portfolio, making it harder to recover. Traditional retirees face this risk over a shorter period, but early retirees, with decades of retirement ahead, need to be particularly cautious.

Strategies to Mitigate Market Volatility:

- Asset Allocation Flexibility**:** Maintaining a balanced portfolio that includes a mix of equities, bonds, and other income-generating assets is crucial. Early retirees should regularly review and rebalance their portfolios to maintain an optimal level of risk and return.
- Cash Buffer**:** Maintaining 1-2 years' worth of living expenses in cash or highly liquid investments can help protect early retirees from needing to sell assets during market downturns, allowing their investments to recover before withdrawals.
- Withdrawal Flexibility**:** The ability to reduce withdrawals or adjust lifestyle expenses in response to market fluctuations is key. Early retirees who live below their means can cut discretionary spending during economic downturns, thereby preserving their investment portfolios.

3. Inflation Risk

Inflation poses a significant challenge for early retirees, as it erodes the purchasing power of savings over time. Over several decades, even modest inflation can greatly reduce the value of a fixed-income stream, forcing retirees to draw more from their portfolios than originally planned.

Strategies to Counter Inflation Risk:

- Invest in Inflation-Protected Assets**:** Including investments that historically perform well during inflationary periods, such as Treasury Inflation-Protected Securities (TIPS), commodities, real estate, and certain types of stocks, can help protect against rising inflation.

- Continue Investing in Growth-Oriented Assets: While bonds and cash are safer in terms of market volatility, growth-oriented assets like equities can help your portfolio outpace inflation. A well-diversified portfolio with a healthy allocation to stocks can provide the long-term growth needed to keep up with inflation.
- Consider Geographic Diversification: Investing in international markets can help mitigate the risk of inflation or currency depreciation in any one country, allowing early retirees to take advantage of global opportunities.

4. Healthcare Costs

Healthcare is a major concern for early retirees, particularly those who retire before qualifying for Medicare (usually at age 65). The lack of employer-sponsored health insurance, rising medical costs, and potential for unexpected healthcare needs make this one of the most pressing issues for the FIRE community.

Strategies to Manage Healthcare Costs:

- Health Savings Account (HSA): Contributing to an HSA while still working provides early retirees with a tax-advantaged way to save for future healthcare expenses. HSAs offer triple tax benefits (tax-deductible contributions, tax-free growth, and tax-free withdrawals for qualified expenses), making them a powerful tool for managing healthcare costs in retirement.
- Private or Marketplace Health Insurance: Early retirees often need to rely on private health insurance or the marketplace exchanges set up by the Affordable Care Act (ACA). Planning for this expense early on, by budgeting a higher annual

amount for health insurance premiums and out-of-pocket expenses, is crucial.

- Stay Healthy: Preventive care, regular exercise, and maintaining a healthy lifestyle can reduce the likelihood of major healthcare expenses in retirement. Early retirees have more time to focus on health and well-being, and prioritizing these areas can help manage long-term healthcare costs.

5. Lifestyle Adjustments and Psychological Challenges

One often overlooked challenge of early retirement is the emotional and psychological shift that comes with leaving the workforce. For many, work provides structure, social interaction, and a sense of purpose. Early retirees must adjust to a new lifestyle that may lack these traditional sources of fulfillment.

Strategies to Maintain a Healthy Early Retirement:

- Find Meaningful Activities: Whether through volunteering, pursuing hobbies, or starting a side business, it's important for early retirees to find ways to stay engaged. The shift from full-time work to retirement can be jarring, and finding fulfilling activities helps maintain mental and emotional well-being.
- Social Connections: Building and maintaining strong social relationships is critical. Many early retirees report feeling isolated, especially if most of their peers are still working. Joining clubs, engaging with community organizations, or cultivating friendships with other early retirees can combat loneliness and provide social stimulation.
- Stay Flexible: Early retirees should be prepared to adapt their lifestyles over time. Circumstances, goals, and interests may evolve, and maintaining

an open mindset allows retirees to embrace new opportunities or challenges without feeling constrained by a rigid plan.

6. Maintaining Financial Discipline Over Decades

Once early retirement is achieved, maintaining the financial discipline that made it possible becomes even more important. Without the structure of a paycheck, there can be a temptation to overspend, especially during the early "honeymoon phase" of retirement when newfound freedom often leads to increased travel or discretionary spending.

Strategies for Maintaining Financial Discipline:

- Create a Realistic Spending Plan: Setting and adhering to a sustainable spending plan is essential. This plan should be based on conservative estimates of investment returns, inflation, and living expenses to avoid depleting retirement funds too quickly.
- Track Expenses and Adjust Regularly: Regularly monitoring spending and comparing it to the initial retirement budget allows early retirees to make necessary adjustments. Staying on top of finances helps prevent overspending and keeps retirement plans on track.
- Set Clear Goals for Different Stages of Retirement: Planning for the "go-go," "slow-go," and "no-go" phases of retirement ensures that spending levels align with activity levels and healthcare needs. Early retirees are likely to spend more in the first decade of retirement, but careful planning can prevent financial shortfalls later in life.

7. Reevaluating Investment Strategies in Retirement

While the FIRE (Financial Independence, Retire Early) approach often focuses on building wealth through aggressive saving and investing during the accumulation phase, the de-accumulation phase—where assets are drawn down to fund retirement—requires a different mindset. Early retirees must regularly evaluate and adjust their investment strategies to account for shifting needs, economic conditions, and risk tolerance.

Strategies for Reevaluating Investment Approaches:

- Shift Toward Income-Producing Investments: As retirees rely more on their portfolio for daily living expenses, a shift toward income-generating investments—such as dividend-paying stocks, bonds, or real estate—can provide more consistent cash flow. This can reduce the need to sell off growth-oriented assets during market downturns.
- Sequence of Withdrawals: Managing the order in which funds are withdrawn from various accounts (e.g., taxable accounts, tax-deferred retirement accounts, or Roth IRAs) can optimize tax efficiency and extend the life of retirement savings. For example, drawing from taxable accounts first may allow tax-advantaged accounts to continue growing.
- Safe Withdrawal Rate: While the traditional "4% rule" is a popular starting point for retirement withdrawals, early retirees should remain flexible, especially during periods of market downturns or rising inflation. Adjusting the withdrawal rate to 3-3.5% or being willing to cut spending temporarily can protect against prematurely depleting assets.

8. Anticipating Future Tax Changes

Tax planning is especially important for early retirees, who may experience fluctuating income levels over their retirement. Given the long retirement horizon, tax laws are likely to change several times, and being proactive in tax planning can help early retirees avoid large, unexpected tax liabilities.

Tax Strategies for Early Retirees:

- Roth Conversions: During the early years of retirement, especially before required minimum distributions (RMDs) begin at age 72, it may be advantageous to convert traditional IRA or 401(k) assets into a Roth IRA. Roth accounts grow tax-free, and distributions are tax-free, offering protection from future tax rate increases.
- Harvesting Capital Gains: Taking advantage of low-income years to harvest capital gains at favorable tax rates can help reduce future tax burdens. Selling appreciated assets strategically can lock in gains without incurring significant tax penalties.
- State Taxes: Moving to states with lower or no income taxes is a strategy some early retirees use to minimize their overall tax burden. Understanding both federal and state tax implications ensures long-term tax efficiency.

9. Managing Lifestyle Inflation

One of the hidden challenges in early retirement is lifestyle inflation. Without the discipline of a steady paycheck and a work schedule, retirees may gradually increase their spending on leisure activities, travel, and entertainment. Over time, this can erode the financial cushion carefully built during the accumulation phase.

How to Combat Lifestyle Inflation:

- Stick to a Budget: Even in retirement, adhering to a clear and realistic budget is key to preventing overspending. Regularly revisiting and updating the budget can help early retirees maintain their financial goals without compromising their lifestyle.
- Differentiate Between Wants and Needs: Creating a hierarchy of spending priorities allows retirees to indulge in experiences or purchases without jeopardizing the sustainability of their retirement funds. Separating discretionary spending from essential expenses ensures that core needs are always met.
- Emphasize Value-Based Spending: Instead of simply spending more as income becomes available, early retirees can focus on aligning their spending with their core values and long-term goals. This approach helps maintain financial discipline while allowing for enjoyment in the areas that matter most.

10. Dealing with Unforeseen Circumstances

Early retirement does not make individuals immune to unforeseen challenges, such as family emergencies, natural disasters, or economic crises. Being financially prepared for unexpected events is crucial to maintaining financial independence.

Strategies for Handling Unforeseen Circumstances:

- Emergency Fund: Even in early retirement, maintaining a liquid emergency fund of 6-12 months' worth of living expenses can provide a financial safety net. This prevents the need to tap into long-term investments during market downturns or in times of crisis.

- Insurance: Early retirees should ensure they are adequately insured, particularly in areas such as health insurance, long-term care insurance, and property insurance. While the FIRE mindset often encourages minimizing expenses, skimping on insurance can lead to significant financial hardships in the future.
- Contingency Plans: It's essential to have contingency plans in place in case investment returns fall short or healthcare costs rise unexpectedly. Early retirees should be willing to make temporary or permanent lifestyle adjustments if needed, such as downsizing a home, returning to part-time work, or reducing travel and luxury expenses.

11. Continuing Financial Education

The financial landscape is constantly evolving, with new investment vehicles, tax laws, and retirement planning strategies emerging regularly. Early retirees must stay informed about these changes to ensure they are optimizing their portfolios and maintaining financial independence.

How to Stay Financially Informed:

- Ongoing Learning: Staying updated through financial newsletters, podcasts, books, and courses helps early retirees make informed decisions as new opportunities and risks arise. Joining the FIRE community or working with a financial planner can also provide guidance.
- Regular Financial Checkups: Conducting periodic reviews of one's financial situation, including net worth, cash flow, and investment performance, is vital to staying on track. An annual or semi-annual financial checkup can help early retirees adjust

their strategies in response to changing circumstances.

- Working with Advisors: While many FIRE adherents take a DIY approach to financial planning, there may be times when professional advice is warranted. Working with tax advisors, estate planners, or financial advisors can provide insights into complex decisions, such as tax-efficient withdrawals, long-term care planning, or real estate investments.

Achieving early retirement through the FIRE strategy is an admirable goal, but maintaining financial independence requires ongoing diligence and adaptability. The extended retirement horizon presents unique challenges, such as market volatility, inflation, and healthcare costs. Early retirees must remain disciplined in their spending, carefully manage their investments, and adjust their strategies in response to changing economic conditions and personal circumstances. By staying informed, flexible, and focused on long-term goals, early retirees can not only sustain their financial freedom but also enjoy the freedom and fulfillment that the FIRE movement promises.

CHAPTER EIGHT

PERSONAL DEVELOPMENT AND WEALTH

This chapter emphasizes the connection between personal growth and financial success, highlighting how developing key life skills can accelerate wealth creation.

The Role of Emotional Intelligence in Wealth Creation

- How Emotional Intelligence (EQ) Influences Financial Success

Emotional Intelligence (EQ) plays a pivotal role in financial success, both in managing personal finances and in broader wealth creation. While technical financial knowledge is essential, EQ adds an often overlooked layer of influence, shaping how individuals interact with money, make investment decisions, manage risks, and sustain long-term financial well-being. EQ refers to the ability to recognize, understand, and manage one's emotions, as well as the ability to understand and influence the emotions of others.

Here is how EQ impacts wealth creation:-

1. Improved Decision-Making and Risk Management

High emotional intelligence enables individuals to make more rational financial decisions, minimizing the impact of emotions such as fear or greed that can lead to poor choices. Emotional intelligence helps people:

- ❖ Avoid impulsive decisions: Those with high EQ are better at delaying gratification, resisting the temptation of short-term wins for long-term wealth accumulation. This ability is crucial in avoiding impulsive purchases, speculative investments, or emotional trading.

- Manage risk effectively: Risk tolerance is often influenced by emotions, but individuals with high EQ can assess risks more objectively. They are less likely to react to short-term market volatility with panic or exuberance, and more likely to stick to their long-term investment strategies.
- Control emotional biases: Behavioral finance highlights how emotions such as loss aversion, overconfidence, and herd behavior can distort financial decision-making. EQ allows individuals to recognize these emotional biases and counteract them by focusing on data-driven, rational choices.

2. Resilience in Financial Setbacks

Setbacks are inevitable in any financial journey, whether it's a market downturn, job loss, or personal financial crisis. Emotional intelligence fosters resilience, enabling individuals to recover from financial adversity more effectively.

- Bounce back from failure: A high EQ individual views financial setbacks as temporary and part of the broader learning process. They are less likely to dwell on mistakes and more inclined to take corrective action to recover.
- Maintain perspective during crises: During times of financial stress, people with strong emotional intelligence can maintain perspective, avoiding panic-driven reactions. They understand that market cycles and personal financial challenges are part of the broader picture and can take a long-term approach to recovery.
- Emotional regulation: EQ allows individuals to manage anxiety, frustration, or fear during

turbulent financial times. This skill is critical for maintaining discipline, sticking to budgetary goals, and avoiding rash decisions that could worsen the situation.

3. Effective Relationship Management in Financial Affairs

Wealth creation often involves collaboration, whether through partnerships, financial planning with spouses, or working with financial advisors. High emotional intelligence enhances relationship management, fostering trust and collaboration in these contexts.

- Better financial communication: High EQ helps individuals communicate more clearly and empathetically about financial matters. This is essential when discussing complex financial topics with partners, family members, or advisors, ensuring alignment of goals and expectations.
- Managing conflicts: Financial decisions can lead to conflicts, especially in relationships or business ventures. EQ helps navigate these conflicts by understanding and addressing the underlying emotions, leading to better resolutions and maintaining financial harmony.
- Leveraging social intelligence for networking: High emotional intelligence also supports better networking and collaboration, which can lead to business opportunities, partnerships, and professional growth. Strong interpersonal relationships built on trust can lead to wealth-building opportunities through joint ventures or mentorship.

4. Building Financial Discipline

One of the key aspects of wealth creation is the ability to consistently save, invest, and stick to a financial plan. EQ supports this discipline by fostering self-regulation and goal-oriented behavior.

- Delayed gratification: High EQ individuals are better able to delay immediate rewards for long-term gains, whether by consistently saving, maintaining a budget, or sticking to an investment strategy.
- Goal-setting and achievement: Emotional intelligence enhances the ability to set clear financial goals and maintain focus on achieving them. High EQ individuals can manage emotions like frustration or impatience that might otherwise derail long-term financial plans.
- Staying focused in the face of temptation: Whether it's spending on luxury items or diverting funds from investments for short-term pleasures, those with strong emotional regulation skills can resist temptations that detract from long-term wealth creation.

5. Financial Independence through Self-Awareness

Self-awareness is a cornerstone of emotional intelligence and is crucial for understanding one's financial habits, tendencies, and relationship with money.

- Recognizing financial weaknesses: People with high self-awareness can identify their financial weaknesses, such as overspending, impulsive investments, or emotional decision-making. Acknowledging these weaknesses allows them to take steps to improve or seek help when necessary.

- Aligning financial behavior with values: High EQ individuals can align their financial goals with their personal values and purpose. For instance, they are more likely to invest in sustainable or ethical ventures that reflect their principles, ensuring that wealth creation contributes to their broader life goals.
- Understanding money mindsets: Emotional intelligence helps individuals understand the psychological factors driving their financial decisions, such as a scarcity mindset or fear of failure. Addressing these deeper emotions enables them to cultivate a healthier, more abundant relationship with money.

6. Stress Management and Financial Well-being

Financial anxiety is a common issue for many, regardless of wealth level. Emotional intelligence helps in managing stress associated with financial matters.

- Reducing financial anxiety: High EQ individuals are better equipped to handle the stress associated with financial responsibilities, from debt management to retirement planning. They use coping mechanisms like mindfulness, problem-solving, and stress-reduction techniques to remain calm and in control.
- Developing a balanced financial approach: Emotional intelligence promotes balance between aggressive wealth-building strategies and the need for personal well-being. High EQ individuals understand the importance of mental and emotional health in sustaining long-term financial success and avoid burnout from relentless financial pursuits.

7. Long-Term Wealth Sustainability

Sustaining wealth requires ongoing financial literacy and emotional intelligence. High EQ ensures individuals not only build wealth but also manage it effectively over the long term.

- Preventing lifestyle inflation: As wealth grows, there is a temptation to increase spending proportionally. Emotional intelligence helps individuals manage lifestyle inflation by distinguishing between needs and wants, allowing them to live below their means even as their income increases.
- Wealth preservation: High EQ individuals are more likely to make conservative and informed decisions that preserve wealth across generations. They recognize the emotional impact of wealth on future generations and can manage succession planning, inheritance, and family dynamics with sensitivity and foresight.
- Legacy planning: Emotional intelligence plays a role in planning for a meaningful legacy. It encourages individuals to think beyond financial accumulation and consider how their wealth can be used to positively impact their families, communities, and causes they care about.

Emotional intelligence is a critical component of wealth creation and financial success. By enhancing decision-making, fostering resilience, improving relationship management, and supporting financial discipline, EQ provides the emotional and psychological tools necessary to navigate the complex financial landscape. Individuals who cultivate high emotional intelligence are better equipped to manage their money, build sustainable wealth, and achieve long-term financial independence while maintaining emotional well-being.

- Using EQ to Improve Decision-Making in Personal and Professional Finance

Emotional intelligence (EQ) plays a critical role in shaping effective decision-making, especially in the context of personal and professional finance. EQ, defined as the ability to understand and manage one's own emotions as well as recognize and influence the emotions of others, is a vital component of financial success. The ability to balance logic with emotional awareness allows individuals to make informed financial decisions that are sustainable in the long term, avoiding impulsive mistakes and fostering better relationships in professional and personal financial contexts. In the realm of wealth creation, leveraging EQ can lead to improved financial outcomes and a more disciplined approach to money management.

1. Emotional Intelligence and Financial Decision-Making

- One of the key ways that emotional intelligence impacts financial decision-making is by helping individuals regulate their emotions when faced with financial challenges. Financial markets, personal investments, and business ventures often come with significant risks and volatility. During these times, emotions such as fear, anxiety, and greed can cloud judgment, leading to rash decisions like panic selling, over-investing in speculative assets, or missing out on opportunities due to fear of failure.
- Through developing strong emotional intelligence, individuals can better manage these emotional impulses, staying calm under pressure and

making decisions based on rational analysis rather than short-term emotional reactions. For instance, a person with high EQ can recognize their emotional triggers, allowing them to pause, reflect, and make decisions based on long-term financial goals rather than reactive emotional responses.

2. Understanding the Role of Self-Awareness in Financial Decisions

- Self-awareness, a core component of emotional intelligence, is crucial for financial decision-making. It involves recognizing one's emotional state, strengths, weaknesses, and values. In the context of personal finance, self-awareness helps individuals understand their relationship with money. Are they risk-takers or risk-averse? Do they tend to spend impulsively or save diligently? By understanding these tendencies, individuals can create financial strategies that align with their personal behavior patterns, making it easier to avoid financial pitfalls and capitalize on their strengths.
- Self-awareness enables leaders to understand how their financial decisions affect their organizations and stakeholders. Leaders with high EQ can evaluate their emotional responses to market changes, company performance, and stakeholder expectations. This understanding allows them to make more strategic decisions that prioritize long-term financial health over short-term gains driven by emotional pressure.

3. Managing Emotional Triggers in Financial Markets

- Financial markets are inherently volatile, and external events can trigger strong emotional reactions. News of a market downturn, for example, might prompt fear-based decisions such as selling off investments prematurely, while a booming market might trigger greed, leading to overinvestment in high-risk assets.

- Individuals with strong emotional intelligence are better equipped to manage these emotional triggers. Rather than reacting impulsively, they can assess the situation more objectively, consult their financial goals, and decide on the best course of action. This ability to stay level-headed during market fluctuations helps to minimize losses during downturns and capitalize on opportunities when they arise.
- For example, during the 2008 financial crisis, many investors panicked and sold their assets at a loss. However, those with higher emotional intelligence and financial literacy were able to remain calm, recognizing that markets would eventually recover. By not giving in to fear, they were able to hold or even buy assets at lower prices, benefiting in the long term.

4. Empathy in Financial Negotiations and Professional Relationships

- Empathy, another pillar of emotional intelligence, is essential in professional finance, particularly in negotiations, stakeholder management, and client relations. Understanding and acknowledging the emotions, perspectives, and needs of others is crucial when engaging in negotiations or managing teams.
- Leaders with strong emotional intelligence can better understand the motivations of their clients, employees, and stakeholders, leading to more effective communication and stronger relationships. For example, in negotiations, being empathetic allows individuals to find mutually beneficial solutions by addressing the underlying

concerns of all parties involved. This approach often leads to better long-term outcomes, as opposed to purely transactional, financially driven negotiations that can damage relationships.

- Empathy can enhance relationships with partners, family members, and financial advisors. Recognizing the financial concerns and goals of a spouse or family member can foster more collaborative financial planning, leading to better outcomes for everyone involved. Similarly, financial advisors who demonstrate empathy can better understand their clients' financial goals and emotional comfort with risk, enabling them to offer more personalized advice that aligns with the client's long-term objectives.

5. Using EQ to Balance Short-Term and Long-Term Financial Goals

- One of the ongoing challenges in both personal and professional finance is balancing short-term financial needs with long-term goals. Emotional intelligence helps individuals manage this balance by keeping short-term emotional impulses in check while maintaining focus on broader financial objectives.
- For example, someone with strong EQ may be tempted to spend money on a luxury item for immediate gratification but, by tapping into their self-awareness and emotional regulation, they can remind themselves of their long-term savings or investment goals. This emotional regulation helps them avoid short-term splurges and maintain financial discipline, which is critical for wealth accumulation.
- In business, leaders who leverage EQ can manage the tension between short-term profitability and long-term growth. They understand the emotional pressures that come

with quarterly performance targets but remain focused on sustainable strategies that drive future financial success.

6. Emotional Intelligence and Financial Resilience

- Financial resilience is the ability to withstand economic shocks and recover from financial setbacks. Emotional intelligence plays a key role in building this resilience. Individuals with high EQ are better equipped to navigate financial adversity, such as job loss, market downturns, or unexpected expenses, by staying calm and approaching problems with a solution-focused mindset.
- By managing their emotions during financial crises, individuals can avoid panic-driven decisions and instead focus on practical solutions, such as re-evaluating budgets, seeking alternative income sources, or consulting with financial professionals. This resilience helps them recover more quickly and maintain long-term financial stability.

7. Leveraging EQ to Build Wealth through Collaboration and Networking

- In professional finance, emotional intelligence is essential for building strong networks and collaborations. Financial success often depends on relationships, whether with clients, partners, or investors. Individuals with high EQ excel in networking because they can build genuine connections based on trust and mutual understanding.
- In collaborative financial ventures, such as partnerships or investment groups, EQ helps individuals navigate interpersonal dynamics,

manage conflicts, and ensure that all parties remain aligned with shared financial goals. These relationships are essential for identifying opportunities, sharing knowledge, and achieving greater financial success.

In both personal and professional finance, emotional intelligence is a powerful tool that enhances decision-making, builds resilience, and fosters relationships that support long-term wealth creation. By managing emotions, balancing short- and long-term goals, and fostering empathy in financial interactions, individuals can make smarter financial choices that lead to sustainable financial success. Cultivating emotional intelligence not only strengthens one's financial acumen but also enhances the ability to navigate the complexities of wealth-building with confidence and clarity.

- Building Relationships That Support Wealth Growth: Networking, Mentorship, and Collaborations

Building wealth is not just about smart investments or financial strategies—it's equally about cultivating the right relationships. Emotional intelligence (EQ), which is the ability to recognize, understand, and manage emotions in oneself and others, plays a crucial role in establishing and nurturing relationships that are vital for long-term wealth creation. By leveraging EQ, individuals can more effectively engage in networking, seek out mentorship, and collaborate with others—all of which are critical for wealth growth. Below, we explore how networking, mentorship, and collaborations can fuel wealth creation and how emotional intelligence plays a key role in each.

1. Networking: Expanding Your Circle of Influence

Networking is one of the most powerful tools in building wealth. It involves forming and nurturing relationships with people who can provide opportunities, share knowledge, and offer support. Whether it's through professional associations, industry events, or personal connections, networking opens doors to resources that can significantly enhance financial success.

The Role of Emotional Intelligence in Networking:

- Building Trust and Rapport: EQ enables individuals to develop trust and rapport more easily. When networking, high emotional intelligence helps people pick up on non-verbal cues, show empathy, and build strong emotional connections with others, which can lead to lasting professional relationships.
- Active Listening: One of the core components of EQ is active listening. Networking is not just about talking about yourself but listening to others, understanding their needs, and finding mutually beneficial solutions. This fosters more meaningful interactions.
- Managing Social Anxiety: Many people feel anxious when meeting new people, but individuals with high EQ can regulate their emotions and remain composed in social settings. This helps them approach networking opportunities with confidence and poise.

Networking Strategies to Support Wealth Growth:

- Join Industry-Specific Groups: Engage in professional associations, social media communities, or local business groups where like-minded individuals share ideas, experiences, and opportunities.

- Attend Events and Conferences: Regularly attend conferences, seminars, and workshops in your field to meet influential people and potential partners. Follow up after the events to solidify connections.
- Focus on Value Creation: Approach networking with a mindset of adding value to others' lives. Whether it's through sharing expertise or offering introductions, reciprocity often leads to long-term beneficial relationships.

By nurturing relationships through networking, individuals can open the door to career advancement, investment opportunities, and collaborative ventures that enhance wealth-building potential.

2. Mentorship: Learning from Those Who Have Succeeded

Mentorship is a key aspect of professional and financial growth. By seeking out mentors who have achieved the kind of success you aspire to, you can gain invaluable insights, guidance, and support that may take years to acquire on your own. A good mentor can help you avoid common pitfalls, accelerate your learning curve, and introduce you to opportunities you might not otherwise encounter.

The Role of Emotional Intelligence in Mentorship:

- Building Strong Mentor-Mentee Relationships: Emotional intelligence enables individuals to form deeper, more meaningful mentor-mentee relationships. It allows mentees to show vulnerability and ask for advice, while also appreciating the mentor's time and expertise.

- Receiving Constructive Feedback: EQ helps individuals receive feedback gracefully, without becoming defensive. This is critical in mentorship, as mentors often point out areas where mentees can improve. High EQ allows mentees to take feedback constructively and turn it into actionable growth strategies.
- Maintaining Long-Term Relationships: Strong mentor-mentee relationships often last for many years. Emotional intelligence helps sustain these relationships by fostering mutual respect, open communication, and understanding over the long term.

Mentorship Strategies to Support Wealth Growth:

- Seek Mentors in Various Areas of Wealth: Look for mentors who excel in different aspects of wealth creation—whether it's entrepreneurship, investing, real estate, or philanthropy. This diversified guidance can help you build a comprehensive wealth strategy.
- Be Open to Learning and Change: A key to benefiting from mentorship is being open to learning new approaches, adopting new mindsets, and being willing to change course when needed. Mentorship is most effective when mentees are adaptable.
- Give Back 10 percent of whatever you receive: As you grow in your career and wealth-building journey, give back by becoming a mentor yourself. Sharing your knowledge and helping others succeed builds stronger networks and enhances your own emotional intelligence through empathy and communication.

Mentorship provides a structured way to learn from those who have already traveled the path you're on, ensuring that your financial decisions are informed by experience and wisdom.

3. Collaborations: Pooling Resources and Ideas for Greater Wealth

Collaborations, whether in business, investments, or creative ventures, allow individuals to pool their resources, knowledge, and expertise to achieve shared goals. Partnerships and collaborations can lead to financial opportunities that would be difficult to achieve individually. They also help diversify skill sets and approaches, bringing new perspectives that fuel innovation and growth.

The Role of Emotional Intelligence in Collaborations:

- Managing Group Dynamics: High EQ helps individuals navigate complex group dynamics in collaborative settings. Being able to manage emotions, communicate effectively, and mediate conflicts are critical for successful collaboration.
- Mutual Respect and Cooperation: Emotional intelligence fosters an environment of mutual respect, where each person's contributions are valued. This is important in partnerships where differing opinions or work styles might otherwise cause friction.
- Flexibility and Compromise: Successful collaborations often require compromise. High EQ enables individuals to be flexible, finding middle ground and maintaining harmony without sacrificing the project's integrity or goals.

Collaboration Strategies to Support Wealth Growth:

- Form Strategic Partnerships: Collaborate with individuals or businesses that complement your strengths and fill gaps in your expertise. Strategic partnerships can lead to co-investments, joint ventures, or business opportunities that accelerate wealth accumulation.

- Share Knowledge and Expertise: Effective collaborations are built on the principle of reciprocity. Be willing to share your expertise and resources with others, and in return, you will benefit from their unique contributions.
- Use Collaborations to Scale: Whether it's in business, real estate, or investments, collaborations often enable participants to achieve greater scale than they could on their own. Pooling resources reduces individual risk and increases the potential for larger returns.

Through thoughtful collaborations, individuals can leverage collective strengths and resources to access opportunities that might otherwise be out of reach.

Emotional Intelligence as the Cornerstone of Wealth-Supporting Relationships:

At the core of building relationships that support wealth growth—whether through networking, mentorship, or collaborations—is emotional intelligence. EQ allows individuals to connect with others on a deeper level, navigate the complexities of interpersonal relationships, and build the trust and rapport necessary for sustained financial success. By cultivating emotional intelligence, individuals can enhance their ability to form and maintain relationships that open doors to new opportunities, foster personal growth, and contribute to long-term wealth creation. Ultimately, wealth-building is not just a solo journey but one that thrives on relationships grounded in trust, empathy, and mutual success.

Time Management and Productivity for Financial Growth

- How Effective Time Management Correlates with Financial Success

Effective time management is not merely a productivity tool; it is a fundamental skill that significantly impacts financial success. In today's fast-paced and competitive world, the ability to manage time effectively can lead to improved financial outcomes, whether for individuals, entrepreneurs, or organizations. This chapter explores the correlation between time management and financial success, illustrating how prioritizing time can enhance productivity and ultimately lead to greater wealth accumulation.

1. Optimizing Resource Allocation

Effective time management allows individuals and businesses to allocate their resources—time, money, and effort—more efficiently. This optimization leads to higher productivity and improved financial results.

- Prioritization of Tasks: By using techniques like the Eisenhower Matrix, individuals can distinguish between urgent and important tasks, ensuring that high-value activities are prioritized. This focus allows for efficient progress toward financial goals, such as saving, investing, and generating income.
- Increased Output: When time is managed well, individuals can accomplish more in less time. This increased output can translate into higher earnings, especially in roles that reward productivity or in entrepreneurial ventures where every moment spent directly affects profitability.
- Cost Savings: Efficient time management can reduce unnecessary costs. For instance,

businesses that optimize project timelines can lower labor costs and increase customer satisfaction by delivering services or products promptly.

2. Enhancing Decision-Making

Time management fosters a more structured approach to decision-making, which is crucial in financial contexts. Quick and hasty decisions can lead to financial mistakes, while effective time management allows for thorough analysis.

- ❖ Better Research and Analysis: Allocating specific time slots for researching investment opportunities or financial planning helps individuals make informed decisions. Properly analyzing options reduces the risk of costly mistakes and improves the potential for returns.
- ❖ Reflective Decision-Making: Time management provides space for reflection. Individuals who take the time to assess their financial decisions—whether it's purchasing a new asset, investing, or budgeting—can avoid emotional responses and focus on long-term impacts.

3. Goal Setting and Achievement

Effective time management is critical for setting and achieving financial goals. Clear goals act as a roadmap, and efficient time allocation ensures consistent progress toward those goals.

- ❖ SMART Goals: Utilizing the SMART (Specific, Measurable, Achievable, Relevant, Time-bound) framework for financial goal setting is enhanced through time management. Setting aside dedicated time to plan and track progress can significantly increase the likelihood of achieving these financial milestones.

- ❖ Routine and Consistency: By establishing routines for financial activities—such as budgeting, saving, and investing—individuals can build consistency, leading to better financial habits and outcomes. Regular reviews and adjustments in strategy contribute to long-term financial growth.

4. Maximizing Income Opportunities

Time management can directly affect the ability to capitalize on income-generating opportunities. Whether through side hustles, investments, or career advancement, how effectively time is utilized plays a crucial role.

- ❖ Side Hustles and Freelancing: For many, managing time effectively allows for the pursuit of additional income streams, such as freelance work or side businesses. By allocating time for these endeavors, individuals can diversify their income, leading to increased financial security.
- ❖ Networking and Professional Growth: Time management facilitates better networking opportunities, which can lead to career advancements and increased earnings. Individuals who schedule time for networking events, professional development, and relationship-building can open doors to new opportunities.

5. Reducing Financial Stress

Effective time management can alleviate financial stress, which can have detrimental effects on decision-making and overall financial health.

- Managing Financial Responsibilities: By organizing financial tasks—such as bill payments, budgeting, and tax preparation—individuals can reduce the chaos often associated with financial management. A well-structured approach allows for timely actions and prevents missed payments or late fees.
- Work-Life Balance: Time management fosters a better work-life balance, reducing stress levels and enhancing overall well-being. Individuals who balance work commitments with personal time are often more productive and make better financial decisions.

6. Leveraging Time for Investment Growth

Investing wisely requires time—both for research and for allowing investments to grow. Effective time management allows individuals to dedicate adequate resources to this critical area.

- Research and Due Diligence: Time must be allocated for researching investment opportunities, understanding market trends, and performing due diligence on potential investments. Effective time management ensures that investors can make educated choices that align with their financial goals.
- Patience and Long-Term Mindset: Investing is often a long-term endeavor. Individuals who manage their time well can cultivate patience, resisting the urge to react impulsively to market

fluctuations. This long-term mindset can lead to more favorable investment outcomes.

7. Creating Passive Income Streams

Time management can play a crucial role in creating and managing passive income streams, which are essential for long-term wealth accumulation.

- Time Investment in Asset Creation: Establishing passive income sources—such as rental properties, dividend stocks, or online businesses—requires an initial time investment. Effective time management allows individuals to research, plan, and set up these income-generating assets.
- Monitoring and Adjustment: Once passive income streams are established, ongoing time management is necessary to monitor performance and make adjustments. This proactive approach ensures that income sources remain profitable and aligned with broader financial goals.

8. Long-Term Wealth Building

Ultimately, effective time management contributes to long-term wealth building by instilling discipline, focus, and strategic thinking in financial endeavors.

- Legacy Planning: Individuals who manage their time effectively can dedicate effort to long-term planning, including estate planning and legacy considerations. This foresight ensures that wealth is preserved and passed down according to one's wishes.
- Continuous Improvement: Time management encourages continuous learning and

improvement in financial literacy. Individuals who allocate time for financial education—through reading, attending seminars, or seeking professional advice—are better equipped to navigate the complexities of wealth building.

Effective time management is integral to achieving financial success. By optimizing resource allocation, enhancing decision-making, maximizing income opportunities, and reducing financial stress, individuals can create a solid foundation for wealth accumulation. In a world where time is often seen as a limited resource, those who learn to manage it wisely position themselves for greater financial prosperity and long-term success. Developing strong time management skills is not only a pathway to increased productivity but also a vital strategy for achieving financial independence and building a secure future.

- Productivity Tools and Techniques to Maximize Wealth-Building Activities

In the pursuit of financial growth and wealth accumulation, time management and productivity are indispensable tools. The way individuals manage their time directly impacts their ability to build and sustain wealth. By integrating productivity tools and techniques, one can streamline decision-making, maximize output, and maintain a focused path toward financial goals. The efficiency gained from applying the right tools not only helps in wealth-building activities but also fosters a disciplined approach to personal and professional finances. Below are some of the key productivity tools and techniques that can be utilized to enhance wealth-building efforts.

1. Time-Blocking and Task Prioritization

- Time-blocking is a technique that involves allocating specific blocks of time to various tasks throughout the day. This structured approach ensures that crucial wealth-building activities, such as reviewing investments, budgeting, and financial planning, are given priority. By assigning dedicated time slots to these activities, distractions are minimized, and tasks are completed with greater focus and efficiency.
- Prioritization tools such as the Eisenhower Matrix can help categorize tasks into four quadrants:

  - Urgent and Important (tasks to focus on immediately),
  - Important but Not Urgent (long-term wealth-building activities),
  - Urgent but Not Important (tasks that can be delegated), and
  - Neither Urgent nor Important (tasks to eliminate).

This method helps individual's focus on activities that have the most significant impact on financial growth, allowing them to manage their time effectively and avoid the trap of "busywork."

2. Automation of Financial Processes

- Automating routine financial tasks is one of the most effective ways to improve productivity. Tools like automated bill payments, savings transfers, and investment contributions can reduce the need for manual intervention and ensure that wealth-building activities continue without interruption. Personal finance apps such as Mint, YNAB (You Need a Budget), and Personal Capital allow users to automate savings goals, monitor expenses, and track investments, freeing up time for more strategic financial planning.

- ❖ Automation also extends to investments, where robo-advisors such as Betterment and Wealthfront automate portfolio management, rebalancing, and tax-loss harvesting. These platforms use algorithms to manage portfolios based on individual financial goals and risk tolerance, ensuring that investment strategies are optimized without constant oversight.

3. Goal-Setting Tools for Financial Growth

- ❖ Setting clear financial goals is essential for wealth-building, and using goal-setting frameworks such as SMART goals (Specific, Measurable, Achievable, Relevant, and Time-bound) can enhance focus and productivity. Tools like **Trello**, **Asana**, or **Todoist** can help individuals break down long-term financial goals into smaller, manageable tasks and milestones. These platforms allow users to create financial to-do lists, set deadlines, and track progress over time.
- ❖ Through regularly reviewing and adjusting these goals, individuals can remain motivated and ensure they stay on track to meet their financial targets. Goal-setting platforms also offer reminders and updates, which help reinforce accountability and keep wealth-building activities at the forefront of daily routines.

4. Using Financial Dashboards to Track Wealth-Building Metrics

- ❖ Financial dashboards provide a centralized platform where individuals can view all their financial information in one place, from investments and debts to savings and net worth.

Dashboards like **Personal Capital** offer users the ability to track their financial progress, view investment allocations, and get insights into cash flow and portfolio performance.

- By having a clear visual representation of their finances, individuals can make informed decisions and quickly identify areas where they need to improve. Dashboards help streamline the process of managing multiple financial accounts, making wealth-building more efficient by reducing time spent gathering information and manually calculating numbers.

5. Mind Mapping and Brainstorming for Financial Strategy

- For individuals looking to develop new wealth-building strategies, mind mapping and brainstorming tools can help organize thoughts, ideas, and opportunities. Apps like **MindMeister** and **XMind** allow users to create visual maps that outline investment strategies, savings goals, and financial plans.
- By using mind maps, individuals can break down complex financial concepts and identify new investment opportunities, diversification strategies, and risk management plans. These tools help in seeing the bigger picture of one's financial goals and can serve as a starting point for developing more detailed and actionable financial strategies.

6. Pomodoro Technique for Focused Financial Planning

- The **Pomodoro Technique** is a time management method that breaks work into intervals (typically 25 minutes of focused work followed by a 5-minute break). This technique can be applied to wealth-building tasks like financial analysis, market research, or investment reviews, ensuring sustained concentration and minimizing burnout. The method also provides a sense of urgency and helps maintain momentum, which is crucial when navigating complex financial decisions.

- Apps like **Focus Booster** and **Pomodone** are designed to help users implement this technique, allowing individuals to maintain a productive pace while tackling essential wealth-building tasks.

7. Budgeting and Expense Management Tools

- Effective budgeting is critical for wealth-building, and personal finance apps offer streamlined solutions to manage expenses and savings. Apps like **YNAB**, **Mint**, and **EveryDollar** allow users to create detailed budgets, monitor spending patterns, and set aside money for future investments. These tools provide real-time data on cash flow, making it easier to identify areas where money can be saved or reallocated toward wealth-building goals.
- In automating expense tracking, users can avoid the time-consuming task of manually updating spreadsheets, which leaves more time for high-value financial activities like researching investments or exploring new business opportunities.

8. Learning Management Tools for Financial Education

- Continuous learning is vital for financial growth, and tools that facilitate self-education can significantly enhance one's wealth-building knowledge. Platforms like **Udemy**, **Coursera**, and **LinkedIn Learning** offer courses on personal finance, investing, and wealth management, helping individuals stay updated on the latest trends and techniques in finance.

- ❖ Through dedicating time to regular learning sessions and using these tools, individuals can sharpen their financial acumen, make better investment decisions, and explore new avenues for wealth creation.

9. Habit-Tracking Tools for Financial Discipline

- ❖ Building wealth requires consistent effort and discipline, which can be nurtured by tracking daily financial habits. Habit-tracking apps like **Habitica**, **HabitBull**, and **Streaks** allow users to monitor and reinforce good financial habits such as saving a fixed percentage of income, reviewing expenses, or contributing to investments regularly.
- ❖ Tracking these habits creates a sense of accountability and encourages users to stay committed to their wealth-building journey, ensuring long-term financial success.

In the fast-paced world of wealth creation, productivity is key to maximizing opportunities and achieving financial goals. By leveraging time-blocking, automation, goal-setting tools, financial dashboards, and continuous learning platforms, individuals can optimize their time and resources to build sustainable wealth. These productivity tools and techniques not only streamline financial management but also foster a disciplined and focused approach to long-term wealth-building activities.

- Creating Systems for Balancing Work, Investing, and Personal Growth

In today's fast-paced world, achieving financial growth while maintaining personal development and professional responsibilities can be a daunting challenge. To navigate this complexity, individuals must establish effective systems that allow for a balanced approach to work, investing, and personal growth. This chapter outlines strategies for creating such systems, emphasizing time management and productivity techniques that support financial success and holistic personal development.

1. Establishing a Vision and Core Values

The first step in creating a balanced system is to articulate a clear vision that aligns with your core values. This vision should encompass your professional ambitions, financial goals, and personal development aspirations.

- Vision Statement: Write a vision statement that outlines your long-term goals in each area—work, investing, and personal growth. For example, "I aim to advance in my career while building a sustainable investment portfolio and dedicating time to lifelong learning."
- Core Values Identification: Identify values that matter most to you, such as integrity, growth, family, and financial security. These values will guide decision-making and prioritization across all areas of life.

2. Time Auditing and Prioritization

Understanding how time is currently allocated is critical for effective management. Conducting a time audit will reveal areas where adjustments can be made for better balance.

- Time Tracking: Use tools like Toggl or Clockify to track daily activities for a week. Categorize tasks into work, investing, and personal growth to visualize time spent in each area.

- Prioritization Matrix: Employ the Eisenhower Matrix to prioritize tasks based on urgency and importance. This helps distinguish between what is essential and what can be delegated or eliminated.

3. Creating a Structured Weekly Schedule

Developing a structured weekly schedule is crucial for maintaining balance among work, investing, and personal growth.

- Block Scheduling: Allocate specific blocks of time each week for focused work, investment activities, and personal development. For example, reserve mornings for high-priority work tasks, afternoons for investment research, and evenings for personal learning or family time.
- Flexible Time Blocks: Incorporate flexibility within your schedule to adapt to unforeseen events or shifts in priorities. This adaptability can help maintain balance without feeling overwhelmed.

4. Integrating Work and Personal Growth

Finding synergies between work responsibilities and personal development can optimize time and effort.

- Professional Development: Seek opportunities for learning and growth within your job. This might include pursuing certifications, attending workshops, or participating in mentorship programs that align with both your career and personal growth goals.
- Skill Development for Investing: Engage in activities that enhance skills beneficial for both your job and investing, such as financial analysis or negotiation tactics. Online courses, webinars, or

reading relevant books can be effective ways to integrate learning.

5. Investment Systems and Routines

Establishing systems for investment activities can streamline the process, making it easier to fit investing into a busy schedule.

- Regular Investment Reviews: Schedule bi-weekly or monthly investment reviews to assess portfolio performance and research new opportunities. This routine helps maintain focus on financial goals and ensures timely decision-making.
- Automation: Automate investment contributions through direct deposit or automatic transfers to investment accounts. This reduces the need for manual intervention and ensures consistent contributions to your financial growth.

6. Leveraging Technology for Productivity

Utilizing technology can enhance efficiency and organization in balancing work, investing, and personal growth.

- Task Management Apps: Use apps like Asana, Todoist, or Trello to manage tasks related to work, investments, and personal development. These tools help prioritize tasks, set deadlines, and track progress.
- Calendar Tools: Employ digital calendars like Google Calendar to integrate work meetings, investment activities, and personal commitments. Color-code different areas for visual clarity and better time management.

7. Building a Support System

Creating a support system can provide accountability and encouragement in achieving balance across various life aspects.

- Networking and Peer Groups: Engage with professional networks or peer groups focused on personal finance, investing, and personal growth. Sharing experiences and strategies can enhance motivation and offer new insights.
- Accountability Partners: Find accountability partner with similar goals, whether it's a colleague, friend, or mentor. Regular check-ins can help keep both parties on track and motivated.

8. Maintaining Mental and Physical Well-Being

Balancing work, investing, and personal growth requires attention to mental and physical health. Integrating well-being practices into daily routines can improve overall productivity.

- Mindfulness Practices: Incorporate mindfulness practices such as meditation, journaling, or deep breathing exercises. These techniques enhance focus and reduce stress, supporting better decision-making in all areas of life.
- Physical Activity: Schedule regular exercise into your routine to maintain physical health and improve mental clarity. Exercise can also serve as a productive break, helping to refresh your mind before returning to work or investment tasks.

9. Regular Reflection and Adjustment

Establishing a regular review process to reflect on your progress in balancing work, investing, and personal growth is crucial.

- Monthly Reflection Sessions: Dedicate time each month to assess what worked well and where adjustments are needed. Reflect on achievements in each area and identify challenges that may require changes in your approach.
- Goal Reassessment: As life circumstances change, it's important to reassess your goals and adjust your systems accordingly. Flexibility is the key to maintaining balance and achieving long-term success.

Creating effective systems for balancing work, investing, and personal growth is essential for sustainable financial growth and overall well-being. By establishing a clear vision, prioritizing tasks, utilizing technology, building support systems, and maintaining a focus on health, individuals can optimize their time management and productivity. This holistic approach not only facilitates financial success but also enriches personal development, leading to a fulfilling and balanced life.

Continuous Learning: The Wealth of Knowledge

- The Importance of Lifelong Learning in Achieving and Sustaining Wealth

In an ever-evolving economic landscape, the pursuit of wealth requires more than just traditional financial strategies; it necessitates a commitment to lifelong learning. This chapter delves into the critical role of continuous learning in wealth creation and preservation, emphasizing that knowledge not only enhances financial literacy but also equips individuals with the skills necessary to adapt and thrive in a dynamic world.

1. Understanding Lifelong Learning

Lifelong learning refers to the ongoing, voluntary, and self-motivated pursuit of knowledge for personal or professional development. It encompasses various forms of learning, including formal education, online courses, workshops, self-study, and experiential learning. By embracing a mindset of continuous improvement, individuals can foster the skills and knowledge necessary to navigate the complexities of wealth management.

2. Adapting to Changing Economic Environments

The global economy is marked by rapid changes driven by technological advancements, market fluctuations, and shifting consumer behaviors. Lifelong learning enables individuals to stay informed about these changes and adjust their financial strategies accordingly.

- Market Awareness: Understanding market trends, economic indicators, and financial products allows investors to make informed decisions. Continuous learning helps individuals stay updated on the latest investment opportunities and threats.
- Skill Adaptation: As industries evolve, the skills required to succeed in the workforce also change. Lifelong learning encourages individuals to acquire new skills or enhance existing ones, making them more adaptable to shifts in job demands and market needs.

3. Enhancing Financial Literacy

Financial literacy is a cornerstone of wealth creation and management. Lifelong learning enhances financial literacy by providing individuals with the tools and knowledge necessary to understand complex financial concepts.

- ❖ Investment Knowledge: By engaging in continuous learning, individuals can deepen their understanding of various investment vehicles, such as stocks, bonds, real estate, and alternative investments. This knowledge allows for more strategic and informed investment decisions.
- ❖ Debt Management: Understanding the principles of debt, credit, and interest rates is crucial for effective financial management. Continuous education in personal finance empowers individuals to manage debt wisely and avoid costly financial pitfalls.

4. Fostering Innovation and Creativity

Wealth creation often relies on innovative thinking and problem-solving skills. Lifelong learning nurtures creativity, enabling individuals to explore new ideas and approaches to wealth generation.

- ❖ Entrepreneurship: For those looking to start their own businesses, continuous learning can provide insights into market gaps, consumer needs, and effective business strategies. This knowledge can help aspiring entrepreneurs develop viable business models and achieve financial success.
- ❖ Investing in New Ventures: Lifelong learners are often more open to exploring emerging industries and investment opportunities, such as technology startups, green energy, and sustainable businesses. This adaptability can lead to profitable investments in high-growth areas.

5. Networking and Building Relationships

Continuous learning often involves collaboration with others, fostering networking opportunities that can enhance wealth-building efforts.

- Professional Connections: Engaging in workshops, seminars, and industry conferences allows individuals to connect with like-minded professionals, mentors, and potential collaborators. These connections can lead to new business opportunities, partnerships, and valuable insights.
- Community Engagement: Learning within community settings can provide access to local resources, investment groups, and support networks. Being part of a learning community enhances one's understanding of regional economic trends and opportunities.

6. Improving Decision-Making Skills

Effective wealth management hinges on the ability to make sound financial decisions. Lifelong learning cultivates critical thinking and decision-making skills.

- Data Analysis: Understanding how to analyze financial data and assess risk is essential for making informed investment choices. Continuous education in data literacy equips individuals with the skills to interpret financial information effectively.
- Evaluating Opportunities: Learning how to evaluate investment opportunities critically allows individuals to discern between sound investments and high-risk ventures. This skill is vital in protecting and growing wealth over time.

7. Cultivating a Growth Mindset

A commitment to lifelong learning fosters a growth mindset, characterized by resilience, adaptability, and a willingness to embrace challenges.

- ❖ Overcoming Setbacks: Wealth building is often fraught with setbacks and failures. A growth mindset encourages individuals to view challenges as opportunities for learning and improvement, ultimately leading to greater resilience in financial pursuits.
- ❖ Continuous Improvement: Embracing a mindset of lifelong learning instills the belief that skills and intelligence can be developed over time. This attitude promotes ongoing personal and professional development, leading to sustained wealth accumulation.

The Wealth of Knowledge

The importance of lifelong learning in achieving and sustaining wealth cannot be overstated. By actively engaging in continuous education, individuals equip themselves with the knowledge and skills necessary to navigate the complexities of the financial landscape. From enhancing financial literacy and fostering innovation to improving decision-making and building valuable networks, lifelong learning is a powerful tool in the journey toward financial success.

To cultivate a mindset of continuous learning, individuals should seek out opportunities for education, remain open to new experiences, and commit to personal growth. By doing so, they not only enhance their own wealth potential but also contribute to a more informed and financially resilient society.

- How to Invest in Self-Education: Books, Courses, Mentors, and Seminars

In an increasingly competitive world, the pursuit of knowledge is one of the most valuable investments individuals can make. Self-education empowers you to adapt to changing environments, enhance your skills, and ultimately build wealth. This chapter explores the various avenues through which you can invest in self-education, highlighting the significance of books, courses, mentors, and seminars in fostering continuous learning.

1. Books: The Foundation of Knowledge

Books have long been a primary source of information and inspiration. Investing in books provides a wealth of knowledge across various subjects, from finance and investing to personal development and entrepreneurship.

- Choose Relevant Titles: Start by identifying books that align with your personal and professional goals. Consider genres like personal finance, investment strategies, leadership, and productivity. Classics like "Rich Dad Poor Dad" by Robert Kiyosaki or "The Intelligent Investor" by Benjamin Graham can provide foundational insights into wealth-building principles.
- Create a Reading List: Develop a structured reading list that prioritizes the most impactful books. Aim to read a mix of genres, including biographies of successful individuals, to gain insights into different paths to success.
- Utilize Book Summaries: If time is a constraint, consider platforms that offer book summaries. These can provide condensed insights from a wide array of books, enabling you to quickly absorb essential concepts.

2. Online Courses: Structured Learning Opportunities

The digital age has made online education more accessible than ever. Online courses offer structured learning environments where you can gain specific skills or knowledge at your own pace.

- Identify Learning Platforms: Explore platforms such as Coursera, Udemy, and Khan Academy, which offer courses on diverse topics, including finance, coding, marketing, and entrepreneurship. Many of these courses are taught by industry experts and can provide valuable certifications.
- Focus on Practical Skills: When selecting courses, look for those that emphasize practical skills and real-world applications. For instance, courses on financial modeling, investment analysis, or negotiation techniques can directly enhance your ability to create and manage wealth.
- Join Learning Communities: Many online courses include access to discussion forums or community groups. Engaging with fellow learners can enhance your understanding, provide networking opportunities, and foster collaboration.

3. Mentorship: Learning from Experience

Mentorship is a powerful tool for personal and professional growth. A mentor can provide guidance, share valuable experiences, and help you navigate the complexities of wealth-building.

- Identify Potential Mentors: Look for individuals who have achieved the goals you aspire to reach. This could be in your industry, community, or even through professional networks. LinkedIn and local business associations can be great resources for identifying potential mentors.

- ❖ Build Relationships: Approach potential mentors with a clear purpose and be respectful of their time. Establish a genuine relationship by expressing your admiration for their work and sharing your goals. A mentor-mentee relationship is mutually beneficial and requires commitment from both parties.
- ❖ Ask for Guidance: Once you have established a mentorship relationship, don't hesitate to ask for guidance. Discuss specific challenges you face, seek advice on strategic decisions, and inquire about resources they recommend for further learning.

4. Seminars and Workshops: Engaging Learning Experiences

Participating in seminars and workshops offers immersive learning experiences that can deepen your understanding of specific topics while allowing you to connect with other learners.

- ❖ Research Relevant Events: Look for seminars, webinars, and workshops related to your areas of interest. Many financial institutions, universities, and industry organizations host events that feature expert speakers and interactive sessions.
- ❖ Network with Attendees: Use seminars as an opportunity to network with other attendees. Building relationships during these events can lead to collaborations, partnerships, and valuable connections that may enhance your financial journey.

- ❖ Engage Actively: Actively participate in discussions and Q&A sessions during seminars. Engaging with speakers and fellow participants can lead to a richer learning experience and help clarify complex concepts.

5. Combining Learning Modalities

A comprehensive self-education strategy often involves combining multiple learning modalities to maximize your knowledge acquisition.

- ❖ Develop a Personal Learning Plan: Create a learning plan that incorporates books, online courses, mentorship, and seminars. Set specific learning goals for each modality, such as reading a certain number of books each month or completing one online course per quarter.
- ❖ Track Your Progress: Use tools like journals or digital platforms to track your learning journey. Document key takeaways, insights, and reflections from each learning experience. This practice reinforces your learning and allows for easier recall in the future.
- ❖ Stay Adaptable: Be open to exploring new learning avenues as your interests and needs evolve. Continuous learning is not static; it requires adaptability to seize new opportunities and insights.

6. The ROI of Self-Education

Investing in self-education has a measurable return on investment (ROI). Enhanced knowledge leads to better decision-making, improved skills, and increased earning potential.

- ❖ Enhanced Career Opportunities: By expanding your skill set and knowledge base, you position yourself for promotions, salary increases, and new job opportunities. Employers often value candidates who demonstrate a commitment to continuous learning.
- ❖ Informed Financial Decisions: Self-education equips you to make informed decisions regarding investments, budgeting, and financial planning. This knowledge can lead to increased wealth accumulation over time.
- ❖ Long-Term Growth: Continuous learning is an investment in your long-term growth. The skills and knowledge acquired will benefit you throughout your career, enabling you to adapt to changing circumstances and seize emerging opportunities.

7. Leveraging Technology for Self-Education

In today's digital age, technology plays a crucial role in enhancing self-education. Leveraging online tools and resources can help streamline your learning process and expand your access to valuable information.

- ❖ Online Learning Platforms: Utilize platforms such as LinkedIn Learning, Skillshare, and MasterClass, which offer a wide range of courses taught by industry experts. These platforms often provide interactive elements, allowing you to engage with course materials more effectively.
- ❖ Podcasts and Webinars: Subscribe to podcasts and webinars that focus on financial literacy, investing, and wealth-building. These formats allow you to consume information on the go and often feature interviews with experts who share their insights and experiences.

- ❖ YouTube and Educational Channels: YouTube hosts a plethora of educational channels that cover various topics, including finance, entrepreneurship, and personal development. Channels like Graham Stephan's and The Financial Diet provide valuable tips and strategies for wealth management.

8. Creating a Learning Community

Building a community of like-minded individuals can significantly enhance your self-education efforts. Learning from peers can offer different perspectives and foster collaborative growth.

- ❖ Join Local or Online Groups: Look for local meet-ups, online forums, or social media groups focused on financial literacy and wealth-building. Engaging with others allows you to share knowledge, ask questions, and gain support in your learning journey.
- ❖ Participate in Book Clubs: Consider joining or forming a book club that focuses on personal finance or business-related literature. Discussing books with others can deepen your understanding and introduce you to new ideas.
- ❖ Accountability Partners: Partner with a friend or colleague who shares similar financial goals. Regular check-ins can keep both of you motivated, accountable, and focused on your self-education objectives.

9. The Role of Mindset in Self-Education

Your mindset can significantly influence your approach to self-education and wealth-building. Adopting a growth mindset allows you to embrace challenges and view failures as opportunities for learning.

- Cultivating Curiosity: Stay curious about new topics and developments in the financial world. A willingness to learn will drive you to seek out new knowledge and skills continuously.
- Embracing Challenges: Rather than shying away from complex subjects, approach them with an open mind. Breaking down difficult concepts into manageable parts can help you gain clarity and understanding.
- Practicing Self-Compassion: Understand that learning is a process that includes setbacks. Be kind to yourself during moments of frustration and recognize that persistence is key to mastery.

10. Evaluating the Effectiveness of Your Learning

To ensure that your investment in self-education yields the desired outcomes, regularly assess the effectiveness of your learning strategies.

- Set Clear Goals: Define specific, measurable, attainable, relevant, and time-bound (SMART) goals for your self-education. Whether it's completing a course or reading a set number of books, having clear objectives will keep you focused.
- Reflect on Learning Outcomes: Periodically review what you have learned and how you have applied it to your financial decisions. Reflecting on your progress helps reinforce knowledge and highlights areas for further improvement.
- Solicit Feedback: Engage with mentors, peers, or course instructors to gain feedback on your understanding and application of the material. Constructive criticism can help you identify blind spots and refine your learning approach.

11. Integrating Self-Education into Your Daily Routine

Consistency is the key when it comes to self-education. Integrating learning into your daily routine can help you maintain momentum and stay committed to your goals.

- ❖ Dedicate Time for Learning: Set aside specific time blocks in your calendar for reading, taking courses, or engaging with mentors. Treat this time as an essential appointment that cannot be overlooked.
- ❖ Utilize Micro-Learning: Incorporate micro-learning techniques by dedicating short bursts of time to learning throughout your day. For example, listen to a podcast during your commute or read an article during your lunch break.
- ❖ Create a Learning Environment: Surround yourself with resources that inspire learning. Designate a quiet space in your home for reading and studying, filled with books, educational materials, and motivational quotes.

The Lifelong Journey of Self-Education

Investing in self-education is a continuous journey that requires dedication, curiosity, and adaptability. By leveraging resources such as books, courses, mentors, and technology, you can build a robust knowledge base that enhances your ability to create and manage wealth.

Remember that the journey of self-education is not solely about accumulating knowledge but also about applying that knowledge to make informed decisions that align with your financial goals. Embrace the wealth of knowledge available to you, actively seek opportunities for growth, and foster a mindset of lifelong learning.

CHAPTER NINE

WEALTH AND HEALTH: ACHIEVING TRUE ABUNDANCE

This chapter explores the connection between physical and financial health, highlighting the importance of holistic well-being in achieving true abundance.

The Relationship Between Health and Wealth

- How physical health directly impacts financial success

The relationship between physical health and financial success is profound and multidimensional. Good health provides the energy, mental clarity, and resilience necessary for pursuing and maintaining financial goals, while poor health can lead to significant financial setbacks due to medical costs, decreased productivity, and long-term disability. In this context, understanding how physical well-being affects financial outcomes is critical for those seeking to build and preserve wealth. Below is a detailed exploration of how physical health directly impacts financial success.

1. Productivity and Earnings Potential

Physical health is directly tied to one's productivity and capacity to earn. A healthy body allows for higher levels of energy, mental acuity, and stamina, which are essential for achieving professional success, managing a business, or optimizing investment strategies.

- ❖ Improved Focus and Efficiency: Individuals in good physical condition tend to experience higher cognitive function, enabling them to focus better, make quicker decisions, and solve problems more effectively. This often translates into better job performance, increased creativity, and enhanced decision-making abilities, which can lead to promotions, raises, and better business outcomes.

- Reduced Absenteeism: Good health decreases the likelihood of taking time off work due to illness or injury. Chronic health issues can cause frequent absences, reducing career advancement opportunities and leading to loss of income. Maintaining health allows individuals to be consistent in their professional and entrepreneurial efforts.
- Work Longevity: A healthy lifestyle can extend an individual's working life. People who take care of their physical health are likely to experience fewer debilitating health conditions as they age, allowing them to stay in the workforce longer if they choose, thereby extending their income-earning years.

2. Lower Healthcare Costs

One of the most direct links between physical health and financial success is the significant cost savings associated with reduced healthcare expenses. Chronic health conditions, hospitalizations, and regular medical care can quickly deplete savings and reduce disposable income.

- Preventive Healthcare and Savings: Individuals who prioritize exercise, nutrition, and regular preventive health check-ups are more likely to avoid expensive treatments for lifestyle-related diseases like diabetes, heart disease, and obesity. The financial benefits of maintaining good health can accumulate over time as fewer funds are spent on medications, surgeries, and long-term care.
- Impact of Medical Debt: Unanticipated medical expenses are a leading cause of personal

bankruptcy in many countries. Even with insurance, the out-of-pocket costs associated with significant health issues can lead to financial strain. By maintaining good health, individuals can reduce the likelihood of facing substantial medical debt and the associated financial stress.

3. Reduced Insurance Premiums

Maintaining physical health can also lead to lower insurance premiums, particularly for life, health, and disability insurance policies. Insurance providers assess risk based on the individual's health profile, including factors such as weight, smoking habits, and pre-existing conditions. Healthier individuals are seen as lower-risk, resulting in more affordable coverage options.

- ❖ Life Insurance: Healthier individuals often qualify for lower life insurance premiums, enabling them to protect their families and wealth at a reduced cost. Conversely, those with significant health issues may face higher premiums or be denied coverage altogether.
- ❖ Health Insurance: Many health insurance plans offer incentives for individuals who lead healthy lifestyles, such as discounted premiums for non-smokers, those with low body mass indexes (BMI), or individuals who participate in wellness programs. This can lead to substantial long-term savings on healthcare costs.

4. Energy and Resilience for Wealth Building

Wealth creation requires sustained energy, focus, and resilience, all of which are supported by physical health. Entrepreneurs, investors, and professionals need both physical and mental stamina to navigate the challenges associated with growing wealth.

- ❖ Stamina for Entrepreneurship: Building a business or pursuing long-term financial goals often involves long hours and high levels of stress. A physically healthy person is more likely to have the endurance to manage the demands of entrepreneurship, from handling complex negotiations to making strategic decisions under pressure.
- ❖ Stress Management: Physical activity and a healthy diet can significantly improve an individual's ability to manage stress. This is critical when navigating volatile markets, making high-stakes decisions, or facing unexpected financial challenges. By reducing stress, individuals are better equipped to stay calm, focused, and rational in their financial endeavors.

5. Mental Health and Financial Decision-Making

There is a close relationship between physical and mental health, and mental clarity is essential for making sound financial decisions. Poor physical health often contributes to mental fatigue, stress, anxiety, and depression, which can cloud judgment and lead to poor financial choices.

- ❖ Clear Decision-Making: Physical health supports mental well-being, enhancing an individual's ability to think critically, plan long-term, and make decisions that align with their financial goals. For example, individuals suffering from stress or exhaustion may make impulsive financial decisions, such as panic selling during market downturns, which can erode wealth.

- ❖ Improved Willpower and Discipline: Physical health routines often cultivate self-discipline and willpower—traits that are also essential for managing finances. Regular exercise, for example, fosters a sense of discipline that can translate into consistent saving, responsible spending, and long-term investing.

6. The Cost of Unhealthy Lifestyles on Wealth

While maintaining physical health can lead to financial success, neglecting it can have the opposite effect, draining wealth and diminishing future earning potential.

- ❖ Chronic Diseases and Financial Drain: Many chronic diseases, such as hypertension, obesity, and diabetes, are linked to poor lifestyle choices and can result in significant financial strain. In addition to the direct medical costs, these conditions can limit one's ability to work or lead to early retirement, reducing lifetime earnings.
- ❖ Disability and Income Loss: Unaddressed health issues can result in temporary or permanent disability, severely limiting an individual's capacity to earn. In the event of a major illness or injury, individuals may have to rely on savings or insurance payouts, which may not be enough to cover living expenses in the long term.

7. Increased Wealth Accumulation through Healthy Lifestyle Choices

Good physical health can create financial opportunities that extend beyond the avoidance of costs. Healthy individuals often accumulate wealth faster due to their ability to consistently work, manage stress, and seize opportunities.

- ❖ Consistent Financial Habits: Those who maintain their health are more likely to engage in consistent financial practices such as regularly contributing to savings and investment accounts, avoiding debt, and creating long-term financial plans.
- ❖ Ability to Take Calculated Risks: Healthier individuals tend to have the confidence and resilience to take calculated risks, whether in their careers, investments, or business ventures. These risks, when managed well, can lead to significant financial rewards.

8. Holistic Wealth and Health Approach

The interconnection between health and wealth underscores the importance of a holistic approach to personal success. Prioritizing health leads to more productive years, higher earning potential, and reduced financial strain from medical costs. In turn, financial success can provide access to resources that further support a healthy lifestyle, such as quality healthcare, nutritious food, and time for exercise and rest.

- ❖ Investing in Health for Wealth: Viewing health as an investment in future financial success can help individuals prioritize healthy habits, such as regular exercise, balanced diets, and stress management techniques. These habits, though sometimes requiring upfront time and effort, pay dividends in the form of increased financial stability and success over time.

9. Health as an Investment: The ROI of Wellness

Treating physical health as an investment, rather than an afterthought, can yield significant returns—both financially and in terms of quality of life. A proactive approach to health, similar to financial planning, ensures that future expenses related to health issues are minimized while maximizing productivity and personal well-being.

- Proactive vs. Reactive Health Management: Investing in preventive care, such as regular health screenings, exercise, and a balanced diet, is analogous to diversifying an investment portfolio. Just as diversification reduces financial risk, preventive health measures lower the risk of chronic diseases, which can be financially draining in the long run. The ROI from good health practices manifests in the form of reduced medical bills, lower insurance premiums, and fewer workdays lost to illness.
- Longevity and Healthspan: A longer, healthier life can significantly impact financial goals. Individuals in good health are able to work longer if they choose, maintain cognitive function well into old age, and continue to grow wealth later in life. Additionally, a healthy lifestyle increases the “healthspan,” or the years one can live without significant physical limitations, which directly correlates to the ability to manage finances and investments without needing to rely on others.

10. Wealth of Time: How Health Extends Your Financial Horizon

Good physical health doesn't just impact immediate financial success; it also extends an individual's long-term financial horizon, providing more time to achieve, sustain, and enjoy wealth.

- The Compounding Effect: Health amplifies the compounding effect, a powerful principle in finance. The longer you remain healthy, the more time your investments have to grow and compound. Whether it's a retirement account or a business venture, the more time you have to invest and manage your assets, the more wealth you can accumulate.
- Delayed Retirement: Healthy individuals often have the option to delay retirement or even engage in part-time work, consulting, or entrepreneurship well into their 60s and 70s. This extended career horizon can provide additional income and allow investments to continue compounding for a longer period, resulting in a more financially secure retirement.

11. Healthcare as a Key Component of Retirement Planning

A major aspect of retirement planning involves preparing for healthcare costs, which can be unpredictable and burdensome without careful consideration. Physical health plays a direct role in reducing the financial load associated with these future healthcare expenses.

- Minimizing Healthcare Expenditure in Retirement: Medical expenses are often one of the largest costs for retirees. Those in poor health are more likely to face frequent doctor visits, medications, surgeries, and even long-term care, which can drain savings. Healthy individuals, by contrast, are better positioned to use their retirement funds for desired activities, such as travel, hobbies, and investments, rather than medical bills.

- ❖ Longevity Planning: For those pursuing financial independence or planning for early retirement, good health allows for more accurate longevity planning. Healthy retirees can budget for an active, fulfilling lifestyle, confident that they won't need to set aside an excessive portion of their wealth for unforeseen medical costs.
- ❖ Long-Term Care Insurance: Individuals who maintain their health can either avoid or reduce the need for expensive long-term care insurance. Those in poor health are more likely to require assistance with daily living as they age, a cost that can quickly deplete financial resources.

12. Stress Management and Its Impact on Financial Decisions

Chronic stress, often linked to poor physical health, can cloud financial judgment, leading to impulsive or poorly thought-out decisions. By managing physical health, individuals can reduce stress and improve their ability to make rational financial choices.

- ❖ Reducing Decision Fatigue: Good physical health, combined with effective stress management, supports clear thinking and sustained energy levels, reducing the likelihood of decision fatigue. Decision fatigue can cause individuals to make shortcuts in their financial planning or to avoid critical tasks such as rebalancing their portfolios or reviewing financial goals. Healthier individuals are more likely to stay disciplined and focused on long-term objectives.

- Resilience in Financial Setbacks: Stress management techniques—like regular exercise, meditation, and proper sleep—help build emotional resilience. This resilience is critical when navigating financial setbacks, such as market downturns, business challenges, or personal financial crises. Healthy individuals are better equipped to maintain a long-term perspective, remain calm under pressure, and make logical decisions during turbulent times.

13. Work-Life Balance and the Role of Health in Sustaining Financial Success

Achieving financial success often requires balancing work with personal well-being. Physical health is essential for sustaining this balance, as it prevents burnout and ensures that individuals can continue to operate at their best over the long term.

- Preventing Burnout: Those who prioritize physical health through regular exercise, adequate sleep, and proper nutrition are better able to maintain high levels of productivity without risking burnout. This is especially important for entrepreneurs and high-level professionals whose financial success relies on sustained effort and long-term focus.
- Maintaining Financial Motivation: Health plays a key role in maintaining the motivation to achieve and sustain financial success. When individuals feel energized and physically well,

they are more likely to remain driven to pursue their financial goals, whether that means growing a business, advancing in a career, or building an investment portfolio.

14. Health as a Family Wealth Strategy

Health is not only personal; it can also be part of a broader family wealth strategy. Good health habits passed on to family members can contribute to their financial success, as well as reduce financial burdens related to caring for ill relatives.

- ❖ Transferring Healthy Habits: Teaching children and other family members the importance of physical health instills habits that will benefit them throughout their lives. Healthier family members are more likely to succeed academically and professionally, make better financial decisions, and contribute to building generational wealth.
- ❖ Reduced Caregiving Burden: Poor health in family members can result in a significant financial and emotional burden. By promoting a healthy lifestyle within the family, you not only improve your own financial success but also help ensure that your loved ones do not require costly long-term care or medical interventions in the future.

15. Health, Wealth, and Legacy Planning

Planning a financial legacy is about more than just accumulating wealth—it's about ensuring the well-being of future generations. Physical health is a critical factor in legacy planning, as it influences the ability to manage and grow wealth over time.

- Managing Wealth for the Long Term: Healthy individuals are better able to manage their estate and make long-term financial decisions that align with their legacy goals. Whether it's managing trusts, mentoring the next generation, or overseeing charitable giving, maintaining good health ensures that individuals remain capable of executing their plans.
- Living a Legacy, Not Just Leaving One: Good health allows individuals to actively participate in the management of their wealth and guide their heirs in financial stewardship. A healthy lifestyle enables individuals to enjoy the wealth they've built, actively contribute to their community, and witness the impact of their financial legacy.

The Synergy Between Health and Wealth

Physical health is an integral part of financial success. A healthy body and mind enable individuals to maximize productivity, reduce costs, maintain resilience, and make sound financial decisions. By investing in health through preventive care, stress management, and a balanced lifestyle, individuals can protect their wealth, extend their working years, and enjoy a higher quality of life.

In turn, financial success provides the resources needed to maintain good health—whether through access to quality healthcare, time for physical activity, or the ability to invest in healthy food and lifestyle choices. This synergy between health and wealth underscores the importance of a holistic approach to life, where physical well-being and financial prosperity reinforce and sustain each other. By recognizing and acting on this connection, individuals can create a sustainable path to long-term success in both health and wealth.

- The Cost of Poor Health on Wealth-Building Potential

The connection between health and wealth is often underestimated, but the impact of poor health on an individual's ability to accumulate wealth is profound. As health deteriorates, the costs associated with medical care, lost productivity, and reduced earning potential can significantly hinder one's financial trajectory. In a broader context, maintaining good health is not just a personal responsibility but an integral part of wealth-building and financial success.

1. Direct Financial Impact of Healthcare Costs

- ❖ Poor health leads to substantial direct financial costs, which can derail wealth-building plans. Medical expenses, particularly for chronic diseases, are one of the leading causes of financial instability. In many cases, prolonged illnesses can result in high out-of-pocket expenses that deplete savings and force individuals to rely on loans or credit, accumulating debt that hinders wealth accumulation.
- ❖ Health issues such as heart disease, diabetes, and obesity often require long-term treatment and medication, driving up costs. Insurance coverage may mitigate some of these expenses, but high deductibles, co-pays, and non-covered treatments still place a financial burden on individuals. In the U.S., for example, medical expenses are a leading cause of bankruptcy, with people losing not only their savings but also their homes and assets.
- ❖ In terms of wealth-building potential, these expenses reduce the amount of money that could otherwise be invested, saved, or used to create other income streams. Individuals who suffer from poor health are less likely to build robust

investment portfolios or achieve significant financial milestones because their resources are funneled toward maintaining their health.

2. Reduced Earning Potential

- Another significant cost of poor health is its impact on earning potential. Health problems can limit an individual's ability to work, either by reducing their working hours or forcing them to take time off for treatment and recovery. This translates into lost wages, missed career opportunities, and in severe cases, permanent disability that takes individuals out of the workforce altogether.
- When individuals experience chronic illness or poor health, their productivity declines, which can affect promotions, bonuses, and job stability. This diminished earning capacity over time compounds the problem, creating a vicious cycle where health challenges reduce income, and the lack of income worsens access to quality healthcare and healthy living conditions.
- For entrepreneurs or business owners, poor health can be catastrophic. Running a business often requires long hours, physical and mental stamina, and the ability to manage stress. If health deteriorates, it can disrupt business operations, lead to losses, and force closures, particularly if the business is heavily dependent on the owner.

3. Loss of Productivity and Financial Opportunity

- Even in cases where poor health does not lead to direct financial hardship, it still undermines wealth-building by reducing productivity. Health issues such as fatigue, pain, or mental health challenges like stress and anxiety can reduce one's ability to focus, make decisions, and seize financial opportunities.

- ❖ Individuals dealing with poor health are more likely to delay important financial decisions, miss opportunities to invest or grow their business, and struggle to manage personal and professional financial responsibilities. This decreased productivity results in missed chances to build wealth, particularly in competitive industries where efficiency and quick decision-making are crucial.
- ❖ On the other hand, those who maintain good physical and mental health are better positioned to take advantage of opportunities, whether it's a new job, investment prospects, or entrepreneurial ventures. Their ability to stay sharp, manage stress, and maintain focus allows them to make timely and informed financial decisions that contribute to long-term wealth.

4. The Long-Term Impact of Health on Retirement Wealth

- ❖ Poor health in the later stages of life has an outsized impact on wealth-building, particularly when it comes to retirement planning. Health-related expenses tend to increase with age, and those who haven't maintained good health throughout their lives face higher medical costs in retirement, reducing the savings they can rely on for leisure, travel, or other life goals.
- ❖ For individuals who suffer from poor health early on, their ability to build a sufficient retirement fund is already compromised due to the financial strain experienced during their working years. Furthermore, if poor health forces early retirement, individuals lose crucial years of income that could have gone toward increasing their savings, pension, or retirement investments. In addition, they may need to start drawing from retirement

accounts earlier than expected, depleting these funds more quickly and leading to a less secure retirement.
- ❖ In contrast, individuals who prioritize health throughout their lives are not only able to work longer if they choose but also can enjoy retirement without the constant worry of medical bills and associated costs. Their ability to maintain wealth and enjoy a financially secure retirement is directly linked to their health.

5. The Psychological Burden of Poor Health on Financial Decision-Making

- ❖ Poor health, particularly chronic conditions, has a significant psychological toll, contributing to stress, anxiety, and even depression. These mental health challenges can cloud judgment and affect financial decision-making. When someone is overwhelmed by health-related stress, they are more likely to make impulsive or short-sighted financial decisions, such as taking on unnecessary debt, liquidating investments at the wrong time, or neglecting financial planning altogether.
- ❖ The mental burden of poor health can also lead to a defeatist attitude, where individuals feel less motivated to pursue wealth-building opportunities or believe they are incapable of achieving financial goals. This mindset can stagnate financial growth and prevent individuals from seeking the financial education, mentorship, or tools needed to reverse their circumstances.

6. Health as an Investment in Wealth-Building

- ❖ To mitigate the costs of poor health on wealth-building potential, individuals must recognize that health is an essential investment. Prioritizing preventative healthcare, adopting healthy lifestyle habits, and managing stress effectively are all critical strategies for protecting one's financial future.

- Investing in health means regular exercise, balanced nutrition, mental health care, and preventive medical checkups. These habits not only reduce the likelihood of chronic diseases and medical emergencies but also improve overall productivity and focus, allowing individuals to pursue wealth-building activities with greater energy and clarity.
- Moreover, employers and businesses that promote health and wellness programs for their employees contribute to both their own long-term profitability and the financial success of their workforce. Healthier employees are more productive, take fewer sick days, and contribute to the organization's success, which in turn benefits everyone's financial future.

7. The Role of Preventive Healthcare in Protecting Financial Stability

- Preventive healthcare plays a crucial role in mitigating the cost of poor health on wealth-building potential. Regular health screenings, vaccinations, and early detection of diseases can drastically reduce the likelihood of developing serious health conditions that lead to expensive medical bills and long-term treatment costs. Many chronic conditions such as heart disease, diabetes, and certain cancers can be managed or even prevented through early intervention. By prioritizing preventive healthcare, individuals not only safeguard their health but also avoid the financial pitfalls associated with untreated health issues.

- Preventive care is often much less expensive than emergency treatment. For example, routine checkups can detect health issues early, allowing for less invasive and less expensive treatments. Conversely, failure to take preventive measures can result in sudden medical emergencies, which can lead to overwhelming medical bills, loss of income due to time off work, and potential long-term disability.
- From a financial perspective, investing in regular health maintenance can be viewed similarly to diversifying an investment portfolio—it's about risk management. Just as one diversifies assets to protect against financial losses, regular health checkups and maintaining a healthy lifestyle protect against the financial drain of unexpected medical issues.

8. The Multiplier Effect of Poor Health on Generational Wealth

- Poor health not only affects the individual but can also have a long-lasting impact on generational wealth. When an individual is unable to build and sustain wealth due to health problems, it limits their ability to leave behind financial resources for future generations. Children and dependents may be forced to take on caregiving responsibilities or financial burdens to support the family member in poor health, reducing their ability to accumulate wealth themselves.
- In some cases, health-related financial strain can lead to the liquidation of assets, such as selling a family home or withdrawing from retirement accounts prematurely. This erodes the potential for wealth transfer, preventing the establishment of a financial legacy that could benefit children and grandchildren.

- Additionally, families impacted by the financial strain of poor health may be less able to afford educational opportunities, limiting the upward mobility of younger generations. This creates a cycle in which poor health not only diminishes wealth in the present but also limits the opportunities for future wealth accumulation within a family.
- In contrast, families who prioritize health tend to have more resources available to invest in education, property, and other wealth-building opportunities for their children, increasing the likelihood of generational wealth transfer.

9. Workplace Health and Financial Prosperity

- Workplaces that support employee health initiatives—such as offering health insurance benefits, wellness programs, and mental health support—are contributing to their employees' financial well-being and long-term wealth potential. A healthy work environment reduces absenteeism, improves productivity, and lowers healthcare costs for both employees and employers.
- Employers who prioritize employee wellness foster a culture of health, which ultimately leads to higher levels of job satisfaction, lower turnover, and increased loyalty. In turn, employees who feel supported in their health endeavors are more likely to remain productive, grow within their roles, and take advantage of career advancement opportunities, all of which contribute to long-term financial success.
- For the individual, participating in workplace wellness programs can help reduce the personal cost of healthcare and support healthier habits that enhance their ability to work efficiently and build wealth over time.

10. The Importance of Mental Health in Financial Decision-Making

- While physical health is often the focus of wealth-building discussions, mental health is equally important in shaping financial success. Poor mental health—whether due to stress, anxiety, depression, or other mental health conditions—can impair decision-making, leading to impulsive purchases, avoidance of financial planning, and neglect of critical investments or savings strategies.
- Chronic stress, in particular, has a profound impact on financial behavior. It can lead to a "scarcity mindset," where individuals feel overwhelmed by their current circumstances and unable to think long-term about wealth-building strategies. This can result in poor financial choices, such as taking on high-interest debt, cashing out retirement accounts prematurely, or neglecting investment opportunities that could build wealth over time.
- Prioritizing mental health is essential for making sound financial decisions. Engaging in stress-relief activities, seeking therapy or counseling when needed, and ensuring work-life balance are all critical strategies for maintaining the mental clarity and emotional resilience required to manage finances effectively.

11. Healthy Habits and Their Compounding Effect on Wealth

- Building and maintaining healthy habits can have a compounding effect on wealth-building efforts. For example, regular exercise and a healthy diet can increase energy levels, enhance focus, and improve overall productivity, enabling individuals to work more effectively and achieve their financial goals. In contrast, poor health habits such as smoking, excessive alcohol consumption, and a sedentary lifestyle can lead to chronic illnesses that drain financial resources over time.

- ❖ Moreover, adopting a proactive approach to health can help individuals avoid the need for expensive medical treatments, reduce insurance premiums, and increase longevity. A longer, healthier life allows for more years of income generation and investment, compounding wealth over time. Additionally, individuals in good health tend to have better mental acuity, enabling them to make more informed and strategic financial decisions throughout their lives.
- ❖ The positive effects of good health on productivity and financial success are cumulative. A healthy person is more likely to maintain consistent work habits, seize new opportunities, and stay engaged in wealth-building activities well into their later years. This long-term commitment to health amplifies their ability to generate wealth and achieve financial independence.

12. The Impact of Health on Entrepreneurship and Financial Independence

- ❖ Entrepreneurs are particularly vulnerable to the financial costs of poor health, as their businesses often depend on their ability to work long hours, manage stress, and maintain peak mental and physical performance. Poor health can derail business operations, cause lost revenue, and force entrepreneurs to step away from their ventures, leading to financial instability.
- ❖ For those pursuing financial independence, maintaining good health is critical. Achieving financial independence requires a high level of discipline, focus, and consistency—qualities that

are difficult to maintain when health issues arise. By prioritizing health, entrepreneurs and individuals aiming for financial independence can ensure they have the stamina and resilience needed to succeed in their financial goals.

- Furthermore, entrepreneurs with strong health are better positioned to innovate, take calculated risks, and drive their businesses forward. Their physical and mental well-being allows them to lead teams effectively, handle stress more efficiently, and make strategic decisions that contribute to long-term business growth and wealth accumulation.

Health as the Cornerstone of Wealth

Ultimately, health is not a separate component of wealth—it is a foundational element. Without good health, the ability to accumulate, maintain, and grow wealth becomes significantly compromised. The financial burdens of medical care, lost earning potential, and reduced productivity all highlight the importance of prioritizing health as a key investment in one's financial future.

By adopting a proactive approach to health, including preventive care, healthy lifestyle habits, and mental health maintenance, individuals can not only avoid the financial drain of poor health but also enhance their wealth-building potential. Health provides the energy, focus, and longevity required to pursue financial opportunities and achieve long-term financial independence.

In the pursuit of wealth, health should never be sacrificed. Instead, it should be recognized as one of the most valuable assets in the wealth-building journey, with long-term benefits that extend beyond mere financial gain to a richer, fuller, and more fulfilling life.

- Practical Steps to Maintain a Healthy Lifestyle for Sustained Productivity and Wealth Creation

The relationship between health and wealth is well-documented. Maintaining a healthy lifestyle has a direct impact on long-term productivity and wealth creation. Healthy individuals are more likely to perform better professionally, make sound financial decisions, and avoid the high costs associated with poor health. Below are practical steps to maintain a healthy lifestyle that not only supports sustained productivity but also enhances wealth-building efforts.

1. Prioritize Regular Exercise for Physical and Mental Health

Engaging in regular physical activity is essential for maintaining good health and increasing productivity. Exercise improves cardiovascular health, boosts energy levels, and reduces the risk of chronic diseases such as diabetes, heart disease, and hypertension, which can lead to expensive medical bills.

- Set a Routine: Incorporate at least 30 minutes of moderate exercise (such as walking, running, swimming, or strength training) into your daily routine. Scheduling workout sessions at the start or end of the day can help you remain consistent.
- Combine Productivity with Movement: For those with busy schedules, integrate exercise into your daily life by taking walking meetings, standing desks, or quick 10-minute workout breaks throughout the day. Regular movement keeps your energy levels high and reduces fatigue, enhancing your productivity.
- Leverage the Mental Health Benefits of Exercise: Physical activity stimulates the production of endorphins and serotonin, which can significantly

reduce stress, improve mood, and sharpen focus. This enhanced mental clarity leads to better decision-making in personal finances and business endeavors.

2. Adopt a Balanced, Nutrient-Rich Diet

Your diet directly influences your physical health, energy levels, and cognitive function. A balanced, nutrient-rich diet supports both mental acuity and sustained energy, enabling better performance at work and more thoughtful financial decisions.

- Incorporate Whole Foods: Focus on whole, unprocessed foods such as fruits, vegetables, lean proteins, and healthy fats. These foods provide the essential nutrients your body needs to maintain energy levels and reduce the risk of illnesses.
- Practice Portion Control and Mindful Eating: Overeating or consuming unhealthy foods can lead to fatigue, obesity, and other health issues. Eating mindfully and maintaining portion control help manage weight and ensure that you are eating to fuel productivity, not out of stress or boredom.
- Stay Hydrated: Drinking enough water throughout the day is critical for maintaining focus and energy. Dehydration can lead to headaches, fatigue, and reduced concentration, all of which negatively affect productivity and decision-making.

3. Prioritize Sleep for Cognitive Performance and Decision-Making

Sleep is one of the most overlooked aspects of health but is crucial for cognitive function, emotional well-being, and decision-making. Poor sleep reduces your ability to think clearly and can lead to poor financial decisions or decreased work performance.

- ❖ Develop a Consistent Sleep Schedule: Going to bed and waking up at the same time each day helps regulate your body's internal clock and improves sleep quality. Aim for 7-9 hours of sleep per night to ensure full recovery and optimal cognitive function.
- ❖ Create a Sleep-Friendly Environment: Ensure your sleeping space is conducive to rest by minimizing distractions such as noise and light, maintaining a cool temperature, and keeping electronic devices out of the bedroom.
- ❖ Practice Good Sleep Hygiene: Avoid heavy meals, caffeine, and alcohol close to bedtime, and engage in relaxing activities such as reading, meditation, or gentle stretches to signal to your body that it's time to sleep.

4. Manage Stress for Sustained Mental Health and Financial Discipline

Chronic stress not only impacts physical health but also impairs decision-making, leading to poor financial choices and decreased productivity. Learning how to manage stress is key to maintaining focus, discipline, and emotional resilience.

- ❖ Incorporate Stress-Relief Practices: Engage in relaxation techniques such as meditation, deep breathing exercises, or yoga to help reduce stress levels. These activities can improve emotional control, allowing you to make better decisions under pressure.
- ❖ Establish Boundaries Between Work and Personal Life: Having a clear distinction between work time and personal time can reduce stress and prevent

burnout. This balance enhances overall productivity and keeps you focused on long-term financial goals.

- Seek Support When Needed: Whether through professional therapy, talking to a mentor, or relying on a support system of family and friends, seeking help can alleviate the mental burden of stress and enable more thoughtful decision-making.

5. Develop Time Management Skills to Optimize Productivity

Effective time management is essential for balancing work, personal well-being, and wealth-building activities. When time is poorly managed, stress increases, productivity decreases, and long-term financial goals may be neglected.

- Use Tools to Stay Organized: Productivity apps like calendars, to-do lists, or project management software can help you stay on top of your tasks and maintain a balance between work, health, and personal life.
- Prioritize Tasks Based on Impact: Focus on high-priority tasks that contribute directly to wealth creation or professional advancement. This reduces wasted effort and ensures that your time is spent on activities that yield the most significant results.
- Schedule Breaks and Downtime: Regular breaks throughout the day improve focus and productivity. Allow yourself time to step away from work to engage in physical activity, relaxation, or hobbies. Downtime is crucial for preventing burnout and maintaining sustained effort in the long run.

6. Focus on Preventive Healthcare

Preventive healthcare is an essential investment for long-term health and financial stability. By addressing health concerns early, you can prevent expensive medical treatments down the road and ensure that health issues do not interrupt wealth-building activities.

- Get Regular Health Check-Ups: Schedule annual physical exams, dental visits, and other preventive health screenings to identify potential health issues before they escalate into larger, costlier problems.
- Maintain Health Insurance: Having adequate health insurance coverage reduces the risk of large medical bills, ensuring that unexpected health events do not derail your financial goals. Regularly review your insurance plan to ensure it aligns with your needs.
- Vaccinations and Screenings: Stay up to date with vaccinations and recommended health screenings based on your age, gender, and family history. Early detection of health issues is often the most cost-effective way to manage long-term health.

7. Create a Work-Life Balance for Long-Term Financial and Health Gains

Balancing work with personal time and self-care is crucial for long-term productivity and wealth creation. Constant overworking can lead to burnout, reduce performance, and negatively impact both physical and financial health.

- Set Clear Work Hours: Establishing clear working hours and sticking to them prevents overextension and allows time for self-care, exercise, and leisure, all of which contribute to maintaining health and productivity.

- Leverage Flexible Work Arrangements: For entrepreneurs or those with flexible job roles, take advantage of remote work, shorter workweeks, or creative time management to ensure your work-life balance supports long-term wealth-building and personal health.
- Engage in Hobbies and Social Activities: Leisure activities and social connections are vital for emotional well-being. Make time for hobbies, family, and friends to recharge your mental health and foster positive relationships that support long-term success.

8. Invest in Mental Health and Emotional Intelligence

Your mental health plays a pivotal role in how you manage stress, set and achieve goals, and make decisions—all critical to financial success. Emotional intelligence (EQ) also improves your ability to navigate complex financial situations, negotiate, and work well with others.

- Practice Self-Awareness: Regular reflection on your emotions and how they influence your financial and professional choices helps improve self-discipline and emotional regulation. Journaling or talking with a mentor can enhance this awareness.
- Develop Emotional Resilience: Resilience allows you to bounce back from setbacks, whether personal or financial. Techniques like mindfulness, gratitude, and positive thinking can help improve emotional resilience.
- Seek Therapy or Counseling: Professional help from a therapist or counselor can provide valuable tools for managing emotional challenges and developing a healthy mindset around wealth, career, and personal growth.

Health as a Foundation for Wealth Creation

A healthy lifestyle is the cornerstone of sustained productivity and wealth creation. By prioritizing exercise, diet, sleep, stress management, and work-life balance, individuals can maintain the physical and mental stamina necessary to build wealth over the long term. Health not only reduces the risk of costly medical bills but also enhances cognitive performance, emotional well-being, and decision-making ability, which are all crucial to financial success. By integrating these practical steps into your daily routine, you can ensure that your health supports—not hinders—your financial goals and overall quality of life.

Investing in Your Health as a Financial Strategy

- Why health is one of your most valuable assets

When discussing financial strategies and wealth creation, health is often an overlooked yet crucial component. Health, however, is one of the most valuable assets you possess; as it serves as the foundation upon which all other aspects of your financial life depend. Without good health, the ability to generate income, make sound decisions, and pursue long-term wealth goals can be severely compromised. Investing in your health is not just about preventing medical expenses—it is an essential financial strategy that enhances productivity, resilience, and overall quality of life.

1. Health Enables Sustainable Income Generation

At the core of any wealth-building strategy is the ability to earn an income, whether through employment, entrepreneurship, or investments. Good health is vital to sustaining your ability to work, be productive, and take advantage of opportunities to grow wealth.

- Physical Capacity for Work: Your physical health directly influences your capacity to perform work, whether in a physically demanding job or a mentally taxing career. Chronic health problems can limit your ability to maintain consistent employment, reduce your productivity, and lead to missed opportunities for promotions or career advancements.
- Mental Health and Cognitive Function: Beyond physical well-being, mental health plays an equally critical role in your ability to work effectively. Poor mental health can lead to decreased concentration, motivation, and decision-making skills, all of which can negatively impact your career and income potential.
- Entrepreneurship and Leadership: For entrepreneurs and leaders, maintaining good health is even more essential. Business ownership requires long hours, resilience, and creativity. Poor health can limit your ability to lead a team, manage business challenges, and scale your enterprise.

2. Health Mitigates Long-Term Medical Costs

One of the clearest financial arguments for investing in your health is the direct reduction of medical expenses. Poor health often results in costly medical treatments, chronic illness management, and lost productivity due to sick days. Proactively maintaining health can significantly reduce these expenses over a lifetime.

- Preventive Care is Cost-Effective: Regular check-ups, a healthy lifestyle, and early detection of potential health problems through preventive care help avoid the expensive treatment of chronic diseases such as diabetes, heart disease, and cancer. The cost of managing these conditions far exceeds the investment required to prevent them.

- Reduced Health Insurance Premiums: Maintaining good health can also lower your health insurance premiums. Individuals who engage in healthy behaviors such as regular exercise, a balanced diet, and not smoking often qualify for lower insurance costs. Moreover, some employers offer wellness incentives, further reducing health-related expenses.
- Avoiding Debt Due to Medical Emergencies: Medical emergencies are a leading cause of financial distress and bankruptcy. By prioritizing your health, you minimize the risk of unexpected medical costs that can derail your financial plans. Building an emergency fund for health-related issues is an important part of this strategy.

3. Health Increases Longevity and Wealth Accumulation

Good health contributes to a longer, more fulfilling life. The longer you live in good health, the more time you have to grow and enjoy your wealth. Investing in your health allows you to maximize the compounding effects of your investments and increase your wealth over time.

- Extending Your Earning Years: Many people plan to retire based on their financial goals, but without good health, they may be forced into early retirement or face limited income in their later years. Maintaining health enables you to work longer if needed, ensuring that you can continue to save and invest without the strain of medical issues.
- Maximizing Compounding Returns: Time is one of the most critical factors in wealth

building due to the power of compound interest. Staying healthy allows you to remain active in the workforce and investments for a longer period, allowing your assets to grow significantly over time. The longer your investments compound, the greater your wealth becomes.

- Quality of Life in Retirement: While it's essential to accumulate wealth for retirement, maintaining good health ensures that you can actually enjoy the fruits of your labor. Good health gives you the freedom to travel, engage in hobbies, and spend time with loved ones during your golden years without the physical limitations of chronic illness.

4. Health Supports Optimal Financial Decision-Making

Health influences your ability to make sound financial decisions, both in your personal finances and business ventures. Poor physical or mental health can cloud judgment, lead to impulsive decisions, or create financial stress that results in poor long-term planning.

- Stress Management and Financial Choices: Chronic stress, often linked to poor health, impairs cognitive function and decision-making abilities. This can lead to poor financial decisions such as overspending, neglecting savings, or making risky investments. By investing in your health, you improve your ability to manage stress and make rational, well-informed decisions.
- Emotional Stability and Wealth Creation: Emotional intelligence and stability are crucial for navigating the ups and downs of financial markets, business challenges, and personal finances. Healthy individuals are more likely to

exhibit patience, persistence, and discipline—qualities that are essential for long-term financial success.

- ❖ Mental Clarity and Business Innovation: For entrepreneurs and business leaders, maintaining mental clarity is vital for creativity, strategic planning, and innovation. Investing in both physical and mental health ensures that you can think clearly, solve problems effectively, and adapt to changing market conditions.

5. Health Enhances Productivity and Efficiency

The healthier you are, the more productive you can be. Health not only gives you the energy and focus to complete tasks efficiently, but it also reduces the time lost due to illness or burnout. Over the long term, increased productivity leads to higher earning potential and more opportunities for financial growth.

- ❖ Consistent Performance at Work: Good health helps you maintain consistent performance, leading to career advancement, promotions, and increased income. High energy levels and mental focus make you a valuable asset in the workplace, allowing you to outperform others who may struggle with health-related issues.
- ❖ Avoiding Burnout: Health is critical for avoiding burnout, which can lead to prolonged periods of reduced productivity, lost income, and disengagement from work. By taking care of your body and mind, you can sustain a high level of performance over time and avoid the financial and career setbacks that come with burnout.
- ❖ Improved Work-Life Balance: Good health supports better time management, allowing

you to balance work with personal life, family, and leisure. A balanced life promotes overall happiness, which has been shown to correlate with higher productivity and better financial outcomes.

6. Health Builds Resilience in the Face of Financial Challenges

Life inevitably presents challenges, and maintaining good health helps you remain resilient in the face of these obstacles. Whether dealing with a market downturn, a career setback, or personal financial stress, good health enables you to stay physically and mentally strong, ensuring you can bounce back and continue working toward your financial goals.

- Resilience in Business and Investing: Entrepreneurs and investors must often navigate uncertainty, market volatility, and personal financial crises. Good health allows you to manage the emotional and physical stress that comes with these challenges, ensuring that you can remain focused and make decisions that align with your long-term goals.
- Adaptability and Risk Management: Maintaining health enhances your ability to adapt to changing circumstances. Whether it's a shift in your career, economic conditions, or investment opportunities, healthy individuals are better equipped to pivot and capitalize on new prospects, mitigating financial risks.

7. Health as a Strategic Investment

Viewing health as an investment is a powerful mindset shift. Just as you invest in stocks, bonds, and real estate to build wealth, investing in your physical and mental well-being provides long-term returns in the form of reduced medical costs, sustained income, and enhanced quality of life.

- ❖ Health as a Wealth Multiplier: Healthy individuals are more likely to experience higher income, better job opportunities, and longer careers, all of which contribute to financial stability and wealth accumulation. The compounding effect of good health mirrors the growth of financial investments, making it an essential component of your wealth strategy.
- ❖ A Long-Term Focus on Wellness: Investing in your health requires a long-term perspective, much like any financial strategy. The time and effort you put into maintaining your well-being now will pay dividends in the form of increased longevity, productivity, and wealth creation in the future.

Prioritizing Health as a Core Financial Strategy

Good health is one of the most valuable assets you can possess, and investing in your well-being should be a fundamental part of any wealth-building strategy. By prioritizing physical and mental health, you can enhance your earning potential, reduce long-term medical expenses, and improve your decision-making abilities. Health enables you to work longer, enjoy a higher quality of life, and remain resilient in the face of financial challenges. In this way, investing in your health not only contributes to personal happiness and fulfillment but also serves as a powerful tool for creating and sustaining wealth over the long term.

- Financial Benefits of a Healthy Lifestyle: Lower Medical Expenses and Increased Earning Potential

Adopting a healthy lifestyle not only enhances overall well-being but also yields significant financial benefits. By prioritizing physical and mental health, individuals can enjoy reduced medical expenses and an improved ability to generate income over time. In the broader context of wealth management and financial strategy, investing in health is a powerful yet often underutilized approach that can optimize financial outcomes. From lowering the burden of healthcare costs to boosting earning potential, the financial rewards of living a healthy lifestyle are substantial.

1. Lower Medical Expenses Through Preventive Health

A proactive approach to health is one of the most effective ways to minimize long-term medical costs. Chronic diseases such as heart disease, diabetes, and obesity are major drivers of healthcare expenses. These conditions are often preventable or manageable through lifestyle choices such as regular physical activity, balanced nutrition, and stress management. By maintaining a healthy lifestyle, individuals can reduce their risk of developing these conditions and avoid the high costs associated with their treatment.

- Reduced Hospital Visits and Medications: Preventive care, such as regular check-ups, exercise, and proper diet, significantly lowers the likelihood of requiring expensive medical treatments or long-term medications. A healthier body has fewer medical issues, leading to fewer hospital visits and less reliance on costly prescription drugs. For example, individuals who maintain a healthy weight and engage in regular exercise are at a lower risk of developing hypertension or type 2 diabetes, which would otherwise require ongoing medication and medical monitoring.

- Lower Insurance Premiums: Health insurance providers often offer lower premiums to individuals who demonstrate healthy behaviors, as they present a lower risk of requiring medical care. Lifestyle changes such as quitting smoking, maintaining a healthy weight, and staying active can lead to direct savings on health insurance. Additionally, many employers and insurance companies offer wellness programs that provide financial incentives for healthy living, such as discounts on gym memberships or cash rewards for meeting fitness goals.
- Avoiding High-Cost Emergency Care: Medical emergencies can be financially devastating, especially if they result from preventable conditions. A healthy lifestyle that includes proper diet, exercise, and stress management reduces the likelihood of sudden medical crises such as heart attacks or strokes, which often lead to exorbitant emergency room bills, surgeries, and long-term rehabilitation costs. By investing in your health, you reduce the risk of these costly emergencies.

2. Increased Earning Potential through Improved Health and Productivity

Good health directly impacts your ability to generate income, as it enhances productivity, focus, and energy levels. A healthy lifestyle enables individuals to perform better at work, pursue career advancements, and maintain consistent employment. In this way, the relationship between health and wealth becomes mutually reinforcing, with health serving as a foundation for higher earning potential.

- Enhanced Physical and Mental Energy: Good physical health boosts energy levels, making individuals more effective in their work. This increased energy allows them to take on more responsibilities, perform at a higher level, and pursue additional career opportunities. For instance, individuals who engage in regular exercise report feeling more alert, focused, and capable of handling demanding tasks throughout the day. This, in turn, can lead to promotions, raises, and other forms of career advancement.
- Reduced Absenteeism: One of the most direct ways a healthy lifestyle influences earning potential is through reduced absenteeism. Chronic illness or frequent bouts of illness can result in missed workdays, which not only affect immediate income but can also harm long-term career prospects. By maintaining good health, individuals are more likely to attend work consistently, contributing to better job performance and stability. Employers value reliable employees, and this reliability often translates into higher earnings and increased career growth opportunities.
- Boosted Cognitive Function and Decision-Making: Mental health is just as important as physical health in influencing financial success. A healthy diet, regular exercise, and adequate sleep improve cognitive function, leading to better decision-making, problem-solving, and creativity at work. These benefits are especially critical for professionals in leadership or decision-making roles, as well as entrepreneurs who must navigate complex challenges. Sound decisions made in the workplace can result in more successful projects, higher income, and a stronger career trajectory.
- Increased Opportunities for Career Longevity: A healthy lifestyle can also contribute to career longevity by preventing burnout and physical decline. Many individuals are forced to retire early

or reduce their work hours due to health issues that could have been prevented through lifestyle changes. By staying healthy, you extend your ability to work and earn an income, which can significantly increase the total wealth accumulated over your lifetime. For those who choose to continue working into their later years, good health allows them to remain active and productive in their careers or businesses.

3. Indirect Financial Gains from Lifestyle Choices

In addition to direct savings from lower healthcare costs and higher earning potential, a healthy lifestyle can lead to several indirect financial gains that contribute to long-term wealth building.

- Improved Mental Well-Being and Financial Decision-Making: Mental clarity and emotional stability are critical for making sound financial decisions. A healthy lifestyle that includes mindfulness practices, stress management, and physical activity can improve emotional well-being, leading to better financial decision-making. Individuals who manage their stress effectively are less likely to engage in impulsive spending or make risky investment decisions driven by anxiety. Instead, they are more likely to approach financial planning with a clear, long-term perspective.
- Higher Quality of Life and Productivity in Retirement: A healthy lifestyle not only impacts earning potential during your working years but also significantly enhances the quality of life in retirement. By staying healthy, individuals can continue to enjoy an active lifestyle in retirement, participate in activities they love, and avoid the financial drain of chronic medical conditions. This ensures that retirement savings are used for

enjoyment and leisure rather than healthcare costs, preserving wealth and improving life satisfaction during retirement.

- ❖ Lower Dependence on Caregiving in Later Years: Individuals who maintain good health are less likely to need long-term care or assisted living services as they age. These services can be incredibly expensive, and minimizing the need for them can lead to significant savings. By investing in health now, individuals can reduce or eliminate the high costs associated with elderly care, thereby preserving their wealth for other uses, such as travel, hobbies, or leaving a financial legacy for their families.

4. How to Invest in a Healthy Lifestyle for Financial Benefits

The financial benefits of a healthy lifestyle are clear, but achieving these benefits requires intentional investment in your physical and mental well-being. There are several key strategies to ensure that health becomes an integral part of your wealth-building plan:

- ❖ Prioritize Physical Activity: Regular exercise is essential for maintaining physical health and preventing chronic illnesses. Whether through walking, running, cycling, or strength training, consistent physical activity reduces healthcare costs over the long term and improves daily energy levels, making individuals more productive and focused at work.
- ❖ Adopt a Balanced and Nutritious Diet: A well-balanced diet, rich in fruits, vegetables, lean proteins, and whole grains, supports both physical and mental health. Avoiding processed foods, sugary drinks, and excessive alcohol consumption not only promotes long-term health but also

reduces the likelihood of developing costly medical conditions.

- Practice Mindfulness and Stress Management: Mental health plays a crucial role in overall well-being. Practices such as meditation, yoga, deep breathing, or journaling can help reduce stress and improve emotional well-being. Effective stress management leads to better financial decision-making and improved job performance, both of which contribute to wealth accumulation.
- Prioritize Preventive Health Care: Regular check-ups, health screenings, and preventive measures, such as vaccinations, help catch potential health issues before they become serious and expensive to treat. Proactively managing your health prevents costly medical emergencies and ensures that small issues are addressed before they escalate.
- Invest in Health Insurance: Health insurance is a critical component of financial planning. By investing in comprehensive health coverage, you protect yourself from the financial burden of unexpected medical expenses. Consider policies that reward healthy behaviors or provide incentives for maintaining a healthy lifestyle.

Work-Life Balance and Financial Abundance

- The importance of achieving a healthy balance between career, personal life, and finances

In the pursuit of financial abundance, the importance of achieving a healthy balance between career, personal life, and finances cannot be overstated. While financial success is often a major life goal, neglecting personal well-being, relationships, or physical health in its pursuit can lead to burnout, dissatisfaction, and even diminished wealth over time. Striking a sustainable balance between these areas is essential for long-term financial stability, personal fulfillment, and overall well-being.

1. The Interconnectedness of Career, Personal Life, and Finances

Career, personal life, and finances are deeply interconnected, and each impacts the other in profound ways. A thriving career supports financial growth, while personal well-being enables sustained success in both career and financial pursuits. Neglecting one aspect often creates a ripple effect of challenges in the others, leading to stress, poor decision-making, and, ultimately, reduced financial abundance.

- Career Success and Financial Health: A successful career is often the primary source of income and wealth-building opportunities, providing the means for financial growth. However, over-investing in a career at the expense of personal life can lead to burnout, reduced productivity, and health issues—all of which negatively impact earning potential. A well-balanced approach, where career goals are pursued with clear boundaries, ensures that individuals remain energized, motivated, and capable of sustaining their financial efforts over time.
- Personal Life and Financial Stability: Personal well-being and healthy relationships are fundamental to financial success. A strong support system, emotional balance, and physical health provide the resilience needed to navigate financial challenges and seize opportunities. Neglecting family, friends, or self-care in favor of financial goals can lead to emotional exhaustion, reduced mental clarity, and poor financial decisions.

Conversely, a fulfilling personal life contributes to better mental health, improved decision-making, and greater productivity, all of which enhance financial outcomes.

- Finances and Work-Life Balance: Financial health allows individuals to achieve a greater work-life balance by reducing stress and providing the flexibility to invest time in both career and personal life. Proper financial planning, budgeting, and smart investing create security and financial freedom, reducing the need for overwork and providing more time for personal fulfillment. Financial stability also enables individuals to take breaks, pursue hobbies, and spend time with loved ones without the constant pressure of financial insecurity.

2. Key Benefits of Work-Life Balance for Financial Abundance

Achieving a healthy work-life balance is not just about avoiding burnout or stress—it has real, tangible benefits for building and sustaining financial abundance. Here are some of the key ways that balance contributes to long-term financial success:

- Increased Productivity and Career Longevity: A balanced life enhances focus, energy, and productivity in the workplace. When individuals take the time to rest, recharge, and engage in activities they enjoy, they return to their work more energized and creative. This higher level of productivity often leads to greater job performance, promotions, and salary increases. Additionally, a balanced approach reduces the likelihood of burnout, allowing individuals to sustain a high level of performance over the course of their careers.

- Better Financial Decision-Making: Emotional and mental well-being are critical for sound financial decision-making. Individuals who are overworked or stressed may make impulsive or short-sighted financial choices. Conversely, those who maintain a balance between work and personal life are more likely to approach financial decisions with clarity and a long-term perspective. This leads to smarter investments, better financial planning, and more disciplined saving and spending habits.
- Sustained Physical and Mental Health: Physical and mental health are essential components of financial success. Those who prioritize their health through exercise, proper diet, and mental well-being are less likely to face costly medical bills, long-term healthcare needs, or loss of income due to illness. Moreover, good health supports the ability to work productively and maintain a steady income throughout life, which is critical for achieving financial abundance.
- Improved Relationships and Networking Opportunities: Personal relationships play a significant role in financial success. Strong family support and a network of friends and mentors provide both emotional and practical assistance during financial challenges. Maintaining a balanced life allows individuals to nurture these relationships, leading to opportunities for collaboration, new ventures, and professional growth. Social connections can also lead to investment opportunities, business partnerships, and career advancements that may not have been available otherwise.

3. Strategies for Achieving Balance While Pursuing Financial Abundance

Achieving work-life balance while focusing on financial abundance requires intentional effort and strategic planning. Here are some key strategies to help individuals strike a balance between career, personal life, and financial growth:

- Set Clear Boundaries: Defining boundaries between work and personal life is essential for balance. This includes setting specific work hours, taking time off for rest, and ensuring that personal time is free from work-related distractions. It also means being mindful of financial goals and setting realistic timelines for achieving them without sacrificing personal well-being. Creating these boundaries allows individuals to be fully present in both work and personal life, leading to better performance and relationships.
- Prioritize Time Management: Effective time management is critical to balancing career, personal life, and finances. By setting clear priorities and organizing tasks, individuals can allocate sufficient time for work, personal activities, and financial planning. Tools such as time-blocking, scheduling, and task management software can help streamline daily responsibilities, ensuring that all aspects of life receive appropriate attention.
- Delegate and Automate: One of the most effective ways to maintain balance is to delegate tasks, both at work and at home. In the workplace, delegating tasks to team members or automating routine activities frees up time for strategic thinking and personal life. Similarly, at home, outsourcing chores such as cleaning or meal preparation can reduce stress and provide more time for personal growth, hobbies, or family. In the realm of finances, automating savings, investments, and bill payments can reduce the mental load and ensure that financial goals are consistently met.
- Align Financial Goals with Personal Values: Pursuing financial abundance should align with

personal values and priorities. When financial goals are aligned with what truly matters—whether it's family, travel, philanthropy, or personal growth—it becomes easier to maintain a healthy balance. This alignment reduces the stress of financial decision-making, as choices are made with purpose and clarity, rather than out of obligation or pressure.

- Practice Self-Care: Prioritizing self-care is essential for maintaining balance. This includes physical activities such as exercise and proper nutrition, as well as mental and emotional practices like meditation, therapy, or journaling. Self-care helps individuals manage stress; stay focused, and maintains the energy needed to achieve both financial and personal goals.
- Plan for Flexibility: A rigid approach to work-life balance and finances can be counterproductive. Life is unpredictable, and the ability to adapt to changes—whether in career, personal life, or finances—is critical for long-term success. Financial plans should allow for flexibility, and individuals should be willing to adjust work schedules or personal commitments when necessary. This adaptability ensures that balance is maintained even during times of transition or unexpected challenges.

4. The Long-Term Impact of Work-Life Balance on Financial Abundance

Achieving a healthy balance between career, personal life, and finances has lasting benefits that extend far beyond immediate financial success. In the long term, balanced individuals are more likely to experience sustained wealth, personal fulfillment, and overall well-being. By maintaining good health, strong relationships, and emotional stability, they are better equipped to navigate the ups and downs of financial markets, career changes, and personal life events.

- Greater Financial Security: A balanced life leads to more disciplined financial practices, such as consistent saving, investing, and careful spending. This financial discipline builds a solid foundation of wealth, providing greater security and resilience in the face of financial challenges. Moreover, the absence of burnout or financial stress reduces the likelihood of costly financial mistakes, preserving wealth for future use.
- Enhanced Personal Fulfillment: Financial abundance alone does not guarantee happiness or fulfillment. A balanced life that includes meaningful relationships, personal growth, and self-care leads to greater life satisfaction. Individuals who achieve financial abundance through balance are more likely to enjoy the fruits of their labor, spending time with loved ones, pursuing passions, and contributing to their communities.
- Increased Career and Financial Opportunities: A balanced approach to career and finances often leads to more opportunities for growth. By maintaining strong relationships, networking effectively, and staying focused on long-term goals, individuals' open doors to new career paths, investment opportunities, and collaborations that they might have missed if overworked or stressed. This creates a virtuous cycle where balance leads to greater financial abundance and vice versa.

5. The Psychological Benefits of Balanced Wealth

Achieving financial abundance through a balanced life offers significant psychological benefits, which, in turn, reinforce long-term success.

- Reduced Stress and Anxiety: When finances are well-managed and balanced with personal life and career, individuals experience less financial stress and anxiety. They no longer live paycheck to paycheck or feel overwhelmed by financial responsibilities. Instead, having a clear plan and balance between work and personal time fosters a sense of control and calm. This leads to better mental health and enables clear decision-making, both in financial and personal spheres.
- Greater Sense of Purpose: A balanced approach to financial abundance includes understanding the "why" behind wealth creation. For many, financial success is not an end in itself but a means to support loved ones, pursue passions, or give back to society. This sense of purpose drives individuals to make thoughtful financial decisions that are aligned with their values, rather than focusing solely on short-term gains. As a result, wealth is used as a tool for personal fulfillment and positive impact.
- Improved Confidence and Motivation: Balancing career, personal life, and finances instills a sense of confidence. Knowing that financial goals are achievable without sacrificing personal well-being empowers individuals to pursue bigger and bolder opportunities. This confidence fuels motivation to continue improving, whether it's through further career development, personal growth, or exploring new financial opportunities like investments, entrepreneurship, or philanthropic endeavors.

6. Creating a Life by Design, Not by Default

The ultimate aim of achieving financial abundance through balance is the ability to design a life that reflects one's true values, aspirations, and desires. When personal life, career, and finances are aligned, individuals can live intentionally, making decisions that lead to greater happiness and fulfillment. This concept of "life by design" has three key components:

- Intentional Living: Financial abundance gives people the freedom to live intentionally, making choices that align with their deepest values and long-term goals. For example, instead of taking a high-paying job that leads to burnout, someone might choose a career path that aligns with their passions and allows for a better work-life balance. This intentionality fosters a more meaningful life and, counter-intuitively, often leads to even greater financial success because individuals perform better when they are fulfilled and engaged.
- Flexibility and Freedom: One of the greatest rewards of financial abundance is the flexibility it affords. Whether it's taking time off to spend with family, traveling the world, or starting a new business, financial security gives people the freedom to shape their lives in accordance with their dreams. This flexibility is crucial for long-term well-being and contributes to a sense of control over one's destiny.
- Legacy and Impact: A balanced life helps individuals think beyond their immediate needs and consider the legacy they want to leave. Financial abundance offers the opportunity to make lasting contributions to family, community, and society. This might take the form of philanthropy, creating generational wealth, or investing in causes that matter. Achieving financial success through balance ensures that individuals can focus on the long-term impact they want to make, rather than being consumed by day-to-day financial pressures.

7. Building Resilience for Life's Financial Ups and Downs

A balanced approach to wealth-building also prepares individuals for the inevitable challenges that come with life's uncertainties. By integrating work, personal well-being, and finances into a cohesive strategy, individuals become more resilient to economic downturns, career changes, and unexpected personal events.

- Financial Buffering and Emergency Planning: Balance in financial planning includes the creation of emergency funds and financial buffers to weather unexpected financial storms, such as job loss, economic recessions, or health emergencies. This level of preparedness allows individuals to avoid financial panic and make measured decisions when life's unpredictability occurs.
- Adaptability in Career and Investment Strategies: Those who maintain a balance between their career and personal lives are better equipped to pivot when necessary. Whether it's transitioning to a new industry, starting a business, or adjusting an investment portfolio to match changing market conditions, a balanced individual is more adaptable and less likely to be derailed by sudden changes.
- Emotional and Mental Fortitude: Financial setbacks can be emotionally draining, but individuals who have built strong personal relationships and prioritize mental and emotional well-being are better able to cope with these challenges. This resilience not only preserves mental health but also ensures that they remain focused on long-term financial goals, rather than reacting impulsively to short-term challenges.

Achieving financial abundance is not simply about amassing wealth—it's about creating a balanced, fulfilling life where career success, personal well-being, and financial security are intertwined. The journey toward financial success becomes more sustainable and meaningful when it is supported by strong personal relationships, intentional living, and a focus on long-term impact.

By incorporating strategies that foster balance, individuals can enjoy financial success without sacrificing health, happiness, or personal fulfillment. Ultimately, this approach ensures that wealth is not only accumulated but also serves to enrich lives, contribute to society, and leave a lasting legacy for future generations.

- How Work-Life Balance Impacts Long-Term Wealth and Happiness

Achieving long-term wealth and happiness isn't solely dependent on financial strategies or accumulating wealth at all costs. It requires a holistic approach that balances work, personal life, and overall well-being. Work-life balance refers to the equilibrium between an individual's professional responsibilities and personal life, and how effectively one can manage time and energy across these domains. Striking the right balance is essential for maintaining not only financial success but also personal fulfillment and mental and physical health.

This section explores how work-life balance influences long-term wealth and happiness, and why it's critical for sustained financial abundance and overall quality of life.

1. The Link Between Work-Life Balance and Financial Success

Contrary to the belief that long hours and relentless focus on work are the only ways to achieve financial success, research shows that work-life balance plays a crucial role in fostering sustainable wealth creation. Overworking can lead to burnout, reduced productivity, and health problems, which in turn may result in lost income or opportunities. On the other hand, a well-balanced lifestyle promotes productivity, creativity, and job satisfaction, which are key contributors to long-term financial success.

Work-Life Balance Improves Productivity:

- Quality Over Quantity: It's a myth that working longer hours automatically leads to higher productivity. Studies show that productivity peaks at around 40 hours per week and declines significantly beyond that. When individuals manage their time effectively, balancing work with relaxation and personal activities, they tend to work more efficiently.
- Enhanced Decision-Making: A well-rested mind is critical for making sound financial and business decisions. Work-life balance allows individuals to approach challenges with clarity and reduces the risk of poor financial choices made under stress or fatigue.
- Increased Creativity and Innovation: Time spent away from work, particularly on personal passions or relaxation can stimulate creativity. This boost in creative thinking often translates to better problem-solving skills and innovative approaches in business or financial planning.

Preventing Burnout for Sustained Wealth Creation:

- Avoiding Burnout: Chronic overworking leads to burnout, which can manifest as mental exhaustion, lack of motivation, and even physical health issues. Burnout not only affects job performance but can also derail long-term financial goals if it forces individuals to take extended time off or leads to poor decision-making.

- ❖ Maintaining Financial Momentum: By maintaining a healthy work-life balance, individuals can continue working at their peak potential over the long term, ensuring consistent progress toward wealth-building goals rather than suffering from the highs and lows associated with burnout and recovery.

2. Work-Life Balance and Its Impact on Personal Happiness

Financial abundance is often pursued as a means to achieve happiness, but wealth alone does not guarantee a fulfilling life. Happiness is deeply intertwined with relationships, personal fulfillment, and well-being—areas that suffer when work dominates life. Work-life balance allows individuals to nurture these aspects of life, creating a positive feedback loop where happiness enhances productivity, and productivity enhances financial success.

Work-Life Balance Enhances Relationships:

- ❖ Stronger Family and Social Bonds: Individuals who make time for family and friends tend to have more meaningful relationships, which are crucial for long-term happiness. Healthy relationships provide emotional support, reduce stress, and increase life satisfaction, all of which contribute to better mental health and more stable professional performance.
- ❖ Work-Life Balance and Personal Growth: Work is not the only source of personal fulfillment. Engaging in hobbies, learning new skills, and pursuing personal interests outside of work contribute to a sense of achievement and

happiness. These activities can also lead to new opportunities, whether they're personal or professional, enhancing both life satisfaction and wealth-building potential.

Increased Mental and Physical Well-Being:

- Mental Health and Financial Success: A balanced life improves mental health, reducing stress, anxiety, and depression. Good mental health enables individuals to think more clearly, make sound financial decisions, and remain resilient in the face of challenges. In contrast, stress and mental fatigue can lead to rash decisions, poor financial habits, or procrastination, which hinder wealth accumulation.
- Physical Health and Longevity: Long-term wealth is also connected to one's ability to enjoy it, which requires good physical health. Those who balance their work with regular exercise, adequate sleep, and a healthy diet are less likely to suffer from chronic illnesses or health-related financial drains later in life. Moreover, healthier individuals are better equipped to stay active in their careers for longer, which can increase lifetime earnings and wealth.

3. Financial Benefits of Prioritizing Work-Life Balance

Beyond the intangible benefits of happiness and well-being, work-life balance has direct financial benefits that contribute to long-term wealth. By focusing on balance, individuals can optimize their performance at work, reduce costly health issues, and ensure they remain productive over a longer period.

Reducing Health-Related Financial Costs:

- Lower Medical Expenses: Poor work-life balance often leads to stress-related illnesses such as heart disease, anxiety disorders, and burnout, which can result in high medical expenses. Investing in a balanced lifestyle helps prevent these issues, reducing healthcare costs over the long term.
- Sustainable Earning Potential: Individuals who maintain good health and emotional well-being are able to stay in the workforce longer, potentially extending their careers and increasing their lifetime earnings. This is particularly important as life expectancy increases and many people aim for longer periods of financial independence during retirement.

Wealth Is a Marathon, Not a Sprint:

- Longevity in the Workforce: Consistent, long-term success is often more lucrative than short bursts of intense effort followed by burnout. Those who manage their work-life balance effectively are more likely to sustain high levels of performance over many years, enabling them to maximize their earnings potential without sacrificing their quality of life.
- Increased Job Satisfaction and Retention: Employees with better work-life balance tend to be more satisfied with their jobs and are less likely to experience high turnover rates. This increases job security, allows for career growth, and often results in higher wages and promotions—contributing to overall financial stability.

4. Strategies for Achieving Work-Life Balance to Promote Financial Abundance

Achieving a healthy balance between work and personal life requires deliberate effort, particularly in today's fast-paced world where the lines between work and personal time are often blurred. Below are some strategies for creating and maintaining balance that leads to financial abundance:

Time Management and Prioritization:

- Set Clear Boundaries: Establish firm boundaries between work and personal time. This might include setting specific working hours, creating a designated workspace, or using technology to disconnect from work outside of those hours.
- Prioritize Tasks: Focus on high-value tasks that contribute most to your financial goals. By prioritizing work that directly impacts your long-term success, you can achieve more in less time, freeing up personal time without sacrificing productivity.

Incorporating Self-Care and Recreation:

- Invest in Health and Wellness: Make time for physical activities, hobbies, and mental health practices such as meditation or mindfulness. These practices help maintain physical and mental health, enabling long-term productivity and financial success.
- Unplug Regularly: Regularly taking time off to recharge is critical. Whether it's short breaks throughout the day, weekends away from work, or extended vacations, disconnecting from work leads to improved focus and creativity when you return.

Nurturing Relationships and Personal Fulfillment:

- Schedule Time for Relationships: Make time for family, friends, and social activities. Investing in relationships provides emotional fulfillment, reduces stress, and improves overall life satisfaction.
- Pursue Personal Interests: Engaging in non-work-related interests fosters personal growth and can also open up new financial opportunities, such as turning hobbies into side income or business ventures.

Work-Life Balance as the Key to Wealth and Happiness

Achieving long-term wealth and happiness is not just about financial success, but about cultivating a balanced life that allows for personal fulfillment, health, and well-being. A strong work-life balance ensures that individuals can continue to be productive and successful in their careers, while also enjoying the fruits of their labor through meaningful relationships, physical and mental health, and personal satisfaction. By integrating work-life balance into wealth-building strategies, individuals can achieve financial abundance without sacrificing their happiness and overall quality of life.

CHAPTER TEN

CRISIS MANAGEMENT: THRIVING IN TIMES OF UNCERTAINTY

This chapter prepares you to navigating financial crises, whether personal or global, and emerging stronger from setbacks.

Preparing for Financial Shocks

- Strategies for building a robust financial cushion against unexpected events

In an unpredictable world, financial shocks such as job loss, medical emergencies, economic downturns, or even unexpected home repairs can severely impact personal wealth and financial stability. Preparing for these unexpected events is crucial for long-term financial resilience and peace of mind. Establishing a robust financial cushion serves as a safety net that protects against potential setbacks and enables individuals to maintain stability during difficult times. Below are key strategies for building this financial cushion, ensuring preparedness for financial shocks.

1. Establish an Emergency Fund

The cornerstone of any financial cushion is a well-funded emergency account. This fund provides liquid assets to cover unforeseen expenses or periods of reduced income. Best practices for building and maintaining an emergency fund include:

- ❖ Aim for 3 to 6 Months of Living Expenses: Financial experts recommend saving enough to cover 3 to 6 months of essential living expenses, including housing, utilities, groceries, insurance, and debt payments. For those with volatile income or in high-risk industries, it may be wise to extend this cushion to 9 or 12 months of expenses.

- ❖ Automate Savings: To make saving for emergencies a consistent habit, set up automatic transfers from your primary account to a dedicated emergency savings account. This removes the temptation to spend and ensures steady growth over time.
- ❖ Keep the Fund Easily Accessible: Ensure that your emergency fund is liquid and accessible in times of crisis. High-yield savings accounts or money market accounts are good options, as they offer interest without compromising liquidity. Avoid tying up your emergency fund in long-term investments or accounts that penalize early withdrawals.

2. Diversify Income Streams

Relying solely on one source of income can leave individuals vulnerable to financial shocks, especially in times of job loss or economic downturns. Diversifying income sources provides an additional layer of security and helps reduce financial risk. Some strategies include:

- ❖ Develop Passive Income Streams: Explore options for generating passive income, such as rental property, dividend-paying stocks, royalties, or peer-to-peer lending. These sources can provide ongoing cash flow even during periods of unemployment or economic volatility.
- ❖ Freelancing and Side Gigs: In addition to your primary job, consider leveraging your skills to generate extra income through freelancing, consulting, or side businesses. This can be an effective way to supplement your savings and build financial security.

- ❖ Invest in Assets that Appreciate: Focus on income-generating investments like real estate, bonds, or dividend-yielding stocks. These can provide reliable income and grow over time, further protecting against financial downturns.

3. Purchase Adequate Insurance Coverage

Insurance is a critical component of any financial shock-preparedness plan. Properly structured insurance policies can protect you from catastrophic financial losses in cases of illness, injury, or property damage. Consider the following types of coverage:

- ❖ Health Insurance: Ensure that you and your family have comprehensive health insurance to avoid massive out-of-pocket medical expenses in case of illness or accidents. Additionally, review and update your policy regularly to ensure adequate coverage.
- ❖ Disability Insurance: This coverage is essential for protecting against the loss of income due to injury or long-term illness. It provides a percentage of your income if you're unable to work for an extended period.
- ❖ Homeowners or Renters Insurance: Protect your home and personal property from theft, natural disasters, or other damage by having appropriate homeowners or renters insurance in place. This can prevent financial setbacks caused by unexpected events like fires, floods, or break-ins.
- ❖ Life Insurance: If you have dependents, life insurance ensures that your family is financially protected in case of your death. This can cover expenses such as funeral costs, outstanding debts, or provide a financial cushion for your family.

- Liability Insurance: Umbrella liability insurance can provide an additional layer of protection if you're sued for accidents or injuries involving others. This coverage can be critical in safeguarding your assets from legal claims.

4. Reduce and Manage Debt

High levels of debt make individuals more vulnerable to financial shocks, as debt repayments consume cash flow that could be directed toward savings or investments. Reducing and managing debt is a crucial step in building financial resilience. Key strategies include:

- Prioritize High-Interest Debt: Pay off high-interest debt first, such as credit cards or personal loans, to reduce the burden of compounding interest. This will free up more money for savings and emergencies.
- Consolidate Debt: If you have multiple loans with high-interest rates, consider consolidating them into a single loan with a lower rate. This simplifies debt management and reduces the cost of repayments.
- Avoid Accumulating New Debt: Practice financial discipline by avoiding unnecessary borrowing. Whenever possible, pay for expenses using cash or savings to prevent the buildup of new debt.
- Establish a Debt Repayment Plan: Create a clear and realistic debt repayment plan, such as the debt snowball or avalanche method, to systematically eliminate outstanding balances.

5. Create a Budget and Live Below Your Means

A well-crafted budget is essential for tracking income, expenses, and savings. Living below your means—

spending less than you earn—ensures that you can consistently save and build a financial cushion. Here's how to maintain financial discipline:

- Track Spending and Identify Opportunities for Savings: Regularly review your spending habits and identify areas where you can cut back, such as discretionary spending on dining out, entertainment, or non-essential purchases. Redirect these savings toward your emergency fund or investments.
- Prioritize Savings in Your Budget: Include savings as a non-negotiable line item in your budget. This ensures that a portion of your income is consistently allocated toward building a financial cushion.
- Reevaluate and Adjust Spending Regularly: Economic circumstances and personal goals can change over time, so it's important to periodically review and adjust your budget to ensure that it aligns with your current financial situation and goals.

6. Maintain a Flexible Investment Portfolio

A well-diversified investment portfolio can help mitigate risks during economic downturns. While it's important to focus on long-term wealth accumulation, preparing for financial shocks requires flexibility in your investment strategy. Consider the following:

- Diversify Across Asset Classes: Diversification reduces exposure to risk by spreading investments across different asset classes, such as stocks, bonds, real estate, and commodities. This helps safeguard your portfolio from volatility in any one sector.

- Maintain Liquidity: Ensure that a portion of your investments is in liquid assets, such as cash, bonds, or money market funds. This provides the flexibility to access cash during emergencies without needing to sell long-term investments.
- Review Risk Tolerance: Regularly assess your risk tolerance and adjust your investment strategy accordingly, particularly as you approach life events like retirement, job transitions, or significant economic shifts. Being overly exposed to high-risk investments during uncertain times can lead to major losses.

7. Plan for Career Flexibility

Building a financial cushion also involves preparing for potential job loss or career changes. In today's rapidly evolving economy, career adaptability is key to maintaining financial stability. Strategies for career resilience include:

- Invest in Skill Development: Continuously update your professional skills to remain competitive in the job market. This includes pursuing certifications, attending workshops, or gaining expertise in emerging fields. Career adaptability allows you to pivot quickly if your current job becomes unstable.
- Network Regularly: Cultivate a strong professional network to open doors to new opportunities. Maintaining good relationships with colleagues, industry peers, and mentors can lead to job prospects, freelance opportunities, or career guidance in times of need.

- ❖ Consider Remote or Gig Work: Remote work and the gig economy offer flexibility and income diversification. If feasible, explore side gigs or part-time remote work that can provide additional income streams.

8. Stay Financially Informed and Updated

Remaining financially informed and aware of economic trends, tax laws, and market opportunities can help you anticipate financial shocks and make proactive decisions. Regularly review your financial plans and adjust based on changes in personal circumstances or the broader economic landscape.

- ❖ Monitor Economic Indicators: Stay informed about key economic indicators, such as inflation rates, unemployment trends, and interest rate changes, to better anticipate potential financial risks.
- ❖ Work with Financial Advisors: A financial advisor can provide guidance on preparing for financial shocks, optimizing your investment strategy, and ensuring that your financial cushion is adequate for your unique circumstances.

Building a robust financial cushion requires proactive planning and consistent effort. By establishing an emergency fund, diversifying income, maintaining proper insurance, reducing debt, budgeting wisely, and staying informed, individuals can create a solid foundation that will protect them from financial shocks and ensure long-term financial security. Proactively preparing for life's uncertainties not only provides peace of mind but also enables greater financial resilience and the ability to thrive, even in challenging times.

- Emergency Planning: Job Loss, Health Crises, and Market Downturns

In life, financial shocks are inevitable, whether due to job loss, health crises, or market downturns. These events can drastically affect your financial stability, and without adequate planning, they may result in long-term setbacks. Effective emergency planning is essential to building financial resilience and ensuring that unexpected challenges do not derail your financial progress. Below are strategies to prepare for and navigate these common financial shocks.-

1. Planning for Job Loss

Job loss can be one of the most disruptive financial shocks, especially if income is the main or only source of household revenue. Preparing for such an event requires both short-term strategies to address immediate needs and long-term planning to mitigate the overall impact.

Build a Strong Emergency Fund

- 6–12 Months of Living Expenses: The first line of defense against job loss is an emergency fund that can cover at least 6 to 12 months of living expenses. This should include essential costs such as rent/mortgage, groceries, utilities, insurance premiums, and debt payments.
- Easily Accessible: Keep these savings in a high-yield savings account or a money market account to ensure liquidity, enabling you to access these funds without penalties or market volatility risks.

Diversify Income Streams

- Develop Side Incomes: Consider having secondary income streams through freelancing, passive income (rental properties, dividends, etc.), or part-time work. These side hustles or investments can serve as a financial buffer if your primary source of income disappears.

- Gig Economy: With the rise of the gig economy, you can also tap into freelance work or consulting services during job transitions to generate income while searching for long-term employment.

Networking and Skills Development

- Stay Market-Ready: Continuously invest in personal and professional development. Having updated skills and certifications can make you more marketable and improve your chances of quickly finding new employment if job loss occurs.
- Maintain Professional Networks: Relationships in your professional and social networks can often be a key resource in times of job loss. Regularly engage with peers, mentors, and industry professionals to maintain a strong support system that can assist with new job leads or freelance opportunities.

Insurance for Income Protection

- Disability and Income Protection Insurance: If job loss is due to injury or illness, having disability insurance can help replace a portion of your income. Income protection insurance is also an option that specifically covers a percentage of your salary if you are unable to work due to unforeseen circumstances.

2. Planning for Health Crises

A health crisis can impose significant financial burdens, especially if it leads to expensive medical bills or extended periods of unemployment. Emergency planning for health-related issues involves safeguarding both your health and financial well-being.

Comprehensive Health Insurance

- Health Insurance Coverage: Ensure you have comprehensive health insurance to cover medical expenses such as doctor visits, surgeries, prescription drugs, and other treatments. Regularly review your policy to ensure it provides sufficient coverage.
- Health Savings Account (HSA): If you have a high-deductible health plan (HDHP), contribute to a Health Savings Account (HSA). HSAs allow tax-free contributions and withdrawals for qualified medical expenses, providing an extra layer of financial security for health crises.

Disability Insurance

- Short-Term and Long-Term Disability Insurance: In the event of a serious health issue that prevents you from working, disability insurance can replace a portion of your lost income. Short-term policies cover temporary disabilities, while long-term policies provide coverage for extended or permanent disabilities.

Long-Term Care Insurance

- Prepare for Extended Health Crises: For severe or chronic conditions that require long-term care, consider purchasing long-term care insurance.

This policy can help cover the cost of extended medical services, home care, or nursing facilities, reducing the financial burden on you and your family.

Emergency Health Fund

- Set Aside Medical Contingency Funds: In addition to having health insurance, it's wise to establish a health emergency fund to cover expenses such as deductibles, out-of-pocket costs, or treatments not fully covered by your insurance plan. This fund can prevent you from going into debt during a health crisis.

Legal Preparation

- Power of Attorney and Living Wills: In the event of a medical emergency where you are incapacitated, have a power of attorney and living will in place. This ensures that your healthcare and financial decisions will be handled according to your wishes, providing peace of mind for you and your loved ones.

3. Planning for Market Downturns

Market downturns are an unavoidable part of the economic cycle, often leading to volatility in investments, decreased asset values, and even widespread economic recession. Being financially prepared for these downturns requires strategic risk management and portfolio diversification.

Diversify Your Investment Portfolio

- Asset Allocation: Diversify your investments across various asset classes such as stocks, bonds, real estate, and commodities. A well-balanced portfolio can mitigate the impact of market volatility, as different asset classes tend to perform differently under various market conditions.

- Global Diversification: Investing in international markets can also spread risk, as economic conditions in different regions can vary. Diversifying into foreign markets may help cushion the blow during domestic economic downturns.

Maintain Liquidity

- Keep a Portion in Cash or Near-Cash Assets: Having a portion of your portfolio in liquid assets like cash, money market funds, or short-term bonds allows you to cover living expenses or seize investment opportunities during a downturn without having to sell long-term investments at a loss.

Rebalance Your Portfolio Regularly

- Adjust for Risk Tolerance: Periodically review and rebalance your portfolio to align with your risk tolerance, particularly as market conditions fluctuate. As you approach retirement or major life goals, consider shifting to lower-risk investments, such as bonds or dividend-paying stocks.

Emergency Investment Strategy

- Stay the Course: Avoid panic selling during market downturns. It's important to maintain a long-term investment perspective, as markets typically recover over time. Having an emergency fund or liquid assets allows you to avoid withdrawing from investment accounts during bear markets.

- Dollar-Cost Averaging: Consider using dollar-cost averaging to buy into the market gradually during downturns. This approach reduces the impact of volatility by spreading out your investments over time, potentially lowering the average cost per share.

Take Advantage of Opportunities

- Market Downturns as Buying Opportunities: If you are financially stable and have adequate liquidity, market downturns can present unique opportunities to invest at lower prices. Well-timed investments during bear markets can lead to substantial long-term gains.

4. Additional General Strategies for Financial Shock Preparedness

Regularly Review Your Financial Plan

Ensure that your financial plan is adaptable to changing circumstances. Periodically assess your savings goals, insurance needs, and investment strategies to stay prepared for any financial shocks. Work with a financial advisor to tailor your plan for maximum flexibility.

Develop a Debt Management Strategy

Debt can exacerbate the impact of financial shocks, particularly if high-interest loans or credit card debt consume a significant portion of your income. Prioritize paying off high-interest debt and avoid taking on new debt unless absolutely necessary.

Income Protection and Up-skilling

Enhancing your career prospects through continuous learning and skill development can also serve as a safeguard against economic shocks. Being adaptable in your career provides more options and increases your chances of regaining stable income if disruptions occur.

5. Estate Planning as a Safeguard for Financial Shocks

One often-overlooked aspect of emergency financial preparedness is estate planning. While typically associated with long-term planning, estate management ensures that your financial affairs are organized and protected in case of unexpected events, such as incapacitation or death. It also helps shield your assets from creditors and unforeseen liabilities.

Establish a Will and Trust

- Comprehensive Will: A will outlines how your assets should be distributed and ensures that your family and dependents are provided for according to your wishes. Regularly updating your will ensures it reflects current circumstances, such as the birth of children or changes in assets.
- Trusts for Asset Protection: Trusts, whether revocable or irrevocable, are legal vehicles that provide additional layers of protection for your assets. A trust can help ensure that your wealth is passed on without probate, and in some cases, protect assets from creditors and legal challenges during a financial crisis.

Designate Beneficiaries and Power of Attorney

- Updated Beneficiary Designations: Ensuring that all your financial accounts, life insurance policies, and retirement funds have up-to-date beneficiaries is crucial. This step ensures that your assets bypass probate and go directly to the designated individuals, saving time and legal fees during a financial emergency.

- ❖ Durable Power of Attorney: In the event that you are incapacitated due to a health crisis or other reasons, having a durable power of attorney allows a trusted person to manage your financial and legal affairs. This is an essential step in ensuring that your financial obligations—such as mortgages, utility bills, or taxes—are still managed during unexpected events.

Consider Life Insurance for Income Protection

- ❖ Life Insurance Policies: Having life insurance is critical to providing financial protection to your family in the event of your death. It helps replace lost income, pay off debt, and cover future expenses such as your children's education or housing costs. There are various types of life insurance (e.g., term, whole, and universal life), and it's important to select one that aligns with your financial objectives.

Review and Organize Your Documents

- ❖ Organize Critical Financial Documents: Make sure important documents like tax returns, loan agreements, insurance policies, and bank account details are well-organized and easily accessible. Having everything in one place reduces stress and helps family members or executors manage your affairs more efficiently during a crisis.

6. Long-Term Strategies for Financial Resilience

While emergency planning focuses on preparing for immediate shocks, building long-term resilience requires a strategic approach that integrates financial goals, risk management, and wealth-building strategies. Adopting a forward-looking mindset can help ensure that your finances remain strong even during future crises.

Diversify Your Income Streams Beyond Investments

- Real Estate Income: Investing in rental properties or real estate investment trusts (REITs) can provide a stable income stream during market downturns. Real estate can often weather economic shocks better than equities or bonds, depending on the market.
- Business Ventures and Side Hustles: Beyond traditional employment and investments, diversifying into entrepreneurial ventures or side hustles can create additional income buffers. This also ensures that you are not solely reliant on the performance of your primary career or the stock market.

Regularly Update Your Financial Plan

- Adapt to Changing Economic Conditions: The financial landscape is constantly evolving. Regular reviews of your financial plan, including your emergency fund, insurance policies, and investments, allow you to adapt to changing conditions like inflation, market downturns, or shifts in the labor market. Work with a financial advisor to adjust your portfolio or update your strategies as necessary.

Invest in Skills and Education for Career Flexibility

- Up-skilling and Continuous Learning: The future of work is rapidly changing due to technological advancements and economic shifts. Regularly investing in your skills and education ensures you stay competitive in the job market and can transition into new industries or roles if your current field experiences a downturn. This future-proofing approach enhances job security, income potential, and long-term financial stability.

7. Stress-Testing Your Financial Plan

To ensure that your financial plan is truly resilient, it's essential to test it against potential worst-case scenarios. This proactive measure allows you to identify weaknesses and address them before a crisis hits.

Run Worst-Case Simulations

- Scenario Planning: Consider running simulations of worst-case financial scenarios—such as losing your job, facing a major medical expense, or experiencing a significant market downturn. Estimate how your emergency fund, insurance policies, and income streams would perform under these conditions. This approach provides clarity on whether your current financial setup can handle significant shocks.
- Adjust Savings and Expenses: Based on the outcomes of your simulations, adjust your savings rate or make changes to your investment strategy. For example, if your analysis shows that your emergency fund would not last through a 12-month job loss, consider cutting discretionary spending to build up savings.

Prepare for Rising Interest Rates or Inflation

- Impact on Debt: Rising interest rates and inflation can increase the cost of debt and living expenses, exacerbating financial shocks. If you have variable interest loans, such as credit card debt or adjustable-rate mortgages prioritize paying these off as soon as possible.

- ❖ Inflation-Protected Investments: Consider investing in inflation-protected securities like Treasury Inflation-Protected Securities (TIPS) or real assets such as real estate and commodities, which tend to hold value or even appreciate during periods of high inflation.

8. Creating a Culture of Financial Resilience in Your Household

Financial resilience is not just an individual responsibility—it is often a family-wide endeavor. Building a culture of financial preparedness within your household ensures that everyone is aligned with common goals, and that collective financial behavior fosters security for the entire family.

Open Communication About Finances

- ❖ Family Financial Meetings: Hold regular discussions about family finances, including savings goals, budgeting, and emergency planning. Engaging your spouse, children, and other dependents in these conversations builds a sense of shared responsibility and promotes transparency regarding financial decisions.

Educating Children on Financial Preparedness

- ❖ Teach Financial Literacy Early: Instilling financial literacy in children from a young age helps build financial resilience for future generations. Teach them about saving, investing, and managing credit so that they can navigate financial challenges more effectively as they grow older.

Develop Joint Emergency Plans

- Emergency Preparedness for the Entire Family: Ensure that all family members know the household's emergency financial plan. Discuss what to do in the event of a job loss, medical crisis, or natural disaster. Having a comprehensive understanding of roles and responsibilities during a crisis reduces confusion and promotes quicker decision-making.

Preparing for financial shocks is not only about responding to crises but also about proactive planning to minimize their impact. By diversifying income streams, building emergency funds, securing appropriate insurance coverage, and maintaining flexibility in your financial plan, you create a robust financial safety net. A combination of foresight, strategic investments, and continuous education ensures that both you and your family can weather unexpected financial storms and maintain long-term financial health. Ultimately, financial resilience is the cornerstone of lasting wealth and security in an unpredictable world.

Thriving in Uncertain Markets

- Opportunities during financial crises: Buying undervalued assets, rebalancing portfolios, and strategic investments

Financial crises, while daunting, present unique opportunities for investors to build long-term wealth. History has shown that economic downturns often result in assets becoming significantly undervalued, providing savvy investors with the chance to acquire quality investments at a discount. Crises also present an opportunity for portfolio rebalancing and making strategic investments that can yield substantial returns once the markets stabilize. This section explores key strategies for identifying and capitalizing on opportunities during financial crises, focusing on buying undervalued assets, rebalancing portfolios, and engaging in forward-looking investments.

1. Buying Undervalued Assets: Identifying High-Quality Investments at a Discount

One of the most significant opportunities during a financial crisis is the chance to purchase high-quality assets at deeply discounted prices. When markets experience a downturn, investor sentiment often turns negative, leading to widespread selling and an overall decrease in asset prices. However, this indiscriminate selling can push the prices of fundamentally strong companies, stocks, and other assets far below their intrinsic value, creating a prime opportunity for long-term investors.

Value Investing: During a crisis, the focus should shift toward value investing—identifying assets that are undervalued based on fundamentals such as earnings, cash flow, and market position. While short-term price declines may impact these assets, their long-term potential remains strong. By buying during market dips, investors can benefit from future recoveries and substantial capital appreciation when market conditions improve.

Blue-Chip Stocks: Historically, many blue-chip companies (established, financially stable companies with strong track records) experience temporary declines during market crises. These companies tend to weather downturns better than smaller or less established firms and are often among the first to recover. Purchasing shares in blue-chip stocks during a crisis provides investors with the opportunity to acquire stakes in well-established businesses at a fraction of their usual price.

Real Estate: Financial crises also impact real estate markets, often leading to decreased property values. For investors with sufficient liquidity, this can be a chance to purchase income-generating properties or land at below-market prices. Over time, as the economy recovers, real estate investments can appreciate in value, providing both capital gains and passive income streams.

2. Rebalancing Portfolios: Adjusting to Align with Long-Term Goals

Another key opportunity during financial crises is the chance to rebalance portfolios. Crises can cause significant deviations from an investor's intended asset allocation, as certain asset classes may lose or gain value disproportionately. Rebalancing ensures that portfolios remain aligned with an investor's risk tolerance, time horizon, and long-term goals.

Rebalancing for Risk Management: During a crisis, stocks typically experience sharper declines than bonds or other safer assets. This shift may result in a portfolio that is too heavily weighted toward safer, low-return investments. Rebalancing involves selling a portion of the over-weighted, lower-risk assets (e.g., bonds) and buying undervalued, higher-risk assets (e.g., stocks) to return the portfolio to its target allocation. This allows investors to maintain their risk exposure while positioning themselves for gains during the market recovery.

Buying Low, Selling High: A disciplined rebalancing strategy enforces the "buy low, sell high" philosophy, which is particularly important during periods of volatility. Rebalancing during a crisis can help capitalize on the low prices of riskier, growth-oriented investments while securing profits from safer assets that may have outperformed during the downturn. Over time, this disciplined approach can improve portfolio performance.

Tax-Loss Harvesting: Crises often present opportunities for tax-loss harvesting, a strategy in which investors sell underperforming assets at a loss to offset gains and reduce their tax liability. These losses can be used to balance taxable capital gains, lowering the overall tax burden. Proceeds from the sale can then be reinvested in similar assets, maintaining exposure to potential market recovery.

3. Strategic Investments: Positioning for Long-Term Growth

While crises can cause short-term turmoil, they also lay the groundwork for long-term growth. Strategic investments during these periods can provide significant returns as the economy stabilizes and recovers. Identifying sectors, industries, and companies poised for growth during and after the crisis is essential for capitalizing on future opportunities.

Sectors Likely to Rebound: During financial crises, certain industries are hit harder than others. For example, consumer discretionary, energy, and technology sectors may experience significant short-term volatility, but these industries often recover strongly when the economy rebounds. Strategic investors should focus on sectors with strong long-term growth potential that may be temporarily undervalued due to market panic.

Emerging Trends: Crises often accelerate the adoption of new technologies or business models. For instance, during the 2008 financial crisis, tech companies that focused on innovation and digital transformation thrived in the aftermath. Similarly, in the wake of the COVID-19 pandemic, industries related to healthcare, remote work technology, and e-commerce saw massive growth. Identifying these emerging trends during a crisis and investing strategically in companies that support or benefit from these shifts can lead to outsized gains.

Private Markets and Alternative Investments: During financial downturns, investors may also consider diversifying into private markets or alternative investments, such as private equity, venture capital, or commodities. These asset classes often operate independently of traditional public markets and may offer attractive opportunities during periods of volatility. Additionally, alternative investments can serve as a hedge against inflation, currency fluctuations, or other risks associated with financial crises.

4. Maintaining a Cash Reserve: Seizing Opportunities Quickly

Having liquidity during a financial crisis is critical for taking advantage of opportunities as they arise. Investors who maintain a cash reserve are better positioned to deploy capital quickly and buy undervalued assets or make strategic investments when prices are depressed. Liquidity for Flexibility: Maintaining an emergency cash reserve ensures that investors are not forced to sell assets during a downturn to cover unexpected expenses. Instead, they can use this reserve to strategically buy assets when opportunities present themselves. Moreover, liquid assets provide flexibility; allowing investors to adapt to changing market conditions and respond to opportunities swiftly.

5. Patience and Discipline: Holding for the Long Term

While buying undervalued assets and making strategic investments during a crisis can be lucrative, it requires patience and discipline. Market recoveries do not happen overnight, and investors need to be prepared to hold their positions over the long term to realize substantial gains. Avoiding Panic Selling: The key to thriving during a financial crisis is avoiding the impulse to sell during market panic. By staying focused on long-term goals and maintaining discipline, investors can weather short-term volatility and emerge stronger once the market recovers.

Capitalizing on Opportunities During Financial Crises

Financial crises, though challenging, present remarkable opportunities for investors who remain calm, disciplined, and strategic. By focusing on purchasing undervalued assets, rebalancing portfolios, and making forward-looking investments, investors can position themselves for long-term success. Crises allow for the acquisition of high-quality assets at discounted prices, the recalibration of portfolios to match risk tolerance, and the opportunity to invest in emerging trends that will drive future growth. Ultimately, the key to thriving in uncertain markets lies in a combination of strategic planning, disciplined execution, and a forward-looking perspective.

- Behavioral Strategies to Avoid Panic and Stay Calm During Market Volatility

Market volatility is an inevitable aspect of investing, but how investors react during periods of uncertainty can greatly impact their long-term financial outcomes. While it's normal to experience anxiety when markets fluctuate, employing behavioral strategies to avoid panic can lead to more measured and rational decisions. This section explores how investors can maintain calm and composure, even when market conditions are unpredictable, and outlines practical strategies for thriving in uncertain markets.

1. Understanding Market Volatility: Expect and Accept Uncertainty

To navigate market volatility, the first step understands that price fluctuations are a natural part of the market cycle. Volatility can arise due to economic factors, geopolitical events, or investor sentiment, and it doesn't necessarily indicate a long-term market decline. Historical data shows that while markets experience corrections, they tend to recover over time. Acceptance: Knowing that ups and downs are part of investing will help you mentally prepare for periods of instability. Instead of seeing volatility as a threat, view it as an opportunity to reassess your strategy and potentially buy quality investments at a discount.

2. Reframe Your Perspective: Focus on Long-Term Goals

One of the most effective behavioral strategies to stay calm during market volatility is to shift your focus from short-term price movements to your long-term financial goals. Successful investing requires a disciplined, long-term perspective, as market timing is both difficult and fraught with emotional pitfalls. Goal-Oriented Mindset: By focusing on long-term objectives—such as retirement, education funding, or wealth accumulation—you can avoid getting swept up in short-term market noise. Market corrections can seem less significant when measured against the broader context of your financial goals. It's important to remind yourself that short-term volatility is often inconsequential over a 10-, 20-, or 30-year investment horizon.

3. Establish a Pre-Planned Strategy: Develop a Written Investment Plan

An effective way to combat panic during market downturns is to develop and adhere to a clear, written investment plan. This plan should outline your investment objectives, time horizon, risk tolerance, and strategies for asset allocation and diversification.
Stick to the Plan: When the market experiences volatility, it's easy to let fear drive decision-making. However, if you've crafted a thoughtful investment plan, it serves as a roadmap, helping you stick to your strategy even in times of uncertainty. By committing to a pre-determined asset allocation and rebalancing strategy, you can mitigate the emotional reactions that often accompany market fluctuations.

4. Embrace Diversification: Reduce the Emotional Impact of Loss

Diversification is a crucial tool for reducing the emotional impact of market volatility. By spreading investments across different asset classes—such as stocks, bonds, real estate, and commodities—you can reduce the risk that any one segment of the market will derail your entire portfolio.
Balanced Portfolios: A well-diversified portfolio often experiences less severe losses during downturns, which can help reduce the emotional stress associated with seeing large declines in your account value. During volatile periods, diversified portfolios typically exhibit lower volatility and are more likely to recover quickly.

5. Limit Media Consumption: Avoid the 24/7 News Cycle

The constant barrage of market updates, sensational headlines, and financial news can fuel panic and lead to rash decisions during times of market volatility. Financial media tends to overemphasize short-term events, fostering a sense of urgency and fear. Media Detox: To maintain a sense of calm, limit your exposure to financial news, especially during periods of high volatility. Instead of checking your portfolio or market updates multiple times a day, set regular intervals to review your investments, perhaps monthly or quarterly. This helps you focus on long-term trends rather than being consumed by short-term movements.

6. Practice Mindfulness and Emotional Control: Manage Stress and Anxiety

Staying calm during market downturns often requires active stress management and emotional regulation techniques. Mindfulness practices, such as meditation, deep breathing exercises, and yoga, can help reduce anxiety and prevent impulsive reactions. Mindful Investing: Cultivating emotional intelligence in investing involves recognizing and managing the emotions of fear and greed. When anxiety levels rise, practicing mindfulness techniques can help you regain control of your reactions, leading to better decision-making. By acknowledging emotions without acting on them, you can avoid making irrational decisions during market volatility.

7. Use Dollar-Cost Averaging: Take Advantage of Volatility

One of the behavioral strategies to thrive during market volatility is to take advantage of dollar-cost averaging. This strategy involves investing a fixed amount of money at regular intervals, regardless of market conditions. Steady Investments: Dollar-cost averaging allows you to purchase more shares when prices are low and fewer shares when prices are high, helping to reduce the impact of market volatility on your overall portfolio. This technique not only helps smooth out the effects of market fluctuations but also alleviates the pressure of timing the market perfectly.

8. Focus on What You Can Control: Expenses and Cash Flow

During periods of market volatility, investors often fixate on things they cannot control, such as market direction or economic conditions. Instead, redirect your focus to factors within your control—such as your spending habits, savings rate, and asset allocation. Manage Personal Finances: By tightening control over your personal finances and increasing savings, you can feel more empowered and less at the mercy of the markets. Having a stable financial foundation also makes it easier to ride out downturns without needing to sell investments prematurely.

9. Rebalance Your Portfolio: Maintain Your Target Risk Level

Rebalancing your portfolio involves adjusting the allocation of assets back to your original targets after market fluctuations cause significant deviations. Regular rebalancing helps ensure that your risk exposure remains aligned with your goals and risk tolerance. Stay Disciplined: During times of volatility, some assets will perform better than others, causing your portfolio to drift from its intended allocation. Rebalancing forces you to sell over performing assets and buy underperforming ones, a process that promotes the time-tested principle of "buy low, sell high." This systematic approach removes emotions from the equation and helps you maintain balance.

10. Consult a Financial Advisor: Get Expert Guidance

When faced with uncertainty, many investors benefit from professional guidance. A trusted financial advisor can provide objective advice, prevent you from making rash decisions, and help you navigate the complexity of volatile markets.
Expert Support: Financial advisors are well-versed in market dynamics and behavioral finance. They can offer perspective during downturns, helping you stay focused on your long-term goals. Having a professional guide also reduces the emotional burden of managing your portfolio, allowing you to benefit from their experience and insights.

Market volatility is inevitable, but how you respond determines your long-term success as an investor. By developing an understanding of market cycles, focusing on long-term goals, and employing behavioral strategies such as mindfulness, diversification, and disciplined investing, you can avoid panic and capitalize on the opportunities that volatility presents. The key to thriving in uncertain markets is maintaining emotional discipline, adhering to a well-thought-out plan, and using volatility as a tool for growth rather than a source of fear.

The Power of Adaptability in Wealth Building

- Developing adaptability as a critical skill for sustained wealth

Adaptability is an essential trait for those aiming to achieve and sustain long-term wealth. In an ever-evolving global economy characterized by technological advancements, shifting market dynamics, and unpredictable economic cycles, the ability to adjust to new conditions is critical for financial success. Wealth-building, much like any other strategic endeavor, requires continuous evaluation and recalibration. Developing adaptability as a skill allows individuals to respond effectively to changes in the market, economy, or their personal circumstances, ensuring their financial strategies remain robust and relevant. This section explores how adaptability is fundamental to wealth creation and offers practical ways to build this skill for lasting financial success.

1. Understanding Adaptability in Wealth Building

At its core, adaptability is the capacity to adjust to new situations, learn from experiences, and develop creative solutions to challenges. In wealth building, this means being able to pivot when financial strategies are no longer working, recognize new opportunities, and adjust one's mindset and approach to align with shifting economic realities.

In contrast to rigid financial planning, adaptable individuals maintain an open mind and view uncertainty as a natural part of wealth-building. They embrace change as an opportunity for growth and use it to their advantage, whether it's exploring new investment opportunities, modifying spending habits, or acquiring new skills that enhance earning potential.

2. The Role of Adaptability in Navigating Economic Cycles

Economic cycles—periods of growth, recession, and recovery—are inevitable, and the financial markets are constantly fluctuating. Individuals who lack adaptability are more likely to panic during downturns or cling to outdated strategies, risking their long-term financial stability. Conversely, adaptable investors and wealth builders understand that economic changes are cyclical and plan for them by developing flexible strategies.

Surviving Recessions and Market Crashes: During periods of economic decline, an adaptable individual does not react impulsively to market crashes or falling asset prices. Instead, they recognize the opportunity to reassess their portfolio, realign with current market trends, and make strategic moves that protect their wealth while positioning themselves for recovery.

Thriving in Growth Phases: Conversely, in periods of economic growth, adaptable individuals do not rest on their laurels. They continue to monitor their investments, adjust strategies as necessary, and seize new opportunities that emerge. Whether it's diversifying into emerging industries, reinvesting profits, or scaling businesses, adaptability ensures wealth continues to grow during favorable economic conditions.

3. Adapting to Technological Disruptions

Technology is transforming every aspect of the economy, from how we work to how we invest. The rise of automation, artificial intelligence (AI), financial technologies (FinTech), and digital currencies have created both risks and opportunities for wealth builders. Adaptability allows individuals to navigate these changes effectively by integrating new tools, platforms, and investment opportunities into their financial strategies.

Leveraging FinTech: FinTech innovations, such as robo-advisors, AI-driven investment strategies, and digital banking platforms, offer modern, efficient ways to manage wealth. An adaptable wealth builder stays up to date on these trends, taking advantage of technology to streamline their financial management, enhance their investment decision-making, and reduce fees.

Adopting Cryptocurrency and Blockchain: As the financial landscape evolves, digital currencies like Bitcoin and

Ethereum, and technologies like blockchain, have gained traction as alternative stores of value and transaction methods. While these markets can be volatile, adaptable investors recognize the potential of these innovations and make informed decisions about their participation, while also balancing the associated risks.

Up-skilling for Future Wealth: Adaptability extends beyond investments to personal development. As industries and jobs evolve due to technological advancements, maintaining a high income may require learning new skills, embracing digital tools, and pivoting to more relevant careers. Individuals who are willing to up-skill and embrace change in their professional lives will have greater earning potential and can adapt their wealth-building strategies to new economic realities.

4. Adapting Investment Strategies for Diversification

In wealth building, diversification is the key to managing risk and ensuring long-term financial success. Adaptable individuals continuously reassess their investment portfolios to ensure they are properly diversified across sectors, geographies, and asset classes.

Adjusting Portfolio Allocations: As market conditions change, an adaptable investor may adjust their portfolio to reduce exposure to underperforming sectors and increase allocations in areas with higher growth potential. For example, during a global economic slowdown, shifting from growth stocks to more stable, dividend-paying companies, or increasing exposure to bonds may provide better returns.

Exploring New Markets: Globalization and emerging markets offer new investment opportunities, but they also introduce volatility and risk. Adaptable investors are open to exploring global markets, including stocks, bonds, and real estate abroad. They understand the importance of staying informed about international markets, trade agreements, and geopolitical events that may impact their investments.

Incorporating Alternative Investments: In addition to traditional investments like stocks and bonds, adaptable individuals may explore alternative assets such as real estate, private equity, commodities, and hedge funds. These assets often behave differently from public markets, offering additional opportunities for diversification and wealth growth.

5. Developing Financial Resilience through Adaptability

Adaptability is not just about recognizing opportunities; it's also about developing the financial resilience to withstand challenges. Resilience is the ability to recover from setbacks, and adaptable wealth builders focus on creating systems that ensure they can bounce back from financial shocks.

Building an Emergency Fund: An adaptable individual knows the importance of maintaining liquidity to survive unexpected events, such as job loss or market downturns. They prioritize building a cash reserve or emergency fund to cover several months' worth of living expenses, providing a financial cushion during periods of uncertainty.

Balancing Risk and Reward: Adaptable individuals are not afraid to take calculated risks, but they do so with the understanding that diversification and risk management are critical to sustaining wealth over the long term. They regularly evaluate their risk tolerance and adjust their financial plans accordingly.

Adjusting Financial Goals: Adaptable individuals also recognize that personal circumstances change over time. Whether due to a shift in career, lifestyle, or family needs, they are willing to adjust their financial goals to stay aligned with their current reality. This could mean saving more aggressively, retiring later, or exploring new income streams as personal or market conditions shift.

6. Cultivating an Adaptable Mindset

Cultivating adaptability requires both mental flexibility and a willingness to learn. Financial markets and personal circumstances can change unexpectedly, and an adaptable mindset allows individuals to embrace uncertainty rather than fear it.

Emotional Intelligence in Wealth Building: One of the hallmarks of adaptability is emotional intelligence (EQ)—the ability to recognize and manage emotions, particularly in high-stress situations like financial downturns. Those with strong EQ are less likely to make impulsive decisions based on fear or greed, instead remaining calm and rational when adapting to new financial circumstances.

Continuous Learning: Adaptable individuals never stop learning. They regularly educate themselves on financial trends, investment strategies, and emerging technologies. By staying informed, they are better positioned to capitalize on new opportunities and avoid common financial pitfalls.

Networking and Mentorship: Adaptability also involves learning from others. Successful wealth builders seek out mentors, network with like-minded individuals, and stay connected to communities that offer new perspectives and ideas. This collaborative approach ensures they remain adaptable in a rapidly changing world.

Adaptability is not just a helpful trait; it is a fundamental skill for anyone seeking to build and sustain wealth over the long term. By staying flexible, open to change, and continuously learning, adaptable individuals can navigate economic cycles, technological disruptions, and personal challenges with resilience and foresight. Whether it's adjusting investment strategies, embracing new technologies, or up-skilling for future growth, adaptability ensures that financial plans remain relevant and effective in an ever-changing world. Ultimately, developing adaptability is essential for sustaining wealth, achieving financial goals, and thriving in uncertain markets.

- How to Turn Crises into Opportunities for Financial Growth and Reinvention

Crises, whether economic downturns, personal financial hardships, or market disruptions, often present formidable challenges to maintaining and growing wealth. However, for individuals and businesses equipped with adaptability, these crises can serve as catalysts for financial growth, reinvention, and innovation. While fear and uncertainty can cause many to withdraw or act reactively, those who harness adaptability as a strategic tool can seize new opportunities, build resilience, and emerge stronger from even the most daunting circumstances.

In this section, we explore how crises can be transformed into opportunities for financial growth, focusing on the role adaptability plays in shifting mindsets, fostering creative problem-solving and positioning individuals to capitalize on new prospects in times of uncertainty.

1. Changing Your Perspective: Crises as Catalysts for Innovation

The first step in turning a crisis into an opportunity is adopting a mindset of adaptability and openness to change. Rather than viewing crises as threats to wealth and stability, adaptable individuals reframe them as opportunities to innovate, grow, and reinvent financial strategies.

Adopting a Growth Mindset: In times of crisis, maintaining a growth mindset is crucial. This involves seeing setbacks as temporary and solvable challenges rather than insurmountable obstacles. Those with a growth mindset actively seek out lessons in adversity and use them to refine their financial plans. For example, during an economic downturn, an adaptable investor might view falling asset prices as an opportunity to buy undervalued investments, positioning themselves for greater returns during recovery.

Rethinking Financial Goals: A crisis often forces individuals to re-evaluate their financial goals and priorities. Adaptability allows for a fluid approach, enabling individuals to reassess their objectives and adjust their strategies in light of changing conditions. For instance, during a personal financial crisis, someone might shift their focus from short-term spending to long-term savings, strengthening their financial foundation for future growth.

2. Identifying Hidden Opportunities amidst Crisis

One of the hallmarks of adaptability is the ability to recognize and act on hidden opportunities that may arise during crises. While market disruptions and economic shocks can cause widespread losses, they also create openings for those who can pivot quickly and identify new investment or business prospects.

Buying Undervalued Assets: Economic downturns often lead to the devaluation of stocks, real estate, and other assets. For adaptable investors with sufficient liquidity, this is an opportunity to buy assets at discounted prices, thereby laying the groundwork for substantial gains when markets recover. Historically, those who invest during bear markets or recessions often see outsized returns when economic conditions stabilize.

Starting or Scaling Businesses: Crises can also give rise to new business opportunities. As consumer behaviors shift, gaps in the market emerge. During the COVID-19 pandemic, for instance, many businesses pivoted to e-commerce or online services, capitalizing on new consumer needs. Adaptable entrepreneurs quickly restructured their business models to meet demand, while others innovated entirely new products or services that catered to the changing environment.

Leveraging Technological Disruption: Times of crisis often accelerate the adoption of new technologies. Adaptable individuals can take advantage of these shifts by investing in or adopting emerging technologies that improve efficiency or create new revenue streams. For example, digital currencies like Bitcoin or FinTech innovations gained prominence during periods of economic uncertainty, opening new avenues for tech-savvy investors and businesses to grow.

3. Reinvention: Pivoting to New Career or Investment Paths

For those facing personal financial crises—whether from job loss, business challenges, or investment losses—adaptability is the key to reinvention. This can involve pivoting to new careers, reskilling, or diversifying income streams to ensure long-term financial stability.

Exploring New Career Opportunities: A personal financial crisis, such as job loss or business closure, can be an opportunity to reassess career goals and explore new paths. Adaptable individuals are willing to learn new skills, shift industries, or explore entrepreneurial ventures. For example, during the 2008 financial crisis, many professionals used the downturn as an opportunity to pursue education in emerging fields like technology or healthcare, ultimately leading to more secure and lucrative careers.

Diversifying Income Streams: Another approach to reinvention is diversifying income sources. Individuals may take on freelance work, start side businesses, or invest in passive income opportunities such as real estate or dividend-paying stocks. By cultivating multiple income streams, adaptable individuals can reduce their reliance on any single source of income and build financial resilience.

4. Strategic Rebalancing: Adjusting Portfolios for Growth

In times of market turbulence, adaptable investors know that maintaining a static portfolio is risky. Instead, they rebalance their investments to align with evolving market conditions, ensuring they can capitalize on new growth opportunities.

Shifting Asset Allocations: During a crisis, certain sectors or asset classes may outperform others. Adaptable investors recognize this and adjust their portfolios accordingly. For instance, during a recession, it may be prudent to shift investments toward defensive sectors like healthcare, consumer staples, or utilities, which tend to be more resilient in downturns. As markets recover, adaptable investors then rebalance back toward higher-growth sectors or assets.

Taking Advantage of Lower Valuations: Crises often lead to widespread declines in asset prices, even in sectors with long-term potential. Adaptable investors take advantage of these lower valuations by buying quality stocks, bonds, or real estate at a discount, positioning themselves for substantial future gains. This strategy, known as value investing, requires the ability to remain calm during market volatility and the willingness to act against the crowd.

Strategic Reinvestment in Innovation: In addition to traditional asset classes, adaptable investors may look to allocate capital to sectors poised for future growth, such as renewable energy, technology, or biotechnology. Even during crises, these innovative sectors often continue to experience significant development and can offer substantial returns for those willing to invest early.

5. Building Long-Term Resilience Through Adaptability

Crises are an inevitable part of any financial journey, but those who develop adaptability as a core strength can build resilience that protects their wealth over the long term. By preparing for adversity in advance and cultivating an adaptable mindset, individuals can not only survive crises but also thrive in their aftermath.

Building an Emergency Fund: One of the simplest but most effective strategies for financial resilience is maintaining a well-funded emergency savings account. This ensures that when a crisis hits—whether personal, such as a job loss, or broader, like a market crash—there is sufficient liquidity to cover essential expenses without needing to liquidate investments at a loss.

Maintaining Flexibility in Financial Plans: Adaptable wealth builders understand that even the best financial plans must be flexible. They regularly revisit and adjust their financial strategies to reflect new information, changing circumstances, and evolving personal goals. This flexibility ensures they are prepared to pivot quickly during times of crisis, whether by shifting investments, rethinking retirement plans, or temporarily cutting discretionary spending.

Staying Informed and Proactive: Finally, building resilience through adaptability requires staying informed about economic trends, market conditions, and global events. Those who remain proactive—whether by continuing their education, consulting with financial advisors, or monitoring market developments—are better positioned to act quickly when crises arise, turning potential losses into gains.

In summary, adaptability is the cornerstone of turning financial crises into opportunities for growth and reinvention. By adopting a growth mindset, identifying hidden opportunities, and rebalancing strategies during uncertain times, adaptable individuals and businesses can capitalize on market shifts, emerging technologies, and undervalued assets. Reinvention, whether through career changes or new income streams, offers additional pathways to long-term success. Ultimately, those who cultivate adaptability not only protect their wealth in times of crisis but also position themselves for future prosperity, proving that adversity can be the foundation of financial opportunity.

- Case Studies of Individuals and Businesses that Thrived Through Uncertainty

In periods of economic instability and financial uncertainty, those who possess the ability to adapt can transform adversity into opportunity. Whether through innovative business strategies, personal reinvention, or taking calculated risks, these case studies illustrate how adaptability can lead to wealth creation and resilience in the face of uncertainty.

1. Jeff Bezos and Amazon: Thriving During the Dot-Com Bust and the 2008 Financial Crisis

Background: In the late 1990s, the internet bubble saw a massive surge in tech companies, many of which failed when the bubble burst in the early 2000s. Amazon, founded by Jeff Bezos in 1994, faced tremendous pressure during the dot-com bust, with its stock price falling from a peak of $106 to under $6.

Adaptability: Despite the collapse of many tech companies, Bezos and Amazon not only survived but emerged as a leader in e-commerce. Bezos's adaptability was evident in his long-term thinking and willingness to pivot the company's strategy. Instead of focusing solely on book sales, Amazon expanded into a marketplace for a broad range of products. Later, Amazon launched Amazon Web Services (AWS) in 2006, which transformed the company into a major player in cloud computing. This diversification insulated Amazon from market volatility and set the foundation for massive future growth.

Thriving Through Uncertainty: Amazon's adaptability allowed it to thrive during the 2008 financial crisis, where many companies struggled. AWS became a significant revenue driver, while Amazon continued to invest in logistics and technology. Bezos's emphasis on customer obsession, innovation, and long-term vision enabled Amazon to capitalize on growing e-commerce trends and solidify its position as a market leader.

Outcome: Today, Amazon is one of the largest companies globally, with diverse revenue streams in retail, cloud computing, entertainment, and more. Bezos's adaptability and forward-thinking have made Amazon a prime example of thriving through uncertainty.

2. Reed Hastings and Netflix: Pivoting from DVD Rentals to Streaming

Background: Netflix, founded by Reed Hastings and Marc Randolph in 1997, originally operated as a DVD rental service by mail. By the mid-2000s, the rise of digital media and the decline of physical rentals threatened Netflix's business model.

Adaptability: Recognizing the potential of online streaming, Hastings began transitioning Netflix from physical DVDs to a digital streaming platform in 2007. This move required significant investment in technology and licensing agreements with content providers, but Hastings saw the future of entertainment in streaming rather than physical media.

Thriving Through Uncertainty: Netflix's adaptability was put to the test again in 2011 when the company faced backlash for raising prices and splitting its DVD and streaming services. Although Netflix's stock plummeted and subscriber growth slowed, Hastings remained committed to the transition to streaming and original content. By 2013, Netflix began producing its own content, with *House of Cards* becoming its first major hit. The company's bet on streaming and content creation positioned it as a dominant player in the entertainment industry.

Outcome: Today, Netflix is a global entertainment giant, with over 200 million subscribers worldwide. The company's ability to pivot from DVD rentals to streaming and original content production exemplifies the power of adaptability in responding to industry disruptions.

3. Sara Blakely and Spanx: Innovating During Recession

Background: In 2000, Sara Blakely founded Spanx, a company specializing in shape-wear, with only $5,000 of her savings. Despite the initial success of her product, the 2008 financial crisis hit the retail industry hard, and many consumers scaled back on discretionary spending.

Adaptability: Instead of cutting back, Blakely used the economic downturn as an opportunity to innovate. She continued to invest in product development and marketing, focusing on creating new designs that appealed to a broader customer base. Additionally, Blakely's adaptability extended to her sales strategies—she leveraged partnerships with major retailers and expanded internationally, positioning Spanx as a global brand.

Thriving Through Uncertainty: During the recession, Spanx's affordable luxury became appealing to women looking for versatile fashion solutions without spending excessively on high-end products. Blakely also embraced the digital revolution, expanding Spanx's online presence and direct-to-consumer sales model.

Outcome: By 2012, Blakely had become the youngest self-made female billionaire. Spanx's success during a challenging economic period showcases how adaptability in product innovation, sales strategies, and marketing can help a business thrive even in recessionary times.

4. Elon Musk and Tesla: Overcoming Multiple Crises

Background: Tesla, founded in 2003, faced numerous challenges, including financial struggles, production delays, and market skepticism. Elon Musk, who joined the company in 2004, personally invested much of his fortune to keep Tesla afloat during the 2008 financial crisis. The company was on the verge of bankruptcy, and many doubted its ability to survive.

Adaptability: Musk's response to these crises was marked by his adaptability and commitment to innovation. Tesla pivoted its focus from high-end luxury electric cars to more affordable models, such as the Model 3, which would appeal to a broader market. Additionally, Musk restructured Tesla's production processes, investing in automation and vertical integration to lower costs and scale operations. Tesla also embraced renewable energy innovations, expanding into battery storage solutions and solar energy.

Thriving Through Uncertainty: Despite near-bankruptcy in 2008 and ongoing financial challenges, Tesla emerged stronger due to its adaptability in production, market positioning, and energy innovation. Musk's vision for a sustainable energy future and his ability to navigate regulatory, production, and financial hurdles enabled Tesla to outpace competitors in the electric vehicle (EV) market.

Outcome: Tesla's stock surged to record highs in the 2020s, making it one of the most valuable companies in the world. Musk's adaptability in steering Tesla through financial crises, market disruptions, and technological challenges has been key to the company's long-term success.

5. Tim Ferriss: Reinventing Career and Wealth Creation After Personal Crisis

Background: Tim Ferriss, the best-selling author of *The 4-Hour Workweek*, experienced multiple personal and financial crises in the early stages of his career. After several failed ventures and struggling with burnout, Ferriss reached a breaking point and decided to radically rethink his approach to work, life, and wealth creation.

Adaptability: Ferriss's personal crisis led him to reevaluate how he defined success. Rather than pursuing traditional career paths, he embraced minimalism, lifestyle design, and entrepreneurship. Ferriss's adaptability manifested in his willingness to experiment with different income streams, from investing in startups to developing online courses. He also pioneered strategies for automating income and outsourcing tasks, allowing him to focus on creative projects that aligned with his values.

Thriving Through Uncertainty: Ferriss's reinvention led him to create a personal brand that revolved around lifestyle optimization, productivity, and financial independence. His innovative approach to career and wealth creation resonated with a global audience, enabling him to grow his brand, invest in high-growth startups like Uber and Shopify, and generate multiple streams of passive income.

Outcome: Ferriss' success demonstrates how personal reinvention and adaptability can lead to financial freedom. His strategies for managing uncertainty, building multiple income streams, and optimizing productivity have influenced millions of entrepreneurs and professionals worldwide.

6. Procter & Gamble (P&G): Innovating During the Great Depression

Background: During the Great Depression of the 1930s, many businesses struggled to survive, and consumer spending plummeted. Procter & Gamble (P&G), one of the leading manufacturers of consumer goods, faced significant challenges as demand for non-essential products dropped.

Adaptability: P&G responded to the economic crisis by adapting its marketing strategy. The company began sponsoring radio shows, including soap operas, which allowed it to reach a broad audience and create brand loyalty during tough times. P&G also shifted its focus to essential household products and expanded its portfolio to include affordable options for cash-strapped consumers.

Thriving Through Uncertainty: By leveraging innovative marketing and focusing on consumer needs, P&G maintained strong sales and brand recognition during the Great Depression. Its radio sponsorship strategy pioneered a new form of advertising that resonated with consumers, and its adaptability in product offerings ensured that it remained a household staple even in difficult economic times.

Outcome: P&G emerged from the Great Depression as one of the most successful consumer goods companies in the world. Its ability to innovate in the face of adversity and adapt to changing consumer behavior is a testament to the power of adaptability in business.

These case studies demonstrate that individuals and businesses that thrived through uncertainty did so by embracing adaptability. Whether through innovation, reinvention, or strategic pivots, adaptability allowed them to seize opportunities, mitigate risks, and ultimately build lasting wealth. The ability to navigate crises with flexibility, creativity, and resilience is a critical skill for anyone seeking long-term financial success.

CONCLUSION

In *The Wealth Architect (Vol2)*, the path to achieving financial independence has been laid out clearly, offering actionable strategies and insights for anyone committed to transforming their financial future. As you apply these principles—building wealth systematically, managing your money with purpose, and aligning your financial goals with your personal values—you'll not only secure your financial freedom but also unlock the ability to live a life defined by your own terms.

The journey to financial independence is not just about accumulating money; it's about mastering the habits, mindset, and strategies that allow you to take control of your future. With discipline, consistency, and a long-term perspective, the roadmap to financial freedom presented in this book will help you break free from financial constraints and empower you to pursue the life of abundance and freedom you desire. Now, the power to design your financial destiny is in your hands.

.

GLOSSARY OF TERMS

A

Active Income
Income earned through direct involvement in a business, employment, or profession. This type of income requires ongoing effort, such as salary from a job, hourly wages, or freelance work.

Appreciation
The increase in the value of an asset over time, often applied to investments like stocks, bonds, or real estate. It can result in capital gains when the asset is sold.

Asset Allocation
The process of dividing investments among different asset categories, such as stocks, bonds, and cash, to optimize risk and reward based on the investor's goals, risk tolerance, and time frame.

Assets

Resources with economic value that are owned by an individual, corporation, or country. Assets can generate income or be converted into cash. Examples include real estate, stocks, bonds, and intellectual property.

B

Behavioral Economics

A field of study that combines psychology and economics to understand why people sometimes make irrational financial decisions and how those decisions affect markets.

C

Capital Gains
The profit realized from the sale of an asset when the selling price exceeds the original purchase price. Capital gains can apply to stocks, real estate, or any other investment.

Cash Flow
The total amount of money being transferred in and out of a business or individual's accounts. Positive cash flow means that income exceeds expenses, while negative cash flow indicates more money going out than coming in.

Compound Interest
Interest calculated on both the initial principal and the accumulated interest from previous periods. This leads to exponential growth over time, making it a powerful tool for wealth-building.

Cryptocurrency
A digital or virtual currency that uses cryptography for security and operates independently of a central authority, such as a government or financial institution. Examples include Bitcoin and Ethereum.

D

Diversification
A strategy that involves spreading investments across various financial instruments, industries, and other categories to reduce risk. Diversification aims to limit exposure to any single asset or risk.

Dividend
A payment made by a corporation to its shareholders, usually in the form of cash or additional stock, as a share of the profits. Dividends are common in companies with a history of consistent earnings.

E

Emergency Fund
A reserve of cash set aside for unexpected expenses or financial emergencies, such as job loss or medical bills. It is recommended to have at least three to six months' worth of living expenses saved.

Estate Planning
The process of organizing and preparing for the transfer of assets after death. It typically includes wills, trusts, insurance, and other legal arrangements to ensure a smooth transition of wealth.

Equity
The ownership value in an asset after deducting liabilities. In the context of stocks, equity refers to shares that represent ownership in a company. For real estate, equity is the property's market value minus any debt.

F

FIRE (Financial Independence, Retire Early)
A financial movement advocating extreme saving and investing, with the goal of achieving financial independence early in life. Individuals who follow the FIRE method aim to accumulate enough wealth to retire decades ahead of traditional retirement age.

Financial Freedom
The point at which a person's passive income and investments generate enough money to cover their living expenses, allowing them to focus on other pursuits without relying on active income from a job.

H

Hedge

An investment made to reduce the risk of adverse price movements in an asset, typically by taking an offsetting position in a related security or market.

I

Impact Investing
Investments made with the intention of generating measurable social or environmental impact alongside a financial return. Impact investors seek to make a positive difference while growing their wealth.

Index Fund
A type of mutual fund or exchange-traded fund (ETF) designed to track the performance of a specific market index, such as the S&P 500, offering broad market exposure with lower fees.

Inflation
The rate at which the general level of prices for goods and services rises, eroding purchasing power. Inflation can reduce the value of money and impact long-term savings and investment returns.

L

Liabilities
Financial obligations or debts owed by an individual or company, such as loans, mortgages, and credit card balances. Liabilities reduce an individual's net worth.

Liquidity
The ability of an asset to be quickly converted into cash without significantly affecting its value. High liquidity assets include cash and publicly traded stocks, while real estate is considered less liquid.

M

Mutual Fund
A pooled investment vehicle that collects money from multiple investors to invest in a diversified portfolio of stocks, bonds, or other assets. Mutual funds are managed by professional fund managers.

N

Net Worth
A measure of an individual's financial position, calculated as the total value of assets minus liabilities. Positive net worth indicates that assets exceed debts, while negative net worth reflects the opposite.

P

Passive Income
Income earned with little to no effort on the part of the recipient. Examples include rental income, dividends, royalties, and interest from savings or investments. Passive income streams allow for greater financial independence.

Philanthropy
The act of giving time, money, or resources to charitable causes to improve societal conditions. Philanthropy can be a key component of a values-based wealth strategy, contributing to long-term social change.

Portfolio
A collection of financial investments, such as stocks, bonds, real estate, and other assets, held by an individual or institution. A well-balanced portfolio is diversified to manage risk and optimize returns.

R

Real Estate Investment Trust (REIT)
A company that owns, operates, or finances income-producing real estate. REITs offer investors a way to earn a share of the income produced through commercial real estate ownership without buying property directly.

Return on Investment (ROI)
A measure used to evaluate the efficiency or profitability of an investment. ROI is calculated by dividing the net profit by the initial investment cost and is expressed as a percentage.

Risk Tolerance
An individual's capacity to endure the volatility or losses that may occur in their investment portfolio. Investors with high risk tolerance are willing to accept greater losses in pursuit of higher returns, while those with low risk tolerance prefer more stable investments.

S

Stocks (Equities)
Shares of ownership in a corporation that entitle the shareholder to a portion of the company's profits. Stocks can appreciate in value or generate income through dividends, but they also carry risk.

Sustainable Investing (ESG Investing)
An investment approach that considers environmental, social, and governance (ESG) factors alongside traditional financial analysis. ESG investing focuses on long-term, responsible investing that benefits society and the environment.

T

Trust
A legal entity created to hold assets for the benefit of

certain individuals or organizations. Trusts are often used in estate planning to ensure the orderly transfer of wealth across generations.

V

Volatility
A measure of how much the price of an asset, security, or market fluctuates over time. High volatility indicates large price swings, while low volatility reflects more stable prices.

W

Wealth Management
A holistic approach to managing an individual's financial portfolio that includes investments, tax strategies, estate planning, and retirement planning. Wealth management services are typically tailored to the unique goals of high-net-worth individuals.

Will
A legal document that outlines an individual's wishes regarding the distribution of their assets after death. A will can also specify guardianship for minors and other final requests.

LIST OF ACRONYMS

AI - Artificial Intelligence
The simulation of human intelligence processes by machines, especially computer systems, used in modern financial tools and platforms.

APY - Annual Percentage Yield
The rate of return on an investment over a year, taking into account compound interest.

CD - Certificate of Deposit
A savings product offered by banks with a fixed interest rate and maturity date, commonly used in low-risk savings strategies.

CFP - Certified Financial Planner
A professional designation for individuals qualified to offer financial planning services, including investment, estate, and tax advice.

CPI - Consumer Price Index
A measure that examines the average price level of a basket of consumer goods and services, commonly used to assess inflation rates.

DCF - Discounted Cash Flow
A valuation method used to estimate the value of an investment based on its future cash flows, commonly used in stock and business valuations.

DGI - Dividend Growth Investing
A long-term investment strategy focused on investing in companies with a consistent record of increasing dividend payouts over time.

DIY - Do It Yourself
A financial strategy or method of handling personal

investments or financial planning without professional assistance.

ETF - Exchange-Traded Fund
A type of investment fund that is traded on stock exchanges, similar to a stock, and typically holds a diversified portfolio of assets.

ESG - Environmental, Social, and Governance
A set of criteria for evaluating a company's operations with respect to sustainability and ethical impacts, increasingly used in investment decisions.

FANG - Facebook, Amazon, Netflix, and Google
A group of high-performing technology stocks that are often seen as leaders in market growth and innovation.

FDIC - Federal Deposit Insurance Corporation
A U.S. government agency that provides deposit insurance to protect bank depositors in case of bank failures.

FIRE - Financial Independence, Retire Early
A financial movement advocating extreme savings and investment strategies to achieve early retirement and financial independence.

GDP - Gross Domestic Product
The total monetary or market value of all finished goods and services produced within a country's borders in a specific time period, often used as an indicator of economic health.

HNW - High-Net-Worth

Refers to individuals or families with a high amount of liquid assets, typically defined as $1 million or more.

HSA - Health Savings Account

A tax-advantaged medical savings account available to individuals enrolled in high-deductible health plans (HDHPs), allowing them to save for medical expenses while enjoying tax benefits.

IRA - Individual Retirement Account
A tax-advantaged account designed to help individuals save for retirement, with various types such as traditional and Roth IRAs.

NAV - Net Asset Value
The value per share of a mutual fund or an ETF, calculated by dividing the total value of all the fund's assets by the number of shares outstanding.

PE Ratio - Price-to-Earnings Ratio
A valuation measure that compares the price of a company's stock to its earnings per share, often used to assess whether a stock is over- or undervalued.

PPP - Purchasing Power Parity
An economic theory that compares different countries' currencies through the cost of a "basket of goods," used to determine exchange rate fluctuations and economic conditions.

P2P - Peer-to-Peer Lending

A method of debt financing that enables individuals to borrow and lend money without going through a traditional financial institution.

REIT - Real Estate Investment Trust
A company that owns or finances income-generating real estate, allowing individual investors to earn dividends from real estate investments without buying properties.

ROI - Return on Investment
A performance measure used to evaluate the efficiency or profitability of an investment, expressed as a percentage of the initial investment cost.

S&P 500 - Standard & Poor's 500 Index
A stock market index that tracks the performance of 500 large-cap U.S. companies, often used as a benchmark for overall market performance.

SEC - Securities and Exchange Commission
A U.S. federal agency that enforces laws and regulations governing the securities industry, ensuring market integrity and investor protection.

SWOT - Strengths, Weaknesses, Opportunities, Threats
A strategic planning tool used to assess internal and external factors affecting a business or investment, widely employed in financial analysis and wealth management.

TAM - Total Addressable Market
The total market demand for a product or service, often used by investors to estimate a company's growth potential.

USD - United States Dollar
The official currency of the United States, often used as a global reserve currency for international trade and finance.

VC - Venture Capital

Financing provided to startups and small businesses with long-term growth potential by investors, often in exchange for equity.

VTI - Vanguard Total Stock Market ETF
A popular ETF that tracks the performance of the entire U.S. stock market, offering diversified exposure to investors.

YTD - Year to Date
A period beginning at the start of the current calendar year and continuing up to the present date, often used in performance reporting.

401(k)
A U.S.-based employer-sponsored retirement savings plan that allows employees to contribute a portion of their salary into investment accounts, often with tax advantages and employer matching.

ADDITIONAL RESOURCES AND REFERENCES

Books on Wealth Building and Personal Finance

1. **"The Millionaire Next Door" by Thomas J. Stanley and William D. Danko**
   An insightful study of the habits and behaviors of self-made millionaires, offering key principles on frugality, disciplined saving, and smart investing.
2. **"Rich Dad Poor Dad" by Robert T. Kiyosaki**
   A classic in personal finance literature, this book compares the financial philosophies of the author's two father figures, offering lessons on wealth-building, entrepreneurship, and financial independence.
3. **"The Intelligent Investor" by Benjamin Graham**
   A timeless guide on value investing, this book teaches you how to invest wisely and minimize risk in the stock market.
4. **"Your Money or Your Life" by Vicki Robin and Joe Dominguez**
   This book focuses on transforming your relationship with money and achieving financial independence through lifestyle design and mindful consumption.
5. **"The Total Money Makeover" by Dave Ramsey**
   A step-by-step guide to managing personal finances, paying off debt, and building long-term wealth with practical, no-nonsense advice.

Online Resources and Financial Education Platforms

1. **Investopedia (www.investopedia.com)**
   A comprehensive online resource that provides articles, tutorials, and financial dictionaries for understanding complex financial terms, investment strategies, and market trends.
2. **The Financial Independence / Retire Early (FIRE) Community**

(www.reddit.com/r/financialindependence)
A vibrant online forum where individuals share stories, strategies, and advice on achieving financial independence and early retirement.

3. **Morningstar** (www.morningstar.com)
A platform offering detailed analysis and research on stocks, mutual funds, ETFs, and other investment vehicles, helping investors make informed decisions.
4. **Mint** (www.mint.com)
A free personal finance app that helps users track spending, create budgets, and monitor financial goals to build wealth.
5. **NerdWallet** (www.nerdwallet.com)
A personal finance website offering advice on credit cards, banking, investing, mortgages, and more, helping readers make smarter financial decisions.

Investment and Financial Planning Tools

1. **Vanguard** (www.vanguard.com)
One of the world's largest investment management companies, offering low-cost index funds, ETFs, and retirement planning resources.
2. **Betterment** (www.betterment.com)
A robo-advisor platform that provides automated investment management services, helping users build portfolios based on their goals, risk tolerance, and timeline.
3. **Wealthfront** (www.wealthfront.com)
Another leading robo-advisor offering low-cost automated investment strategies, designed for long-term wealth building.
4. **Personal Capital** (www.personalcapital.com)
A hybrid platform combining automated tools and human advisors to help with wealth management, investment planning, and retirement readiness.

Tax Planning and Legal Advice Resources

1. **IRS.gov (www.irs.gov)**
   The official website of the Internal Revenue Service provides comprehensive information on tax laws, filing taxes, deductions, credits, and more for U.S. taxpayers.
2. **TurboTax (www.turbotax.com)**
   A popular tax preparation software that guides users through the process of filing taxes, helping them find deductions and maximize their returns.
3. **LegalZoom (www.legalzoom.com)**
   A trusted source for creating legal documents related to wills, trusts, and business formation, LegalZoom offers resources for estate planning and business structuring.
4. **Estate Planning.com (www.estateplanning.com)**
   An informative platform dedicated to estate planning, with tools and resources for creating wills, setting up trusts, and organizing long-term financial plans for families.

Podcasts and YouTube Channels on Personal Finance

1. **The Dave Ramsey Show (Podcast)**
   Dave Ramsey offers practical financial advice, focusing on debt reduction, budgeting, and wealth building through disciplined financial habits.
2. **The BiggerPockets Podcast**
   A leading real estate podcast that educates listeners on real estate investing, wealth-building strategies, and financial independence through property ownership.
3. **Afford Anything (Podcast)**
   Hosted by Paula Pant, this podcast explores how to make smart financial choices, invest wisely, and live a financially independent lifestyle.

4. **Graham Stephan (YouTube Channel)**
A YouTube channel where real estate investor and personal finance expert Graham Stephan shares advice on investing, frugality, and financial independence.
5. **The Financial Diet (YouTube Channel)**
A channel that provides tips on budgeting, managing debt, saving money, and building wealth, especially geared toward young adults and millennials.

Financial Calculators and Tools

1. **FIRE Calculator (www.firecalc.com)**
A specialized tool for calculating when you can retire based on your savings rate, investment returns, and desired retirement lifestyle.
2. **Bankrate (www.bankrate.com)**
A resource for calculating mortgage payments, credit card debt payoff, and investment growth, providing a clear picture of financial progress.
3. **Compound Interest Calculator (www.investor.gov/additional-resources/free-financial-planning-tools/compound-interest-calculator)**
Use this tool to visualize how your investments grow over time with the power of compounding.
4. **Net Worth Calculator (www.personalcapital.com)**
A feature of the Personal Capital platform that allows users to calculate their net worth by tracking assets and liabilities in real-time.

Educational Courses and Certifications

1. **Certified Financial Planner (CFP) Certification (www.cfp.net)**
For those interested in advancing their financial

planning knowledge, the CFP certification provides a structured and comprehensive education in personal finance and wealth management.

2. **Coursera: Financial Markets Course by Yale University (www.coursera.org/learn/financial-markets)**
   A highly rated online course that covers the fundamentals of financial markets, including stocks, bonds, and derivatives, taught by economist Robert Shiller.
3. **Udemy: Personal Finance Masterclass (www.udemy.com/course/personal-finance-masterclass)**
   An affordable, practical course offering actionable tips on budgeting, saving, investing, and achieving financial independence.
4. **Khan Academy: Finance and Capital Markets (www.khanacademy.org/economics-finance-domain/core-finance)**
   A free educational platform offering tutorials on economics, finance, and investing basics for students at all levels.

OTHER BOOKS BY THE AUTHOR

1. The Wealth Architect (Vol 1): *Building a Life of Unstoppable Riches.*

2. How Ordinary People Can Achieve Extraordinary Wealth: *Rich Habits, Rich Life.*

A short, polite request

If you enjoyed this book, please consider leaving a review on Amazon. Your feedback helps other readers discover the plan. Thank you.

www.ingramcontent.com/pod-product-compliance
Lightning Source LLC
LaVergne TN
LVHW052112210926
848482LV00025B/542

9781069622310